To Jill

all the best

BrandDigital

Simple Ways Top Brands Succeed in the Digital World

Allen P. Adamson

Foreword by David Kirkpatrick,
Senior Editor, Internet & Technology,
Fortune Magazine

palgrave
macmillan

BRANDDIGITAL

Copyright © Allen P. Adamson, 2008.

All rights reserved.

First published in 2008 by PALGRAVE MACMILLAN® in the US—a division of St. Martin's Press LLC, 175 Fifth Avenue, New York, NY 10010.

Where this book is distributed in the UK, Europe and the rest of the world, this is by Palgrave Macmillan, a division of Macmillan Publishers Limited, registered in England, company number 785998, of Houndmills, Basingstoke, Hampshire RG21 6XS.

Palgrave Macmillan is the global academic imprint of the above companies and has companies and representatives throughout the world.

Palgrave® and Macmillan® are registered trademarks in the United States, the United Kingdom, Europe and other countries.

ISBN–13: 978–0–230–60604–3
ISBN–10: 0–230–60604–0

Library of Congress Cataloging-in-Publication Data
Adamson, Allen P.
   Branddigital : simple ways top brands succeed in the digital world / by Allen P. Adamson.
     p.   cm.
   ISBN–13: 978–0–230–60604–3 (hardcover)
   ISBN–10: 0–230–60604–0 (hardcover)
   1. Branding (Marketing)   2. Brand name products.   3. Internet marketing.   I. Title.
HF5415.1255.A33   2008
658.8'27—dc22

                                              2008017390

A catalogue record of the book is available from the British Library.

Design by Letra Libre, Inc.

First edition: August 2008
10 9 8 7 6 5 4 3 2 1
Printed in the United States of America.

I would like to thank my colleague, Betsy Karp, for her dedication and her tenacity. She brought great insight, intellectual capital, and creativity to the project and, once again, has been an incredible partner. (*She* would like to thank her husband, children, step-children, and parents for their support and motivation, and her new granddaughter, Amelia, for helping her keep life in perspective.)

Contents

v

Acknowledgments

This book is based on more than one hundred interviews with the best and the brightest brand professionals. Everyone I spoke to in preparation for this book was exceedingly generous with their time, personal knowledge, and insights. Every conversation expanded my understanding and grasp of the changes that digital technologies are having on the way brands are built and supported. Each interview was truly enjoyable. My first acknowledgment of thanks goes to the smart people listed at the end of this section. I thank you very much for your invaluable contributions.

Next I want to thank Charlie Wrench, Landor's Chairman and President, for giving me the encouragement and freedom to tackle the challenge of writing a second book. His clever suggestion, that digital tools do not change but rather magnify everything we know to be true about building powerful brands, became an organizing principle for the book.

I am also extremely grateful to all my Landor colleagues worldwide who enthusiastically shared their expertise, their thinking, and their time, with a special tip of the hat to Amanda Peterson for her help with defining the vernacular of the digital age.

I want to especially thank Leonie Derry, who managed to keep both Landor and the book-writing process going at the same time. Additionally, I'd like to thank my Landor team in New York—Diane Ashley, Richard Brandt, Mich Bergesen, Joan Bogin, Richard Ford, Karen Floyd, Ken Runkel, Executive Director Katie Ryan, and Dan

Wadleigh. This team of dedicated people contributed to the thinking that went into the project, offered contact information and, most important, kept the office humming while I was busy with the book.

A thank you, too, goes to the Landor marketing team—Lee Aldridge, Sean King, Anna Kowalak, Mindy Romero, and Hayes Roth for their help in getting *BrandDigital* successfully launched into the marketplace—and Bina Kijmedee and Chuck Routhier for their spectacular cover design. And, of course, my digital team here at Landor for their dedication to creating the BrandDigital website—Nicky Hardy, Susan Griffiths, Adam Waugh, Warren Harrison, and Ann Evans.

A special thanks to my editor, Airié Stuart, for her suggestion that I write a second book and her ongoing enthusiasm and support for the initiative.

Finally and most importantly, I want to thank and dedicate this book to my family. My nine-year-old son, Josh, who could easily spend his whole day online (if we let him) and my daughter, Elissa, who at age five continues her love affair with her online Webkinz pets. Saving the best for last, my wife, Madelyn, who reminds me that each day is a gift to be cherished and used wisely.

Interviewees and contributors

Virginia Alber-
   Glanstaetten
Arturo Aranda
Tim Armstrong
Tom Asacker
Susan Avarde
Hashem Bajwa
Damian Baradona
Barbara Basney
Scott Bedbury
Tom Bedecarre
Mark Beeching
David Bell
Jeff Bell
Bruce Benson
Elliot Berger
Simeran Bhasin
David Blyth
Matthew Brown
David Camp
Susan Can
Albert Cheng
David Churbuck
Jon Cook

Debra Coughlin
Kevin Crociata
Jim Cuene
Chris Curtin
Britta Dahl
Lee Ann Daly
Avi Dan
Amrita Das
Sam Decker
Suzy Deering
Michael Donahue
Jason Dowdell
Lee Doyle
Alan Dye
Esther Dyson
Mark Edmonson
Ben Edwards
Chas Edwards
Gary Elliott
Ian Ewart
Leslie Ferraro
Ilana Finley
Giunero Floro
Heather Frahm

Peter Friedman
Tom Friedman
Adam Gerber
Brian Gies
Bob Gilbreath
Marc Giusti
Philip Gladman
Damon Gorrie
Robert Greenberg
Robin Harper
John Harrobin
Junji Hase
Bridgette Heller
Dale Herigstad
Peter Himler
Peter Hirshberg
Donna Hoffman
Joshua Hoffman
Nigel Hollis
Andy Horrow
Brett Hurt
Jeremy Hutchison
Drew Ianni
Michael Jacobs

Doug Jaeger
Trevor Kaufman
Kevin Lane Keller
Noah Kerner
Robin Kietlinski
Larry Kimmel
Ian Kirk
David Kirkpatrick
Russ Klein
Joel Lambertson
Cleve Langton
Lisa Lanspery
Bob Liodice
Mike Lundgren
Maria Mandel
Tim Mapes
Pamela Mazzocco
Joe McCarthy
Phil McIntyre
Carl Mela
Bill Melton
Michael Mendenhall
Jeffrey Merrihue
Russ Meyer
Courteney Monroe
Kelly Mooney
Alison Moore
David Moore
Doug Moore
Caroline Morgan
David Muir

Joe Muran
Jim Nail
John Nardone
Susan Nelson
Jim Nichols
Alex Norman
Rob Norman
Nick Nyhan
Kathy O'Brien
Allen Olivo
Betsy Olum
Scott Osman
Stewart Owen
Shelly Palmer
John Partilla
Simon Pearce
Ellen Perelman
Doug Pippin
Bob Pittman
Faith Popcorn
Robyn Putter
Jim Radosevic
Geoff Ramsey
Mark Read
Lauren Reiss
Rita Rodriguez
Julie Roehm
David Roman
Tom Roope
Rob Rosenblatt
Randall Rothenberg

Peter Sachse
Jonathan Sackett
Becky Saeger
Shafi Saxena
Scott Schiller
Brad Scott
Adam Selig
Scott Siegler
Mark Silva
Kristin Sloan
Harold Sogard
Airié Stuart
Joe Stitzlein
Steve Sullivan
Rory Sutherland
John Sykes
Ronnie Talati
Michael Tchao
Joe Torpey
John Vail
Joan Voight
Barry Wacksman
Trevor Wade
Jennifer Walsh
Ian Wood
Nima Yassini
Steve Zales
Shelley Zalis
Strauss Zelnick

Foreword

David Kirkpatrick,
Senior Editor, Internet & Technology,
Fortune Magazine

Recently I took a much-anticipated business class transatlantic flight with British Airways. I had been smitten by its advertising, with seductive descriptions of flat beds and cosseting treatment. But when I stretched out to sleep on the plane, I was surprisingly uncomfortable. Even though I hadn't paid for the $8,600 ticket myself, I felt burned.

But I didn't just grumble. Instead, I fired up my account on Twitter, a free micro-blogging service on which users can send out short texts on any subject to hundreds of people around the world. "British Airways' 'new' business class very disappointing," I wrote, in the telegraphic language that characterizes Twitter. "Bed too short, privacy lacking, service so-so. Unlikely to fly it again." The brand had, quite unexpectedly, failed to live up to my expectations.

As evidenced by my "tweet," as Twitter posts are called, in today's world there was no reason I had to take my experience lying down, so to speak. An amazingly powerful panoply of digital tools is available to anyone who wants to share an opinion about anything. Yet, too many people in business have yet to recognize how profoundly this is changing the marketing and branding landscape. That's why this book by Allen Adamson is so welcome and necessary. The fundamentals of brand building, from listening to and learning from customers, to relevantly meeting their needs, have been magnified in a world of digital communications and consumer empowerment.

Managing a brand in the digital era is like wrestling an Anaconda in a crowded room—or worse, on a swaying subway train at rush hour. No matter how well you think you can restrain the beast on your own, others are inevitably going to reach over and help you. The companies that cultivate brands best take this as a given. They invite feedback, criticism, and innovative ideas from the users of a product or service. Adamson calls today's consumers "de facto collaborators in the brand-building process." If British Airways had, when I landed, sent me an e-mail or otherwise invited me to give them my response to the trip, perhaps I would have refrained from complaining openly to a large group of potential customers. Alas, they did not.

There is one bedrock explanation for why the relationship between businesses and their customers is so different in the digital era: It's the technological touchstone called Moore's Law—a well-proven theory about the evolution of semiconductor technology first propounded by Intel co-founder Gordon Moore back in 1965. He said that the power of the computer chips underlying all digital products gets exponentially greater over time while their price more or less stays the same. As digital tools have thus gotten cheaper and more powerful, more communications power has been put into the hands of people—a process that shows no sign of abating. That formula has led to the emergence of a succession of amazing tools that take advantage of those chips—from the PC to the Internet to the cell phone to new services like Twitter, Google, MySpace, or Facebook. We are still just beginning to understand how radical are the implications.

Adamson makes many statements in *BrandDigital* that would seem absurd were we not all intuitively familiar with these changes wrought by Moore's Law. Here's one of the most striking ones: "Consumers can track and monitor corporate behavior with the same speed and fluidity that corporations can track consumer behavior." That summarizes one of the most remarkable transformations society has ever seen. It's a fundamental realignment of market power, caused by the levelling influence of the Internet. Another profound notion is encapsulated in a line Adamson quotes from Lenovo's David Churbuck. Speaking about those who shepherd brands and company images, he avers, "Time is not on your side." If you don't move quickly to respond to the new consumer power, your brands could rapidly weaken.

One of Adamson's central and most useful images is that of the "back fence." This quaint image may evoke small-town America, but it also aptly symbolizes where every consumer now stands. After my recent ill-fated airline experience, I stood at the equivalent of a back fence where I could speak not to my next door neighbor but to literally hundreds of similarly talkative people who listen to me on Twitter, and the potentially thousands more who listen to them. Speaking of one of today's most important developments—the stunning rise of social networks—Adamson calls them "equivalents of Wisteria Lane." That is, of course, the setting of the somewhat dark and gossip-driven suburban America of the hit ABC series *Desperate Housewives*. Social networks are powerful drivers of gossip and viral communication, Adamson writes: "When someone whispers it has the potential to turn into a verbal tsunami." I'm so convinced of the potential of social networks like Facebook to change social life, business, marketing, and even politics that I'm writing a book about it myself.

To hear Adamson tell it, being an effective branding and marketing organization these days is a lot like being a responsible and caring person. In this world of pell-mell change and topsy-turvy power relationships, those who would operate with the top-down, hierarchical, imperial methods of old are unlikely anymore to succeed. The word that kept leaping to my mind as I read Adamson's engaging stories from today's brand marketplace was "humility." But the good news, he tells us, is that even the biggest businesses can still apply these new tools of openness and humility to build brands of tremendous strength and durability. Just look at GE, or at Hewlett-Packard's PC business.

We are still only in the early stages of the changes Adamson outlines here. One fundamental statistic shows how much transformation is still to come—and how much opportunity remains for smart marketers to take the reins of their brands. In 2007, 21 percent of total media consumption in the U.S. was digital, but only 8 percent of total advertising spending was. The behavior of the marketing and branding industry clearly hasn't yet caught up to the behavior of the American consumer.

If you're intent on catching up, this book should help. My copy is heavily underlined. I'd be surprised if anyone engaged in any way with stewardship of a business or brand does not find useful insights throughout.

Toward the end of *BrandDigital* Adamson lists a few basic principles, which leap off the page. "First and foremost, stand back. . . . Forget about the way you used to buy media or made your branding decisions. . . . Watch, listen, and learn. . . . Consumer behavior should be your guiding light." It may not be easy, but there really is no choice.

Why This Book?

Awaiting Real Sales from Virtual Shoppers
Google Set to Track Ad Audiences
When Beauty Is More than a Click Deep
Making Social Connections and Selling Cookies
At Starbucks, Songs of Instant Gratification
The Soap Pioneer Plows the Web
A Web Site for Pet Lovers and Marketers Who Love Them

The headlines above, be they from the digital or analog media files, have long been buried amidst the thousands of other headlines about life in the digital lane. I won't dare call it the fast lane because it's beyond fast. No thesaurus—neither digital nor analog versions—offers a single word that describes how rapidly, quickly, or swiftly communication technology is evolving and the significant impact this change is having on our lives. It's almost impossible to open a newspaper or a trade journal, watch the news or, more to the point, click on a website, blog, or podcast without seeing some new development in the digital space of which good marketers must be aware. Of course, as good marketers we must always be aware of what's going on. It's an implied part of our job descriptions. But to be even better marketers we must also read through, around, and between the headlines to determine which are based on truth and/or have long-standing consequences.

My intention in writing this book was not to have it serve as the seminal academic text on the digital revolution or even to demonstrate how new forms of communication are affecting the world in general. I have written this book to help those in the business of building brands determine which of the previous headlines to heed, and to help them clarify what matters in the long term and what doesn't. Part intellectual curiosity, part wanting to figure it out for the benefit of my clients and colleagues, I decided it was time to take everything we've been hearing, reading, and personally experiencing and put it into the context of branding as it's been practiced for the last half century or so. I am a branding professional and I see the world from this perspective. I'm not a technology guru by any stretch of the imagination (just ask my children). I figured if I could make sense of the digital arena and how the best marketers are using digital tools to build and manage their brands, anyone could.

It's become obvious from talking to a great many people in the business that my questions about the digital world are the same questions clients ask their agency partners all the time. How should social sites, like Facebook or MySpace, be used as part of the branding mix? What should marketers know about search functionality? Will you get better return on the development costs of television ads if you reformat them for YouTube? How do you create a successful viral campaign? How effective is consumer-generated content? What happens if someone writes a lousy review of your product on his blog and the story is picked up by CNN? Do you need a special agency to do the digital stuff? How do you keep all this new stuff integrated with the traditional stuff? How do you figure out what technology to use to reach one audience versus another? Should you throw everything you know about branding out the window?

The questions about how to use digital tools to build brands are as ubiquitous as the new media choices, the new terminology, and the decisions that brand organizations must make as they go forward into the new age. I will answer only one of these questions right now—the last one (the others will be answered, to the extent they're answerable, as you read through this book): Do not throw everything you know about brands and branding out the window. The fundamental truths about building brands remain the same.

As you read on, you'll appreciate that these truths have actually taken on more significance than ever. Yes, technology is changing at breakneck speed, as are the behaviors generated by this technology. This doesn't mean you should rush to judgment as far as your branding decisions are concerned. There's a lot to take in and become familiar with, but in learning more about how it affects brands and branding, you'll be better able to apply what you *already* know. This book was written to explain in simple terms the dynamics of the digital era that influence the way good marketers must think about building brands—dynamics that will enable them to build even better brands. While this requires a mental shift, it's not as draconian a change as some might think. Although it wasn't all that easy to pull together and assimilate this information, I've made it an easy read. Given how little time people have these days, I felt this was important.

WHO SHOULD READ THIS BOOK AND WHY?

People like me should read this book: The folks who have spent the better part of their careers working with brands—creating them, managing them for brand organizations or agencies, teaching classes about them. We understand brands: what makes them thrive, and what makes them fail. What we don't understand to the extent that we should is how to take advantage of digital technology and the behaviors it engenders to make brands stronger and more valuable to organizations and to consumers. Yes, we read blogs, and quite a few of us, myself included, write blogs. We have profiles on MySpace or Facebook or LinkedIn. Some of us can upload videos onto YouTube and have our virtual say during CNN's political debates. We can operate webcams and use them to have conversations with our parents in Florida. We can send text messages and converse with our preteens about media without appearing like total nerds. What we don't know is how to integrate all of these activities into our branding responsibilities. Not a whole lot of people do. Those that do, and do it well, are highly sought after. These were the people I turned to as I set out to write this book so I could share what they have to say. My objective was to make it possible for anyone who reads this book to become highly sought after, or, at the very least, comfortable inside their digital skins.

People *not* like me should also read this book. Those who now design sophisticated digital applications, like interstitials and streaming videos, those who grew up viewing digital technology in the same way as the group I just described grew up with music—as its vehicle for self-expression. Generally speaking, these are the younger folks in the marketing world who can explain with casual indifference what mash-ups and widgets and wikis are. Digital technology is merely an extension of their opposable thumbs. They don't see Wi-Fi as sci-fi. Building websites, starting blogs, developing RSS feeds, knowing how to measure and analyze click rates, and how to optimize search engines come naturally. What those in this group may *not* fully comprehend is the fundamental process of how good brands get built. They grew up with technology but not as it applies to the principles of branding. As such, they may not be aware of what it takes to manage a brand and ensure that it thrives rather than fails. Some of them do know this, and these folks are as highly sought after as those in the first group, who understand both branding and how to work competently in the digital world. These, too, are the people you'll hear from in this book.

LOOKING BACK: HOW THE DIGITAL MARKETING LANDSCAPE TOOK SHAPE

Like most business people in the early 1990s, I enjoyed my first years of life online. I enjoyed it because in very large part I could understand it. At this point on the digital timeline, we used our computers and a few simple software applications to make office life easier and more efficient. We arranged meetings, sent e-mails, and submitted timesheets. Easy stuff. Sure, our tech guys had to drop by on occasion to explain one thing or another. They were our in-house equivalent of Best Buy's Geek Squad, long before there was a Best Buy. In my case, if there was a problem—if I forgot my password or how to log in to the company website for job numbers—the geek was me. But this soon became rote, and we also learned how to troubleshoot.

Those of us who considered ourselves early adopters of digital technology also enjoyed the second round of life online, which began during the mid- to-late 1990s. We understood eBay and Google and Amazon. These were brands built without brick and mortar, but the business models developed by their "cyber-preneur" founders made sense. Each of these companies was built on a solid foundation. In other words, each had a realistic plan for making money. Like many others back then, I helped them make money. I began shopping for books on Amazon and buying grocery basics from another early online business called FreshDirect. Like some people, I wasn't uncomfortable sending my charge card numbers out into the ether. It might have been my confidence in having American Express as my partner online. I felt secure using the card and knew that if anything bad happened, they'd take care of any charges that weren't mine. I knew I'd have protection as a consumer. Nothing bad ever did happen, except that I bought more books than I had time to read, and eventually all financial services companies guaranteed protection when customers

5

bought something online. Given that a good number of early websites were transactional in nature, ensuring security and protecting against identity fraud has become an essential factor in any online transaction business model.

Suffice it to say, the companies that made digital buying and selling simple to understand, easy to use, and offered worthwhile products and services were the ones that became more and more successful. Their online functionality made lots of activities more convenient. Bob Pittman, founding member, Pilot Group, Co-founder of MTV, and former COO of America Online and AOL Time Warner, put it this way: "It all starts with the consumer. I'll adopt it if it makes my life easier or more convenient in some way. The Internet does stuff I already do, but it allows me to do it in a more efficient way. Mail versus e-mail. Paying bills. Researching vacation spots down to being able to see my hotel room. Reading news. Renewing subscriptions. Looking up telephone numbers and getting driving directions. The Internet is a box that makes it more convenient to manage my life." Bob went on to say that the companies that enjoyed the earliest successes on the Internet were the first to fully understand how to use the technology to make the things we already do easier. This, in its digital guise, is one of the essential truths of smart branding: Find a relevantly different way to make life more convenient for consumers, and they'll seek you out. Companies that recognize how the Internet, or anything digital, can make something we already do genuinely more fun, easier, or more convenient will succeed. I'll get to this in more detail later on in the book. In the meantime, just a bit more historical perspective.

There was a certain period, again in the late nineties, when I and many others began to think that perhaps we had no understanding of life online. While advertising and branding firms were in the early stages of developing the skills to deal with the now-burgeoning dot.com space, there was something else going on. Twenty-something-year-old kids would come into our offices with enormous amounts of venture capital, truckloads of dollars, and ask us to help them build out a brand idea. As a professional brander, I personally took as professional an attitude as I could toward assessing these opportunities. I tried really, really hard to get my head around how a company—with no long-term business plan, with no sense of how money was going to be made, and with no infrastructure other than a cool website—could become a brand. Don't get me wrong. Thinking we must be missing something, we did our best with these optimistic folks. But, as we all know, it wasn't the brand professionals who were missing something. It was the kids with lots of venture capital. To build a brand you need a tangible business strategy to succeed. All the branding tactics in the world couldn't help, no matter how cool their ideas appeared to be. They missed this seminal point, and pop went the bubble. Enough books have been written about this. No more commentary is necessary.

But let's get back to reality. It was between shopping for books, music, and groceries online that people in the business of building brands began to recognize the growing implications that digital space had on their jobs. As we came to the end of the 1990s, more and more well-respected brands—L.L. Bean, Charles Schwab, GE—were establishing some degree of an online presence. To return to Bob Pittman's point, while it was essential for these brand organizations to determine their objectives in being online, it was the job of branding professionals to get up to speed on how to use the Internet to help build brand value. At this point on the digital timeline, most of the activity had to do with basic website design and functionality. This is in no way meant to diminish the significant nature of these initiatives; quite the opposite, in fact. Even back then, the best brand organizations recognized that online space was a venue with enormous potential to extend the scope and scale of, as well as to reinforce, their customers' brand loyalty. They appreciated that for this to happen their online initiatives had to reinforce what consumers already associated with the brand. In other words, the same rules that applied to offline branding had to be followed online, specifically extending delivery of what the brand promised to this new space. The way this manifested itself in those early days was primarily a function of, well, basic functionality. By that I mean, how fast a site downloaded, or how easy it was to navigate and find the icons required for users to click from content point A to content point B. The design of the site had to reflect what people already associated with the brand: the tone of voice, the arrangement of content, where the Help button was. If a brand was known for fast response to customer needs, for example, the site couldn't take forever to download, and the toll-free number had to be prominent enough to find and read without a magnifying glass. Strategic alignment with the brand promise meant careful consideration of the graphic elements or the amount of copy on a page. It meant placing pertinent copy above the "fold," where people could read it without having to move the cursor down. The online space was a totally new dimension for both consumers and marketers. But it became apparent pretty quickly that the functionality of a website had to communicate as much about the brand's persona as television ads, direct mail, or events and promotions.

The primary challenge for brands with an early Internet presence was to determine exactly how the brand promise should be brought to life online. L.L. Bean, for example, known as much for its comfortable outdoor clothing as for the comfortable voices of its customer service representatives, made sure that functions related to ordering and getting information were easy for online shoppers. Its check-out instructions were intuitive to follow, as befitting the brand, and its re-

turn policies were clearly stated. Charles Schwab, known for serving
the smart do-it-yourself trader, had to make sure this promise manifested itself on its website. I spoke to Becky Saeger, currently Executive Vice President and Chief Marketing Officer at Charles Schwab,
who talked about the Internet in the late 1990s:

> Most of what companies used the Internet for at that time was of a transac-
> tional nature. In 1997, Schwab dealt with clients who wanted to manage
> their own trading transactions. We made it convenient and easy for people
> to do so. It's what our clients wanted and expected from us. Given this,
> Schwab.com, as a branding tactic, was perfectly aligned with the delivery of
> this expectation. In some respects, we were a technology company. We were
> able to give our clients a wonderfully efficient platform for doing what they
> enjoyed doing. We've since evolved from being a transactional, functional
> brand to having deeper relationships with clients that allow us to meet and
> facilitate more of their financial needs. As the social and technological im-
> plications of the Internet have evolved, our brand has evolved, as well.

The evolution of the Internet from a primarily transactional
medium to one of relationship building has been a huge shift, and
this is one of the significant themes covered in this book. It was just
ten years ago that companies were beginning to get a glimpse of how
and why they had to integrate traditional go-to-market tactics with
digital tactics in order to support the brand promise. Consumers
were beginning to encounter and experience branding applications
in far more places and in more ways than ever before. The customer
journey with a brand—all the places customers touched the brand—
while not necessarily longer, was becoming much more random and
not always easy to follow. It quickly became apparent that online interactions with the brand had to feel as comfortable and familiar to
consumers as offline interactions if a brand story was to hold up as
credible. What made this more important was that the new experiences consumers were having with brands in the digital world were

interactive. These customer touch points were two-way: I act, and I expect the brand to react the way I expect it to. The concept of a virtual dialogue with the consumer was beginning to emerge, and new skills were required within organizations to ensure this dialogue exuded "brand-ness," the qualities associated with the brand. As a result, new "interactive" divisions were beginning to be created in major corporations and within a number of agencies. However, more often than not, these divisions were marginalized. The discipline was too new and the people who inhabited these techie departments spoke a language most others in the organization couldn't or didn't want to understand. Traditional media continued to rule the branding roost. With a few exceptions, these new interactive divisions were considered noisy, occasionally pesky, third- or fourth-tier applications in a world in which the most glamorous branding application was the 60-second TV spot.

I spoke with a number of people who remembered those days as being as exciting as they were frustrating. Drew Ianni, now Chairman, Programming & Senior Global Analyst of ad:tech Expositions, a company that hosts international events for global marketers, was at @mosphere, the interactive division at BBDO, in 2000. "The late 1990s, even the year 2000, were very formative years in the history of digital branding," Drew told me. He continued:

> We were doing things like banners, conventional now but innovative for that time period. The first banner ads were placed in 1994. The challenge was that people were not just learning how to use the Internet for marketing; they were still exploring new ways to use the Internet, in general. There were new platforms for digital marketing emerging every day, but there were no budgets for digital. It was too experimental for most people to take seriously. I could understand people not quite getting it in those early days. Then, all of a sudden, it was the year 2000 with lots of new applications and lots of new learning about online marketing. I remember sitting at a table reviewing a budget for

a major new product being launched by BBDO. I went down the line items on this $320 million budget, and still no line item for interactive marketing. What totally blew me away was that this $320 million budget was for a major wireless company! Irony of ironies, we were launching a digital product, and we were still fighting for the legitimacy of digital marketing. Perhaps, the greater irony was that the launch was directed at 16- to 24-year-olds, and a major part of the budget was for television. Even then we knew these kids didn't watch TV the way their parents did. As early as 2000, patterns of media consumption were changing and media budgets continued to be focused on TV.

Drew said he finally got $800,000 for the interactive component of the campaign. Looking back, maybe the greatest irony of all was that in 2000 you could have done extensive Internet marketing for $1 million, a mere drop in any budget bucket.

Well, we're getting close to being a decade beyond the year 2000. The simple truth is that, while agencies and brand organizations are still behind in the adoption of digital branding, they're quickly coming to realize that digital is not an option. It's a must-have. No matter how great an agency's strategic expertise or how talented its creative team, it's of limited value to its clients and to its customers unless it embraces digital thinking. People are using personal, portable, digital means of communications. Brands need to be where the people are, and they need to get there first. Organizations that don't understand the significance of digital technology and the scope of digital resources its related behavior play in their branding are sure to lose out to the competition. A number of agencies have lost major clients as a result of not being up to speed in digital-speak and its associated skill set. When I spoke to Bob Liodice, President and CEO of the Association of National Advertisers (ANA), he told me that digital advertising was one of the underlying themes of the 2007 ANA Conference. "Media has been changing steadily for several years and consumers have been changing their behavior as a result. With eight out of ten consumers online, agencies and brand organizations are, quite frankly, the laggards in the equation. Digital technology cannot be marginalized as a way of reaching and connecting with consumers. By its very nature, it promotes connections and extends the brand conversation. That's what building a brand is about. It's no longer a matter of *if* consumers will change their behavior, but how fast and whether we can keep up."

There's no dearth of information about how online marketing budgets have increased exponentially since Drew and his colleagues fought for a legitimate piece of the pie. According to a recent five-year forecast by Forrester Research, online advertising budgets are set to reach $26 billion by 2010. The Forrester forecast suggests that search applications will be the primary driver behind the changes, representing a whopping $11.6 billion. (If you don't believe me, Google the study.) When asked, as part of the research study, 47 percent of marketers said they would fund increased online spending by upping total media spending. Polled about the efficacy of one media channel over another, 53 percent of responders said they believed television spending would be less effective; 53 percent said print classified ads would be less effective; and 46 percent said newspaper advertising would be less effective. While not quite ready to dismiss traditional media (and they shouldn't), media professionals are quickly learning more about how to determine where people are getting their information, who these people are, and where brand organizations should be putting their money.

To paraphrase the old saying, the only thing that's consistent about this new digital branding space phenomenon is that it will keep changing. We don't need headlines to tell us this. We're as much the participants in this new age of branding as everyone else. The professionals who build the brands use personal, portable means of communications as much, if not more, than the consumers they're trying to reach. It might be wise to know as much, if not more, about the topic than they do.

SIMPLE TRUTHS, NOT PREDICTIONS

I spoke to a great many people when researching this book. Opinions abounded along with myriad predictions about how brands and brand building would be affected by digital tools and behaviors. As one might expect, given that predictions are largely shaped by one's perspective and personal experience, there were very few that overlapped. This book is not based on predictions. It's based on what everyone, no matter what their role or responsibility in the industry, has agreed upon. While each had his or her own view of the digital space—depending on where they sat within an organization, in strategy development or creative execution, in managing a corporate brand division or in managing a communications agency— all conversations on the topic reflected a simple, single, undeniable reality. This reality was, perhaps, most concisely articulated by Charlie Wrench, who is chairman and president of Landor. I use his quote not because he is my boss (although it can't hurt), but because what he said encapsulates all the thoughts on the topic beautifully. "The digital world has not changed the principles of branding but rather has magnified everything we know to be true about building a great brand. The tenets we've always followed have been made more visible by digital technology. The importance they play in our work has only become more obvious."

Digital technology has *not* changed the basic principles of brand building. What once was necessary to do our jobs is still necessary. Whether one refers to it as a channel, a medium, a discipline—whether one considers it a novelty, a mystery, or just another fact of life—the digital world, if anything, has served to redefine the scale of power of the essential truths of branding. Expressed in every interview for this book was the idea that the technological devices that marketers have at their disposal amplify and clarify the tools of our trade—from the way we go about learning what's relevant to our customers, to the products and services developed as the result of our findings. The personal, portable, online arena makes clear that the rules of good branding are unassailable.

Here's what I mean. It's a branding truism that the best brands are based on powerful, yet simple, consumer insights. In fact, one of the only sustainable competitive advantages a brand organization has is getting a terrific insight about its customers that it can call its own. Way back when, for example, coffee was known more for its ability to wake us up than its ability to bring us together to chat over lattes, the brand managers for Maxwell House had an insight that differentiated the brand from its competition and rocketed it to the top of the category list where it remained for years. This simple yet compelling insight was that people had trouble brewing consistently good-tasting coffee. One day it was too bitter, another day too weak, the next day too strong. They took this insight to their coffee genies who developed a brew they promised would be "Good to the Last Drop." It was. A nation of grateful coffee drinkers immediately grasped the simple idea behind the promise and was duly rewarded with the perfect cup of coffee seven days a week. American Express had the brilliantly clear insight that even the most experienced travelers became nervous at the thought of losing their money while abroad or, worse, having their pockets picked at some exotic destination. "Don't leave home without it" became the serious, yet simple idea that travelers worldwide took to heart, and took with them in the form of American Express charge cards and Traveler's Cheques. Much more recently, Sergey Brin and Larry Page, the young founders of Google, had what now seems like an obvious insight—the fast proliferating amount of information becoming available as a result of the Internet was overwhelming to people. They responded to this perception by deciding to "organize the world's information and make it universally accessible and useful." Had it been that obvious, it would have been two different techies with billions in the bank in charge of a company that, according to ComScore, does about four hundred billion searches a year. Suffice it to say, their insight has made searching for information a billion times easier.

Today, because of the magnifying effects of digital technology, marketers can see much more clearly what consumers are thinking, what they're experiencing, and what they're actually doing relative to the buying process. This fly-on-the-wall perspective gives them the ability to develop insights that are far more compelling and that can yield far more effective solutions. The Internet and all things digital have amplified what consumers are saying and doing about the things that irk them and the things that make them happy relative to life, to brands, and to everything else, for that matter. As marketers, we have unimpeded access to customers' thoughts and actions—whether they're posted on blogs, on corporate websites, on the "Walls" of social networks, or on industry discussion and review boards. Search, and ye shall find. Everything is out there under one big magnifying glass.

Concurrently, another truth in branding that has been magnified in the digital arena is that success is far sweeter when you deliver the right message to the right people at the right time. Digital technology has sharpened our focus. We can target the people who really want the things we offer. (And, conversely, they can refine their searches for goods, services, and information. They can find us more easily when they want something.) We now have the ability to observe at a more granular level where people are picking up branded messages and which messages are the ones closing the sale. Testing aficionados are in their glory. They can test, and use the results of their testing, more efficiently. The value of data as a brand-building tool has been magnified tenfold, if not more. We have unparalleled access to real time information about what people search for, what they buy, where they buy it, and how they make their purchase decisions. We have facts and

15

figures about consumer likes and dislikes—good old demographics, and new demographics sliced and diced and tested in ways we never imagined. Brand organizations adept at the use of existing data are just getting up to speed on how to take advantage of the new data sources.

Smart companies have always been able to pretty much figure out what matters to a somewhat well-defined group of consumers. Digital tools are allowing them to fine-tune the "pretty much" and the "somewhat." In fact, it's becoming hard to miss what matters most to the people who matter most to our brand success. We have never before had the opportunity to get so much real-time insight, and with such clarity, relative to how consumers behave and what's important to them. Nor have we had the opportunity to respond to what we've learned so quickly and with such a degree of relevance. This leads to another truth about branding that has been magnified in the digital arena: the need for a company to establish and hold onto a point of relevant brand differentiation if it wants to succeed in the long term.

While many think that creating awareness is the first step to building a strong brand, the fact remains that it's necessary to determine what meaningful difference you want your brand to represent in the minds of consumers before you start shouting about it. Digital tools shine a very bright light on what one brand stands for compared to all the other brands on the shelf and provide reasons why consumers should care. These tools serve to magnify the differences among brands, as well as to accelerate the pace at which people can compare and discover the qualities or benefits that separate one brand from another. Consumers can access so much information so easily that comparing and contrasting has become a natural part of the buying process, if not a habit. And, while it's always been true that people can more easily connect with brands that distinguish themselves by expressing an emotional reason to believe their promise rather than touting a fact or figure, laddering up to an emotional point of difference has become a far greater success factor in the online space. Face value has little value at all. With noise and clutter amplified, with digital technology flattening the competitive playing field, companies are recognizing that basing a brand's difference on something other than a functional benefit—bigger, faster, stronger—has become an increasingly important factor in standing out from the crowd. Promises are profuse. With millions of eyes and ears as judge and jury, brands must now promise and fulfill a higher-order need to maintain their place of honor in the minds of consumers. This is as true for the most basic commodity products, like tissues and laundry detergent, as it is for brands that more readily lend themselves to emotional engagement, like entertainment and beauty. The ability to get clothes cleaner is no longer a meaningful enough promise on which to maintain category leadership.

Brand organizations are also just beginning to understand the power that digital tools play in opinion sharing. It's a truth that talk value in brand building is significant. The Internet and other digital devices have made the spreading of opinion as virulent as viral communication can get. This is both a wonderful opportunity and one that must be carefully monitored. Moms who live continents apart can share their stories about how a particular diaper rash remedy worked wonders on their toddlers' tushes. In less than a day a million moms are out buying the goo. A cook in Caracas raves about a certain kind of frying pan, and all of a sudden there's a worldwide shortage of this type of frying pan. People pass along their views and in an instant, these are views with global ramifications. Al Gore understood this very well in relation to his *Inconvenient Truth*. Digital technology was, in very good part, responsible for the increase in awareness of our planet's environmental challenges, and, in equal part, has been responsible for corporate and individual responses to this challenge.

However, as I said, the same digital opinion sharing that can cause a brand's stock to rise can cause it to fall just as quickly. When one mom tells another who tells another about a toy that poses a choking threat, it's definitely not fun and games for the manufacturer, especially when the general media picks up the word being spread, which happens more often and with less filtering than ever before. The degree to which brand organizations, politicians, and anyone in the public domain must listen to what's being said about them has been magnified to the Nth degree.

While the assets and liabilities of talk power have been magnified in general, the role that good storytelling plays in brand building has also been reinforced by digital technology. From the woman who wanted to know where the beef was and ended up at Wendy's to the man who couldn't believe he ate the whole thing and ended up with an Alka-Seltzer; from the Bud Lite frogs to the Geico gecko, consumers love brand stories well told. They used to hang out and laugh about them at the water cooler. Digital tools have become *virtual* water coolers. Brand stories are passed along, talked about, complemented, and spoofed with glee and velocity (which, by the way, is not always a bad thing, as I'll talk about later). Creativity has never gone out of style, but the value of brilliantly creative ideas and fabulous creative execution has been blown up and blown out of the water by digital technology. The screens may be smaller, but the bigger the ideas the bigger the return on creative investment.

Perhaps the most important truth about building a great brand is that in order to succeed you must deliver what you promise. Digital is a two-way street. Just as we can see consumers with more clarity, consumers can see brands with equal clarity. Corporate behavior has been made highly visible, and the ability to see whether a company's products and services meet consumer expectations has been magnified. Made equally visible are all corporate actions, from the way employees are treated to the company's philanthropic initiatives. In the digital world you are who you are, not what you say you are. There is no place to run and no place to hide. Digital technology has, without question, made it possible for everyone on the planet to observe a brand's actions and judge whether it's meeting its promissory obligations. McCann Erickson's motto, "The Truth Well Told," might well be expanded to "The Truth Well Told and Delivered." Brand organizations must make good on their brand promises like never before. They must deliver the goods and services with nary a slip.

It's been said by many that digital technology has put consumers in control. Every good marketer knows consumers have always been in control. Now, however, there are more ways for consumers to report on what they experience. The control they've always had has been greatly enhanced. Brand organizations, if they're smart, must take more of a controlling interest in what consumers experience and the things they say and do as a result. I had a fascinating conversation with Faith Popcorn, author and influential trend forecaster and CEO of her company, Faith Popcorn's BrainReserve, who talked to me about what she called the "goodness factor." "Companies are under a microscope," she said. "Consumers have the ability to look at what they're up to with a greater degree of scrutiny. What they're looking for is how good the companies are, meaning is the company honest? Is it environmentally aware and responsive? What are its corporate practices relative to its hiring or philanthropic activities? As the world gets more frustrating and more complex, the demand for goodness from institutions is growing. I believe the digital age will force companies to behave with more integrity and truthfulness than ever before."

This is not a bad thing. Digital technology allows us to learn more about how corporations and other institutions are behaving. From interviewee to interviewee there was almost unanimous agreement that digital technology serves up information on an order of magnitude that is bigger, louder, and plainer than day. The technological tools and the behaviors consumer responses engender enable marketers to get better information about customers, to reach consumers exactly when and how they'd like to be reached, and to deliver products and services that are better as a result of the received input. Because of its magnifying effect, digital technology allows, if not forces, brand professionals to do what they do with greater speed, greater accuracy, greater efficiency, greater creativity, and greater honesty. That's the truth. And that's what this book is about.

A DIGITAL LANGUAGE

There's an entirely new lexicon for the things we use and things we do in the digital world. A list of the most utilized words and phrases will follow in a moment. I think it's critical, however, to start with two words that are not new, by any means, but that must be clarified: the words **brand** and **branding.** The difference in meaning between these words is the difference between success and possible failure, in both the analog and digital worlds.

A brand is something that lives in your head. It's a promise that links a product or service to a consumer. Whether conjured up as words or images or emotional responses, brands are the mental associations that surface when you think or hear about a particular car, a cookie, a computer, a set of skis, a toy, a beverage, a bank, a search engine, a charitable organization, a celebrity, or even a country. To put it in the context of this book, when a brand's name comes up in conversation, the mental cursor in your head clicks on the brand's file name, and all the associations you have with the brand are downloaded into your brain.

Branding, on the other hand, is what companies and their partners do to get consumers to think about and form associations with the brand. Among the most basic branding applications are logos and colors, packaging and signage. Then there's advertising, which should not be confused with branding. It's a branding application. Advertising used to be mostly of the television, print, direct mail, outdoor signage, and radio variety. As a result of technological advances, advertising now includes a great number of digital formats; some of them include banner ads, online classified ads, online videos, text ads, and e-mail ads. There are many others, but you get the idea.

In addition to those mentioned above, branding applications also include websites, public relations, events and promotions, retail environments, consumers' customer service experiences, music and sound effects, not to mention the design and functionality of the product you're trying to brand. If something doesn't work the way consumers expect it to, they have had a bad brand association. If consumers experience your brand by touching it, viewing it, or hearing it in any way and it relates to your brand, it's a branding application. The best brand organizations ensure that wherever and however consumers interact with their brands, the consumer experience is consistent with the promise of the brand. Branding applications must deliver on what the brand wants us associate with it. If they don't, they're useless at best, and in some cases harmful to the brand's reputation, and ultimately, its value. This is another of the fundamentals of building brands, which has absolutely not changed.

Today, in addition to what's now being referred to as "traditional branding," there are a variety of new branding applications that have emerged as a result of digital technology. Some are created and controlled by brand professionals, and some aren't. The online advertising and promotions, the mobile messaging, and the initiatives that integrate both traditional and digital formats are, for the most part, created by brand organizations and agencies. In some cases, agencies have requested advertising content ideas from consumers. (This is another topic I'll cover later on in the book.) One of the most significant changes brand organizations must deal with, however, are the branding applications that take place outside their purview. These are blogs, product reviews—requested and not—word of mouth generated within online communities, and the branded consumer-generated content that shows up on YouTube and eventually on CNN, Fox, and Comedy Central. Remember, if a consumer views it, hears it, or experiences it, and it relates to your brand, it's a branding application, whether or not you're responsible for its existence.

Consumers create branding applications, whether or not they even know they're branding applications. The key to successful branding in the personal, portable digital marketplace is to get a better understanding of how these branding applications should or shouldn't be integrated into the overall branding mix in order to generate positive consumer associations with a brand and mitigate negative associations. Having said that, let's go on to the more technical terminology.

Here is a list of the terms that anyone in the business of brands today must be familiar with. My objective in putting it first is to make sure we're all operating from the same playbook.

Avatar: The persona a Web user creates to participate in a virtual world, such as Second Life. In most cases an avatar's appearance can be created and then changed as desired. Avatars communicate with one another within virtual spaces via simultaneous text and/or speech.

Banner ad: An online promotional advertisement, typically rectangular in size, analogous to a print advertisement. Clicking on a banner ad generally takes the viewer to the sponsor company's website. The two primary types of banner ads are display, which is static in nature, and rich media, which allows user interaction.

Blog: Originating from the phrase "Web log," much like a captain's log, most blogs are akin to personal journals or diaries. Other blogs may be more like magazine columns, editorial in nature, and focus on a particular area of interest such as politics, sports technology, culture, or business. The term also refers to websites that feature personal thoughts or musings on various subjects. A blog can contain the ideas or opinions of any person (or organization) who wants to share these ideas or opinions with others. Terms like "vlog" (video Web log), "moblog" (mobile web log) and "flog" (fake blog, in which the writer masks his or her true identity), tend to crop up in media analysis of online trends.

Content management: This refers to the management of information on a website. A content management strategy is the plan by which an organization determines which information is required for its site, how often the information should be updated, how it should be edited, how long it should remain on the site, and how or whether users can contribute to the site. A content management system is the system software that is developed to manage the process of creating, updating, approving, and posting information on the site.

Information architecture: This is the navigational structure of a website: the layout and flow of information. It's the discipline of determining the best and most brand-appropriate way to present information so that it meets user needs and expectations. Information architecture is a template that portrays how a user will move through the site, how many pages the site will have, and how users will link from one page to the next. It shows how many elements appear on each page of the site and prioritizes the importance of the information and, thus, its placement on an individual page and within each section of the site.

Long tail: This is a phrase coined by Chris Anderson in an article in the October 2004 issue of Wired magazine. The "long tail" refers to the way online commerce and culture has changed the distribution curve of products and services. As a result of Internet dynamics, products or services with low demand or sales volume can now collectively comprise a market that exceeds the best sellers at the "head" of the market. The Internet provides enormous opportunities for smart niche organizations to capitalize on buying behavior of fragmented market groups.

Mash-up: This term originally referred to the combination of two audio or video entities to create a new entity. For example, when the disc jockey, Danger Mouse, combined Jay-Z's Black Album with the Beatles' White Album to create the Grey Album he created a mash-up. The term now covers a broader array of "mashing" two elements together (often copyrighted material) to create a newly configured idea, generally in the form of advertising communications. A consumer who takes an existing television advertisement and changes the music or images in some way has created a mash-up. However, the term is also used to describe a Web page or application that integrates elements from difference sources such as Flash Earth (a zoom-able mash-up of Google Maps and Microsoft's Virtual Earth, Yahoo! Maps, Ask.com or NASA Terra.)

Podcast: This refers to an audio file downloaded from a website. This file can be played on demand using an iPod or any other MP3 player.

QR Codes: The "QR" in this term refers to quick response. Much like the one pictured on page 25, it is similar to the UPC code found on grocery and other retail items which are scanned at the cash register. QR codes found on products can be read by cell phones and will directed to branded Web pages to give the user more information. While not widespread in the United States, almost

"Quick Response Code"

every cell phone produced in Japan has the ability to read and recognize QR codes and, as such, play an integral part in the marketing and branding strategies. Consumers can scan these codes with their cell phones and get information on events and promotions, reviews, and detailed product information.

RSS: This is a cold acronym for the friendly term "really simple syndication." It refers to the immediate digital delivery of information from a syndicated source, like a news, magazine, or industry site, to another site.

Search engine marketing: This refers to all of the activities designed and implemented to improve the user experience relative to online search referrals and results.

Search engine optimization (SEO): This refers to the strategies and techniques used to optimize a user's online search referrals and results. It is the assessment of a website's design, content and information to ensure that search engines such as Google, Yahoo!, or Ask.com can pull up the most relevant information possible for those searching for something online. There are two subsets to SEO: "paid" search which refers to service and product advertising which is paid for by the advertiser and appears in search results as a result of "key words" being bought by the advertiser; and "natural" search which refers to the free results which come about as a search engine picks up words naturally in its perusal of the Web.

Second Life®: Second Life is a 3D virtual world developed by Linden Lab inhabited by online avatars, or "Residents" – personas created by users of the site. Since opening to the public in 2003 its popularity has grown exponentially and it is inhabited by millions of Residents from around the globe. Many companies have created marketing initiatives within Second Life, including Adidas, MTV, Reuters, CBS, Harvard University, Coca-Cola, and Colgate. The site can be found at www.secondlife.com.

Social networks: This refers to the online sites such as MySpace, Facebook, and LinkedIn, on which like-minded people gather virtually to share their cultural and educational interests, their resumes, their political views, and their opinions of products and services, along with information about their lives, in general.

Twitter: This is a free online service that allows friends, family and co-workers to stay connected through the exchange of quick, frequent messages. It has been incorporated as a widget on Facebook, the iPhone and other interactive media devices.

User-generated content or video (UGC, UGV): This refers to any information created by consumers rather than marketers in response to a product or service. It includes product reviews, advertising, and videos. A number of marketers have used UGC as a branding tactic with mixed success.

Web 2.0: This term began as a reference to software releases. The first release of a software product is generally referred to as 1.0. Improvements are then released as 1.1, 1.2, 1.3, and so on. A major software overhaul is referred to 2.0. The term now refers to the ubiquitous use of the Internet as an integral part of life by a majority of the world's population as opposed to its relatively low level of adoption just a few years ago.

Widget/Gadget: This is a simple online application that allows people to add or edit information or graphic elements to Web pages, or to link or upload this information to other sites on the Internet.

Wiki: From the Hawaiian word, wiki-wiki, which means fast, a wiki is a type of software that allows immediate viewing and editing of online documents. It enables multiple people to edit the same document while viewing changes.

Word of mouth: This refers to information that is spread spontaneously from one person to another. In marketing, it refers to information about a product or service that is spread from one consumer to another. In the interactive arena, digital tools have increased the potential for information to be spread from person to person more quickly than ever before. Word of mouth is also referred to as "buzz marketing," that is, consumers create a buzz about a product or service. In this case, viewers find some online content so amusing, titillating or inspiring that they pass it along to their friends and colleagues. It's consumer-propelled public relations.

PART ONE

The Truths of Branding Magnified

1

The Importance of Gaining Superior Consumer Insight

When I was in college I spent summers as a waiter in a country club. While there wasn't a great deal of communication between me and the folks at the tables to which I was assigned, they did thank me or ask where I went to school. Other than these polite two-sentence exchanges, I did my job and kept to myself, which suited me just fine. I got to make great money (for a college kid), and, at the same time, got to listen in on some pretty interesting conversations. It wasn't eavesdropping; the club members were talking openly in front of me. For all intents and purposes, I was a fly on the wall. There was no way for me *not* to listen. Just the same, I used my position as a fly on the wall to great advantage. At that point in my life, I wanted to grow up to be the one sitting at a table in a country club, not the one waiting on tables. I became a sponge for information. I wanted to know what these people did for a living, what business deals they were working on (okay, even pick up a stock tip or two), learn about the best places to get a good buy on a waterfront home, find out where they skied, what their investment strategies were, what their political views were—and maybe even if they had daughters who might be interested in dating a hardworking communications major. Essentially, I was gaining insight about these people: where and how they lived, where they bought their bespoke suits, the types of cars they drove, the boats they owned, the golf clubs they used, and the investment firms they trusted.

A segue isn't really required here, but digital technology allows marketers to listen in on the millions of conversations taking place online every minute of every day among participants sitting around a global table. They can listen to what's being said on blogs, on category review sites, on product review sites, within social networks, and on any other digital venue in which people can have their say. And there are a lot of them—venues *and* people having their say. The Internet has magnified both the extent of these conversations and the level of volume. Given the perceived sense of anonymity, people feel comfortable sharing everything. It's like a virtual psychiatrist's office. Marketers can listen in on conversations about everything happening—online or off, on the record and off: Celebrities, the weather, politics, books, music, movies, car insurance, mortgage rates, terrorist activities, environmental issues, feeding their families, feeding the people in Darfur; how to get a date, get rid of a mate, name a baby, diaper a baby, deal with a mother-in-law; and the companies, products, and services they love, hate, would do business with, would consider doing business with, would hands-down recommend, would wish only ill will upon; and everything else marketers have been researching and focusing on as long as there have been companies, products, and services. Suffice it to say, if anyone is talking about it, everyone else can hear it and weigh in with an opinion.

The other thing that has been magnified in the digital space is not just how people talk, but how they behave, specifically when it comes to their buying habits and activities. Marketers can observe in real time what people are searching for, their buying process, the way they compare and contrast products or services or prices, where they go for advice, the offers they deem relevant and those they don't, the specific features of a product that interests them, and which sites they return to for additional information or purchases. The ability to watch what people do, not just what they *say* they do, has become an incredible boon to marketers as they go about gaining insight about their customers and prospective customers. Randall Rothenberg, who is the President and CEO of the Interactive Advertising Bureau, told me about "Marketing Media Ecosystem 2010," a research study co-sponsored by the American Association of Advertising Agencies, the Association of National Advertisers, and Booz Allen. "The data that surprised me most," he said, "wasn't that *Fortune* 1000 marketers stated that gaining an understanding of social networking or media capabilities were among the top priorities. It was that 80 percent said that gaining behavioral targeting capabilities was their number two priority and that 88 percent stated that the *number one* priority was using technology to gain better consumer insights. It's apparent that marketers see interactive tools as a critical component to getting a more granular understanding of consumers, their interests, needs and desires."

The ability to not just digitally listen but to digitally watch consumers in action has significantly sharpened the quality of the insights that brand organizations use in generating business and branding strategies. It's a must-have. Longish story short: The first thing any brand organization must do to be successful is to get insight about the people they want as customers. This is one of the fundamental truths about building a great brand. The better quality the insights are, the better the chances of meeting consumer needs and expectations, and, ergo, the better the chances of becoming a powerful brand. Digital technology is responsible for magnifying our understanding of what is on people's minds.

The marketplace, as Thomas Friedman discussed in his book *The World is Flat,* has become virtually flatter still as a result of digital technology, with words and actions audible and visible from one end of the planet to the other. As a matter of fact, in his new version of the book *The World is Flat 3.0,* Tom titles one of his chapters, "What Happens When We all Have Dogs' Hearing?" He spoke to me about his premise:

> In the digital space everyone's whispering but the whispering is magnified. It's like we've all developed dogs' hearing. The challenge is that because there is so much going on out there it could become overwhelming to marketers. The key to gaining meaningful insight about your audience is to be able to distinguish between the whisper of information that's legitimate and defensible and the information that will take you down the wrong path. Marketers, politicians, anyone or any institution using the Internet to get insight into how people think or feel must develop what I call "judgment algorithms." The information is there for the taking, but ultimately you're the one responsible for determining what's trustworthy. There is a future for trusted sources of information, for trustworthy aggregators of information. The Internet as a means of getting raw information is becoming more perfect. But it's still a matter of judgment as to what's applicable to your needs.

The Internet has made searching for information easier, and it *is* getting more perfect. It is without a doubt one of the digital tools that has been responsible for the seismic shift in the way brand organizations get information and form insights about consumers. As a branding tool, search functionality has significantly magnified the online words and deeds of consumers. It may be one of the best ways to get real-time insights about consumers since Procter & Gamble's Dawn brand team sent researchers into homes across the country to watch how housewives washed dishes. Search, as a way of getting insight, has enhanced the opportunity for brand organizations to hear directly what matters most to people and to determine if their words complement their actions. Search has allowed us, as marketers, to see more clearly whether we're spending millions of dollars developing things our intended audience has been yearning for or whether we're directing branding dollars and communications to the entirely wrong audience.

Search most definitely allows marketers to collect "raw information." It's a science, a very complex science. Perhaps even more complex, however, is the art required to take the data that comes out of the mystical black box, as many in the industry call it, and apply personal judgment based on practical experience. Good marketers know that data is good. Being able to assess the value of data in relation to a business strategy is better. The magic of search for brand organizations is that it has made mining for data about consumer behavior more efficient and more economical. The practical magic of search, however, is that it gives brand organizations a greater body of facts, figures, and mathematical algorithms over which to wave their sound judgment wands. Search is getting more perfect, and this is wonderful. What's more valuable, however, is that search is forcing marketers to learn how to optimize their consumer insights to better meet their business objectives.

Among the people I spoke to about the ABC's of search was Heather Frahm, one of the experts at Catalyst, a company that specializes in search marketing strategies, research, and analysis. From my relatively naïve perspective, I asked her to tell me where search fits into the brand-building process. Without a moment's hesitation she said, "At the very beginning. You must integrate a search strategy into the first draft of your overall marketing strategy. How are you going to know how to position your brand or create effective campaigns if you don't know exactly what people are searching for?" I asked her to elaborate. "Today, search is one of the primary ways consumers get into all phases of the buying cycle. In fact, 40 percent of all online search activity is related to someone's seeing an ad or a promotion, an article or a news story about a new product, and wanting more information about it. It's become a universally automatic response to go to the Internet, log onto a search engine, and expect answers. The right answers. Smart marketers use search as the incredible learning tool it is, and they use it at the start of a project, not as an afterthought. It makes no sense to get a team started on the creative strategy without taking search into consideration." She gave me an example:

> Let's say your company sells prescription medication for hypertension, which some consumers refer to as high blood pressure. By studying search results on the topic before you do anything else, you can see which terminology people use and in what context they use it as they go about their online searching. In this case, at a very simplistic level, are they trying to learn more about 'hypertension' or 'high blood pressure,' or do they refer to the condition by some other term altogether? Finding this out can be the simple difference between someone getting information about your brand versus your competitor's. Data derived from search also allows you to track what happens after someone clicks from one place to another, whether they go to one particular Web page, whether they immediately jump to another, or spend time perusing a bunch. It also allows you to see what activities take place after they land at these destinations. This helps you assess the intent of the search. You use what you learn in order to be able to position your message appropriately at the appropriate time in a buying cycle. Your brand campaign should be built on this insight, and not developed before you get it. More than this, because post-launch content has to be in sync with everything else, you've got to be ready for consumers to search for additional information within minutes of their being exposed to the initial campaign material. This has to be worked in up front. Search has given us the ability to see what consumers actually do in real time, by the millions. We can observe their behavior and use the information to reward their search efforts with relevant information. A good search strategy is critical to a brilliant branding strategy and the subsequent creative execution. Who wouldn't want to put their marketing dollars where they belong?

Who, indeed? But the secret to a good search strategy is found between the lines. Thousands of lines of code and data. As I said in the introduction to this book, you must be able to read between the lines of all you hear and see and read to determine what's relevant to your brand, and, ultimately, to your business. You must be able to make sense of the thousands of possible information algorithms that relate to what an individual might be looking for or concerned about at any given point in time. This is one of the complexities of the undertaking for which most brand organizations turn to other organizations, like Catalyst, for guidance. While it isn't necessary to go into great detail on exactly what these search experts do, it is necessary for marketers to have a fundamental knowledge of how search works in order to incorporate it into their branding tool kit. In short, there are two basic search categories: paid and organic. Paid is paid. Anyone with something to sell can buy search terms and place ads that relate to these terms. A search engine will pick up these ad links and offer them up within the overall inventory of responses to a search inquiry, albeit on a separate section of the response page. While this is definitely applicable to branding strategy, it's more important to understand how a search engine processes organic content to generate these mystical algorithms related to online human behavior. Organic content includes everything from brand websites, brand-sponsored pages on social sites like MySpace and Facebook, and all other online locations on which your brand name might appear, such as blogs, product review sites, industry or general media sites. Some of this content can be controlled by the brand, some absolutely not. The Web is, if anything, democratic. Anyone can say anything about your brand if they want to, which is a chapter unto itself. Suffice it to say, the possible brand-related algorithms are endless.

Be that as it may, there are three basic things a search engine does as it goes about serving up answers associated with organic content.

The first thing it does is "spider" the Web. This is just what it sounds like. The search engine—be it Google, Yahoo, Ask.com, or any other—sends a number of virtual spider tools crawling across the Internet looking for words or phrases related to the search request. As they crawl along, the spiders pick up these words and phrases, which they then put into the search engine's database to be indexed. It's the responsibility of search professionals to make sure that sites over which the brand has control—specifically a corporate website or brand-sponsored MySpace page—are designed so that spiders can "see" the words and phrases the brand organization wants them to see as clearly as possible and in the context in which they want them to be read. Going back to the example Heather provided, if you sell hypertension medication, you want to make sure that your brand-controlled content includes the exact words and phrases the consumers you're interested in attracting use to describe this condition at various points in the buying cycle. Are they trying to learn about the symptoms? Are they looking for side effects of the medication itself? Are they comparing the cost of your medication to the cost of a competitor's medication? All are good questions, and all are key to gaining insight about your target audience. Search strategy starts with making sure your site has the right code words.

When I talked to Jen Walsh, the Digital Media Director for General Electric, she told me that her team completely overhauled GE.com, introducing all new content, design, and technology because they knew the website could be a much stronger brand and messaging platform for the company. "Simple navigation, clean design, and clear use of language and terminology are the underpinnings of the site," she told me.

Our former site had over three thousand pages. This one has five hundred pages, but each serves a distinct purpose. We streamlined the navigation and spent a good deal of effort each month telling GE's story through our homepage features. In addition, we have worked to ensure that search terms link people directly to what they are looking for immediately. There are no vague words or plays on words. Aviation links you to information on aviation. Electronics gets you to electronics, lighting to lighting. What's more, because we get a lot of traffic from outside the United States, we were careful in the redesign to include global headers to help people find their way to local sites in local languages. Everything we did added to the credibility and value of our brand.

I spent time exploring GE.com, and discovered it was as simple to find what I was searching for as Jen described. I also found the content to be incredibly well organized, which is part and parcel of the second step in the search engine process. Search engines categorize online content. They "read" the content at the most literal level for its relevancy to a particular search inquiry. Obviously, it's critical that the search engine understands your branded content the way you intended it to be understood. Your primary objective is to give people who are searching for something in particular a relevant response to their query. When Gillette launched their Gillette Champions promotion featuring Tiger Woods, for example, the company created a specific Web page to explain the promotion. This page was added to the other pages on the brand's site, which includes topics like product information, shaving tips, and corporate news. The search-savvy people at Gillette made sure that any search engine reading the Web page about the Gillette Champions promotion read it as just that: Here's everything you need to know about this exciting event. It's not that the company was afraid that some pre-pubescent golfer would end up on the Gillette information page about razor burn; it's just that it wouldn't have been all that meaningful to the young shaver; he wanted to read about Tiger Woods. To get insight about people, you need to understand their intent. When you give them exactly what they're looking for in return, it makes them feel pretty good about your brand. Not a bad equity-building opportunity.

The third thing a search engine does as it spiders through the information is to evaluate the level of authority or credibility that specific content has among people who are searching for answers on a particular subject. Of the millions of pages on the Internet, these are the pages or sites that turn up most often as germane to specific queries. Search engines also determine which sites are most often linked to from other sites. What trail do people follow in their search for precisely what they want, and where do they end up, having found exactly what they're after? You want your online content to be deemed authoritative by the search engine. You also want anything that prompts a link to your site to add to your brand's credibility, as Jen Walsh said of the GE site, not to detract from it. Having your branded content show up most often as the most applicable response to a search query is a very cost-effective way to build brand awareness, not to mention esteem. Having it turn up in a manner totally at odds with your brand promise is neither cost effective nor valuable in any way at all.

Another person I spoke to about how search has magnified the importance of getting good customer insight before starting any branding venture was John Nardone, a co-founder of Modem Media, one of the earliest and still most prescient digital marketing firms, and now with [x + 1] marketing. John told me that when it comes to the value of search as a branding tool, you've got to think about the old adage, "garbage in, garbage out." More specifically, what John said was:

> You must be clear from the start how you want to use search to help you meet specific business objectives. Your search strategy should clearly articulate the value that consumers are meant to derive from each keyword. This will give you guidance for what you should measure. The old metrics associated with successful search had to do with the number of clicks or the amount of traffic

a site received. This can give you a quantitative baseline of sorts, but you have to consider carefully the three or four key online search-related interactions connected to your business strategy if you want maximum benefit.

For example, one client reevaluated its search strategy after making an initial decision to optimize a single action rather than taking into consideration multiple consumer value points. The company was in the business of helping people lose weight by providing motivation and support from others in the same situation. It originally thought that people who searched for its name would be best served by linking to its website's "Meeting Finder" button where they could sign up for membership. The company established this consumer search activity as a metric for success and invested time and money making the initial click-to-landing page interaction simple and friendly. The company found, however, that while there were plenty of people who used search functionality to find meeting locations in their vicinity, this wasn't necessarily the behavior that was driving people to sign up. It learned that first routing consumers through product information and an explanation of benefits and membership options was more effective than having them go directly to a "location" finder. It was a valuable insight on the part of the brand organization. It led them to reevaluate which search interactions had the greatest effect on their business, and they began the work of putting them into place.

Among the other activities that search experts undertake to help brand organizations get insight about their customers is mapping what I refer to as conversational points of entry. There are lots of ways to talk about the same topic, and keeping a close eye on consumer discussions makes this evident. In a space where conversation is king, it's critical to identify the conversations most pivotal to gaining insight about what matters most to which audience. As Rob Norman, CEO of GroupM Interaction, said, "We're now in the position to hover on the backyard fence of millions of conversations. The key is to determine which conversations are relevant to what you sell. If you're in the food category, for instance, you can tap into and potentially add value to discussions that range from product ingredients, to what foods are healthy, to what do I feed my family for dinner, to what should we do about feeding people in Darfur."

This goes back, in some part, to monitoring the words or phrases people use to get at the information they want. But it also has to do with the many diverse and valuable points at which a brand can engage with consumers and become an appreciated member of the dialogue. Search generates lots and lots of information. But it also opens up doors to branding strategies an organization might not have considered; opportunities for a search engine's mathematical algorithms to intersect with the searcher's judgment algorithms. Tim Armstrong, President of Advertising and Commerce at Google, North America, put this in greater perspective:

Customers today actually have the power to help organizations expand their brand's meaning. The Internet allows real engagement between companies and customers and the customers are more than happy to provide insight about how a brand can be more useful to them. We're finding that there are more ways for a brand to play a part in peoples' lives, and it's consumers who are helping open the doors to these opportunities. Here's what I mean. Let's say I'm on the brand management team for a certain type of toothpaste. I'd want to have content on the Internet that brings people together to discuss basic oral care or the benefits of fluoride protection. That's obvious. Now, let's say a fifty-year-old woman goes to iVillage, a great website, and wants to get information about improving her overall health as she gets older, including her oral health. Toothpaste brand managers may not have appreciated the opportunity to engage in a conversation about oral care as it applies to the health of baby boomers until the iVillage user brought it to their attention. They might not have realized they could be part of a chat about oral care for babies until some curious dad went looking for ideas on parenting websites. When a kindergarten teacher goes in search of curriculum for her little charges, it's a chance for the brand team to be made aware that a placing an animated video on YouTube about how to brush your teeth might be a sensational learning tool and a dynamite brand builder. Brand organizations are just starting to realize that the ability to monitor what people are genuinely interested in enables them to expand the meaning and relevancy of their brand.

Tim went on to tell me about a meeting he had with the digital brand team at a major brewing company. Google had done a study for the company to determine the number of digital places people could connect with their brand. When he asked those at the table to take a guess at how many opportunities they had to engage with their target, the answers were in the one-or two-digit range: nine places, thirty-five places, and so on. When Tim explained that the study had uncovered 192,000 places on the Internet where the company could take part in a meaningful dialogue with its customer, the team was floored.

General Mills is a company well respected for its ability to gain insights about consumers and to use these insights to better serve up breakfast, lunch, and dinner the way people want them. In the 1960s the organization discovered that moms wanted to spend more time with the family and less time in the kitchen. With that in mind, its Betty Crocker brand introduced the "Helper" line of products, Hamburger Helper and Chicken Helper among them. When the company recognized that people knew they should eat their veggies, but that preparing fresh peas, carrots, and spinach was time-consuming, Green Giant scientists came to the rescue by finding a way to lock in the freshness of vegetables by freezing them and packaging them ready to cook and serve. True to character, General Mills also took an early interest in learning how to enhance its offerings to consumers by taking note of the different ways food was being talked about online. The brand once again turned insight into innovation, using its professional judgment to align its digital initiatives with its overall business strategy the brand's business.

Doug Moore, Vice President of Advertising and Media at General Mills, told me the company launched a successful new community

43

site called EatBetterAmerica.com after it realized that there were all sorts of online discussions among baby boomers relative to the friction between knowing you *should* eat better and *wanting* to eat better. "We used this insight to create a community site for boomers that would alleviate this friction," Doug said. "EatBetterAmerica.com was designed to make healthy eating and staying healthy a pleasant, even fun experience. The site is filled with practical content, but based on what we learned about this target, it was designed with a little sense of humor. Usually healthy eating is the big finger wag. It's the rules you have to follow. Baby boomers don't take well to finger-wagging tactics. EatBetterAmerica.com is about 'I want to' instead of 'I should do.'"

EatBetterAmerica.com is not linked to any particular brand. In fact, as General Mills used its findings to learn more about this market segment, the company realized it would make more sense to create the site as an open platform, allowing other companies to add content. This adds credibility and trustworthiness to the site and to the General Mills brand. In addition, by monitoring how consumers behave online from one group to another, General Mills discovered that baby boomers prefer their online experiences to be more Mac-like than PC-like. That is, they want to click on an article or a link and have it download instantly without having to wait for a PDF file to download. Data indicated that while this segment likes to spend some time exploring the Internet, they mostly want to get in, get what they're after, and get out.

I've been to the EatBetterAmerica.com site a few times, and each time I've found something different to read about and some interactive device to engage with. There's a section called "Body Explorer," for instance, where you can drag a type of food, say broccoli or a doughnut, to a dimensional profile of the human body and drop the food onto the profile. You then see the pros and cons of eating this type of food. You can observe the effect it has on your body,

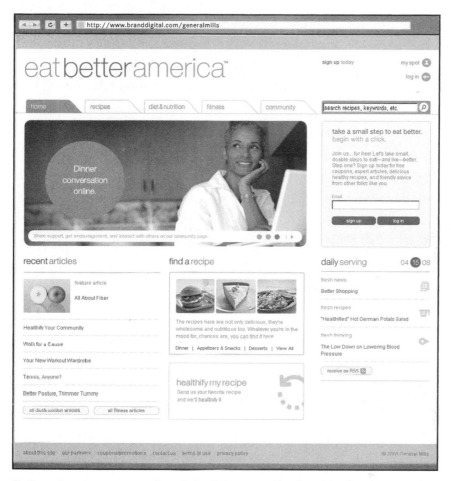

EatBetterAmerica.com, a non-branded website created by General Mills, connects with consumers on the critical issue of maintaining a healthy lifestyle.

what nutrients it provides or doesn't. Another simple tool is called "Healthify." Readers submit recipes, and the Healthify function demonstrates how to make the recipe healthier by adding or substituting various ingredients. EatBetterAmerica.com doesn't just give boomers a way to Healthify their own lives; but also to join a health-conscious community. Everything on the site makes you feel a little smarter, but it is General Mills who has done all the hard work. Their original insight has benefited boomers and the brand alike.

As in all brand initiatives, there are lots of digital opportunities to create customer experiences across multiple channels and dimensions. It's critical to the bottom line for marketers to determine which points of touch will yield the greatest return on investment. One of the beauties of the Internet is that while it allows real-time monitoring of consumer behavior, it also allows real-time testing of where and how and why consumers react to one idea instead of another. This adds to the value of the insights gained from digital searching. Digital technology makes for the perfect environment in which to create and test hundreds of messages against multiple audiences within a finite amount of time. This means a fundamental shift in the way brand strategy might be developed. A number of folks I spoke to who worked with major brand organizations told me they'd started moving away from one big annual planning session, one big idea, and one big media schedule in order to accommodate on-the-fly opportunities that became apparent as a result of ongoing testing. Testing and managing data have become far more sophisticated over the last five years. Assessment models allow precise targeting against individual users and for specific digital devices. Testing and measuring, as it relates to brand strategy, has evolved almost as quickly as the digital space itself. It's had to. Shelley Zalis, Founder of OTX, an acronym that stands for online testing exchange, talked to me about some of the changes in her area of expertise.

The way we used to test and measure was much more linear. Technology has blown the doors off traditional research methods by allowing us to interact with, and ultimately engage, consumers in the very ways they think and act. Technology has helped us create richer, more immersive, and contextual survey environments. This results in more focused, thoughtful, and useful responses. There's as much art as there is science in the research enabled by technology and, when done well, it yields more instinctive and honest responses. Ultimately, because consumers have enthusiastically embraced how technology allows them to communicate and express themselves, research companies have no choice but to do the same to truly help their clients understand where consumers are coming from.

As Shelley said, agency research departments and independent research companies like OTX *don't* have a choice when it comes to using the same technology consumers are using to gain valuable insights about these consumers. Digital tools help marketers listen better, and observe more clearly. Almost overnight, there have been some fascinating new tools developed to help gauge and measure what's being said and done online, the objective being, of course, to help give brand organizations a competitive advantage relative to their customers' behavior. Measurement tactics now include things like video diaries and video blogs. Researchers use semiotics (the science of signs and signals) as well as ethnographics (how culture influences behavior) and geotargeting (the process that allows marketers to direct messages to people in specific geographic locations). WPP, a global marketing communications firm and parent of Landor, has a unit called Buzzmetrics that studies word of mouth and how it spreads in the digital world. The field of biometrics has grown to the extent that consumers are literally wired to devices that can monitor their heart rates, brain waves, and eye movements in response to branded stimuli. Return on investment has been a part of the branding equation since day one. It used to be one of the inherent costs of business that it was necessary for marketers to buy the attention of people they didn't necessarily want to talk to, mixed along with the people they did. That's the un-beauty of mass marketing. As the digital age advances, it seems marketers will have the chance to buy the attention of only the most valuable audiences. It's not a reality yet, but it seems we're getting close. Adam Gerber, Chief Marketing Officer of Quantcast, a company that focuses on delivering more precise audience measurement of digital media, offered a hypothetical (but potentially very real) example of what's possible.

> Let's say you're a large appliance retailer, and you have a phenomenal database. You've kept good records of people who bought washing machines and dishwashers. Given your knowledge of appliances, you know exactly how long one brand of appliance is apt to last versus another. This is incredibly valuable if you want to reach out to someone just before their appliance needs to be replaced. Even better, let's say you've been collecting data about how to best reach these customers and others who could be considered "look-alikes," consumers who connect with media in the same way, be it via the Web, a specific website, a mobile phone, or through e-mail or direct mail. When you can map how people are actually connecting to brands on top of knowing their buying behavior or brand preference, it makes your ROI that much better.

In my first book, *BrandSimple,* I wrote about the Nikon brand, specifically its understanding that getting good consumer insight is critical before launching into a market—in the case I cited, the point-and-shoot market. In order to expand into this space, Nikon wanted to get insight about how to overcome its reputation as a camera brand solely for professional photographers without damaging its equity among loyal Nikon users. The company's insights, gathered in the days before the digital search age, allowed them to successfully "de-niche" their niche brand image by proving how even the average consumer could take fabulous pictures automatically. Fast forwarding to the digital age, specifically the digital camera age, Nikon looked to digital technology to help get insight about how to market its new digital Nikon D40. In their forward-thinking strategy, the company let consumers do the lion's share of the talking as part of the initiative.

Michael Jacobs, Executive Creative Director of MRM, an interactive agency that works with Nikon, gave me an overview of the campaign called "Picturetown." "Nikon wanted to get more learning about the concerns people had about digital cameras," he said.

> It saw an opportunity to harness both the power of consumer testimony and the power of the Internet as a way of gaining insight. The company sent representatives to Georgetown, South Carolina who handed out two hundred of its D40s to ordinary people, amateur photographers who represented a range of consumer segments. They told these folks to take pictures, and that's exactly what they did, by the hundreds. The Nikon representatives also told these amateur photographers to report back what they learned about the D40. From one person to the next, they reported back how easy the camera was to use. The lack of shutter delay meant they could just keep shooting and shooting and get the photos they wanted. They liked the big screen and the fast auto-focus. They talked, and Nikon listened. Using the information they gave us, we were able to understand exactly how to market the camera. As a branding tactic, we made a video in partnership with Flickr, an online photography site, which integrated the stories they told and the pictures they took. The video was titled "Picturetown," and it became the focus of the Nikon launch for the D40, anchoring and integrating the online and offline branding.

Nikon did more than make Picturetown the focus of its D40 launch. It made stunningnikon.com/picturetown/ the centerpiece of its search optimization efforts directing anyone in search of information about digital cameras to the site. The beauty of the site—and it is literally beautiful—is that it is an absolute delight to interact with. Lisa Baxt, Senior Manager of Communications for Nikon, talked about the significance of the site:

> The site, stunningnikon.com/picturetown/, plays a primary role in the campaign, as it's the destination where consumers can immerse themselves in the Picturetown experience. On the site, consumers meet the real inhabitants of Picturetown, view their actual pictures, and experience the Nikon D40 through their eyes. The site is an opportunity for consumers to become truly engaged with the townspeople and see how the D40 transformed their

In its Picturetown initiative, Nikon harnessed the power of the Internet and the power of consumer insights to help them market their new D40 camera.

picture-taking abilities. Nikon has received positive feedback from the residents of Georgetown, South Carolina as well as from consumers who have seen and reacted to the site. When you can put cameras in peoples' hands and let their experiences tell the story, it resonates.

The site has continued to evolve and support Nikon's consumer-centric, communications approach by creating an environment in which engaging the consumer with real-world scenarios is the goal. Since October 2006, Nikon has been following twelve photo enthusiasts, "Passionate Shooters," who are using the Nikon D80 digital SLR in order to communicate how this camera assists them in capturing the images and experiences they are passionate about. There is also an organic element to the campaign as these enthusiasts have shared their pictures on photo communities, including Flickr, and have received a huge amount of interest and positive feedback. Nikon understands the power of the digital marketplace to both gain and leverage consumer insight. It also understands the power of its brand. As Lisa said, "It's a bold statement to let the consumers talk about the cameras, but it communicates just how confident Nikon is with its products." Visit the site and you'll see and hear why people are so enthusiastic about Nikon cameras. It's a perfect example of how one brand is using consumer insight and the magnifying effects of the digital marketplace to masterfully support its communications goals.

Not simply apropos of Nikon, I would add to Tom Friedman's comment that as marketers we've been given dog's hearing the fact that we've also been given an eagle's eyesight. The ability to hear and see what's going on in the world, and specifically as it relates to our business, has been amplified, magnified, and enhanced in many ways by digital technology. The digital tools available to us as marketers, most significantly search, have fundamentally changed the way we can manage brands. The digital space, in general, has magnified one of most important truths about building great brands: If you want to succeed, it's critical to gain insights about what consumers want, what they talk about when we're not in the room, and how they really behave. It's a judgment that needs no algorithm.

2

The Importance of Relevant Differentiation

In a former life I worked at an agency called Benton and Bowles, where I was assigned to the Dawn dishwashing liquid account. I was elated. Not because I spent a lot of time washing dishes, but because I finally had the opportunity to work with Proctor & Gamble. I say "finally" because P&G was, and continues to be, brilliant at building brands. In the past, when I had been assigned to work on a brand account that competed with a P&G brand, I knew it would be a challenge. I looked forward to seeing how P&G did what it did, hopefully being able to add my own two cents' worth of brilliance. Among the many things at which the company excels is its ability to delve into what consumers think and feel about specific subjects and to draw great insights from its efforts. It takes these insights and uses them as the basis for product development and branding strategy. When it came to washing dishes, the insights the company drew from its copious research, which included visits to kitchens across America to literally watch housewives wash dishes, was that grease is the enemy.

Once grease gets into the dishwater it sticks to everything, making the chore frustrating and counterproductive. The pots and pans and plates and utensils seem to get dirtier, not cleaner. This, in turn, makes the chore more time consuming. This insight was given to the scientists at P&G, who were given the directive to see if they could come up with a better solution to the problem. The solution that emerged from the lab was Dawn, a product that gets rid of grease in dishwater.

Proctor and Gamble had identified a functional benefit, a tangible quality that could truly differentiate the product from all of the other dishwashing liquids on the shelves. It was a benefit that would enable consumers to get dishes cleaner faster, a product difference that was meaningful to the people who spent time washing dishes. More than this, P&G could own the claim that Dawn was specifically formulated to eliminate grease from dishwater. It was proprietary. The brand team took its insight, its newly formulated product, and its relevantly different promise and captured it in the single evocative sentence, "Dawn takes grease out of your way." With this simple idea driving its success, Dawn enjoyed many years at the top of its product category.

This was the first chapter in the success story. Another of the things at which P&G excels is not resting on its laurels. We all know that products come and go and consumers are fickle. After a few years, as the number of dishwashing products increased in variety, as promises of superiority filled the airwaves, P&G recognized it was time to move its brand's point of relevant differentiation up a notch. Not move away from Dawn's functional benefit, but to take this functional difference "up the ladder" in order to be able to express it in a way that transcended function. To retain its place in the category, to *stay* meaningfully different in the minds of consumers, P&G knew it had to communicate its brand's promise in a way that demonstrated it understood why greasy dishwater was frustrating to people. In other words, it had to show signs of empathy. Coming at the functional benefit from an emotional point of view would enable the brand to connect with its customers at a deeper level, to build a relationship with them based on a shared appreciation for what makes dishwashing so exasperating. By articulating its promise as a more emotional point of view, P&G could maintain its stronghold on its brand's relevantly different promise, critical in the fast-expanding product category.

The Dawn team had discovered that taking grease out of the way was a definite tangible advantage. But, because dishwashing liquid is nothing more than a commodity, how could P&G credibly communicate the Dawn promise in a way that would help it build a relationship with its customers on an emotional level? The P & G brand team, which excelled at all things brand, excelled at laddering up. The challenge in this case, however, was to be able to figure out how high up the ladder the Dawn promise could go and still legitimately connect to the functional difference without stretching plausibility. The P&G team knew that if it went too far up the ladder and promised that using Dawn would create a life-altering scenario, "BS" meters would be on full alert. The team determined that the subtle suggestion that Dawn's grease-cutting abilities would enable people to get out of the kitchen faster and do the things they'd rather be doing, like spending time with the family, reading a book, or enjoying an evening out with friends was a viable option. Inferring that life is more pleasurable when dishwashing is faster and easier was a position on the ladder Dawn could own and that consumers could believe.

This new and improved promise was terrific for two very important reasons. First, it was flexible enough to be used as a conversation starter with a broader range of target audiences. Second, it was more durable and sustainable than Dawn's original functional promise. It would last longer and be more easily defensible against the constant barrage of products and promises from competitors. In a world of the new and improved, the brand team had identified a platform from which it could not only hold onto Dawn's leadership position, but build on it.

The best brand organizations know that a brand promise that transcends functionality gives it a longer and stronger shelf life, figuratively speaking, and sometimes, literally. A better mousetrap is only a better mousetrap until something even better comes along. Differentiating your brand on a functional benefit is not only good, it's a requirement. But if you can take this benefit up the ladder it's even better. Flexible, scalable, and sustainable are fighting words in the branding world. And their importance has only been made more obvious in the digital world. It's not just that the supermarket, the department store shelves, and the airwaves have become increasingly crowded; it's the Internet and every other venue in which consumers who have become inundated with the sights and sounds of branding pick up information. The irony of this newest type of clutter is that it all exists within the same framework—the digital box on your desk. Yes, television and print still play a part, but most of the sights and sounds—the words, the pictures, the fruits of HTML, the flash, the banners, the blogs, the games, and the gadgets—happen in one confined space. Given that so many people spend so much time with digital means of communication, the challenge for a brand to stand out is becoming much more difficult. The truth that a company must establish a forceful, sustainable point of relevant differentiation in order for its brand to succeed has been magnified within this space.

Susan Nelson, Executive Director of Consumer Insights at the Landor office in San Francisco talked about this. "The digital space has basically put everything there is to see and know about a brand under a high-power microscope," she said. She continued:

> Every branding channel, whether it's online or off, is being driven by an incredible amount of energy. Consumers are not just bombarded with more

communication and information from more sources; they can selectively access information more readily. They can deduce in an instant what makes one brand of soap or shampoo different from another. They read reviews. They read blogs. They read news about product recalls. Everything is out there. More than that, everything is accelerated in the digital space. If something misfires, a company has no time to plan a course of action. It's got to be ready to react. In fact, it used to be that brands started with a slow build, and if anything went wrong, there was a slow crash. Today, with the accelerated, amplified transmission of information, brands can be built faster than before, especially if they get positive spin from the Internet crowd and it's then spun out to the mass media. Having said this, a brand can crash just as fast.

There is a colossal amount of energy being driven by digital means of communication. Brand organizations are beginning to realize that in order to stand out as meaningfully different in the minds of consumers they've got to spend equal amounts of energy in non-digital and digital environments to define something that can stand up to the forces of digital nature. It's also becoming apparent that once a brand organization identifies a functional attribute it can call its own, it's increasingly necessary to take it higher up the ladder for consumers to be able to understand why it's really different and any better. Apple, with its amazing skills at building brands, recognized that touting the functional superiority of its iPod was going to give it limited shelf life as a brand leader. These days, the amount of time a brand can be a winner based on its gigabyte capacity is almost no time at all. With the pace of technological advances and the amount of noise generated about one product's superiority over another, Apple staked its claim on a higher rung. Wouldn't it be terrific if you could store hundreds of your favorite tunes in cool little device and take it with you wherever you go? Yes, it would. It *is*. And I love being part of this cool crowd with our white earbuds listening to our favorite tunes as the subway car swings and sways us to our destinations, or as we jog along the paths of Central Park. Its coolness factor has helped Apple sustain its brand difference and expand its product line better than any promise of basic functionality could.

On the subject of ladders, I'd like to share an interesting conversation I had with Stewart Owen, Chief Strategic Officer of ad agency mcgarrybowen. "It's one thing to get people emotionally involved in their tennis shoes, or their car, or their beer or soft drink," he told me, "but for classic consumer goods, or commodity services like banking or insurance, laddering up is a tricky proposition. You can't pick something that's so far up the rungs that people can't ladder back down to the connection it has to your brand. A brand ladder has to have rungs all the way up and all the way down or it's not a useful ladder. When you're looking to find a simple point of difference on which to base your brand, especially when the objective is to stand out in the vast digital marketplace, whatever you come up with must link back to the actual product functionality. What the product does for me, how it benefits me. The trick is not to get so far up the ladder that you can't figure out how to get back down."

P&G knew it could take its Dawn brand up the ladder because consumers already associated the dishwashing liquid as a product that could get dishes cleaner in a shorter amount of time because it dissolved grease in dishwater. P&G also knew how far up the ladder it could go without getting into the ozone. Its promise that life would be more pleasurable as a result of your being able to get through the chore of washing dishes was believable, and it tied back directly to the product's function. I spoke about this concept with Donna Hoffman, a co-director of the Sloan Center for Internet Retailing at the University of California in Riverside, where she and her colleagues study how and why people relate to brands. During our conversation we talked about elevating a brand's functionality to a more emotional level and some of the things she's observed in her work: "Brands are inherently emotional things. A brand is not owned by the people who manufacture it, it's owned by the people who think about it. The customers. It's the responsibility of brand managers to tap into some essential human need that a certain group of consumers think about and share. One of the beauties of the digital space in terms of building a brand is that it's interactive. People can engage with other people, and they can engage with brands. This presents a huge opportunity for brand organizations to more profoundly connect with consumers on an emotional level. Digital tools can bring a higher-level brand benefit to life in a way that very few branding tools can. The key is to know how to take advantage of these tools to build brand relationships around a shared need."

One of the examples Donna gave me was about how tissues—one of the most commonplace products—differentiated itself. How, you might ask, is it possible to differentiate a brand of tissues on a higher-order benefit than the ability to contain sneezes or control germs? Kleenex showed how it can be done with its "Let it out" campaign. In 2007, Kimberly Clark's Kleenex brand managers looked at the digital environment and asked how the company could use the digital space in the way it should be used: to connect people around the Kleenex brand promise. Where was the emotionally connective tissue in tissues? More than this, how far up the ladder could the brand go without losing sight of the brand's functional promise, the ability to control sneezes and germs better than any other brand of tissue? Well, how about its ability to staunch the tears that run down your face as you laugh hysterically at a story told by your best friend? What about the ability to wipe away the tears at a wedding, a funeral, or a kindergarten graduation? How about the tissue that slows the tears as you relate a sad story to a therapist? Maybe it's the tissue used to wipe the dirt from your son's gleeful face after his first Pee-Wee football win.

Tissues are very helpful during all the times in our lives when we express ourselves. Times when we "let it out" over a poignant memory, during a celebratory moment, or simply when we tell our parents how much we love them. Our eyes and noses run for a variety of reasons. One reason is that, as human beings, we share with others, and our sharing makes us feel better—and the outpouring of tears is the result of this process. Tissues play a part in any cathartic moment, moments when we "let it out." This is the rung on the ladder on which Kimberly Clark decided to land and from which it could launch branding in alignment with its functional benefit. When you "let it out" you feel better.

The Kleenex brand team understood the power of the Internet and made it an integral part of its branding strategy. It created a "Let it out" tour, during which a very good "listener" and his comfortable blue couch traveled the country stopping in cities to pose emotion-provoking questions to passersby on the street. "What would you say to your mom if she were here?" "What makes you laugh out loud?" "How far would you go for your hometown sports team?" The video-taped responses were used as the basis for television spots and as the foundation for the Kleenex website. Visitors to the site can download the videos but, perhaps more germane to the brand idea, can create and upload their own videos in which they "let it out" about one emotional moment in their lives or another. "How I told my boyfriend I loved him." "How I feel about my brother." "This is me at my son's first T-ball game." "This is what happened when I changed my hairdo." The videos, both those created on the Kleenex tour and those created by the Kleenex-using public, are genuinely funny and sad and expressive. Some have become so popular with visitors to the site that they've been sent along to YouTube and have found homes on My-Space and Facebook profile pages. The site designers, appreciative of the fact that some folks are camera-shy, created a blog where people can "Let it out" with words or song lyrics. As a natural branding extension to the "Let it out" campaign, there is also a Kleenex promotion that allows people to share their personalities by designing custom tissue boxes. The Kleenex team identified a way to take a very functional benefit up the ladder in order to further differentiate the brand in a sea of commodity products. More than that, it took advantage of digital tools to get people to share the value the Kleenex brand played in their lives. In an environment as complex and wild as the digital environment, these actions are nothing to sneeze at.

While Kleenex is a relatively recent entry to the list of brands that have made it to YouTube, there is another brand that made the list almost immediately after there *was* a YouTube. That brand is Dove. A product of Unilever, Dove was launched in 1957 as a beauty bar. The company differentiated the brand by means of its moisturizing benefit. Dove would not dry out your skin the way soap did because it was, in fact, not soap at all. The original branding, which was created by Ogilvy and Mather, was based on the functional claim that "Dove doesn't dry your skin because it's one-quarter cleansing cream." This promise, supported by claims from dermatologists, made Dove an icon brand. Unilever used this functional benefit as the basis for its branding until around the year 2000, when the company decided to extend the brand's name to other related products. The Unilever marketing team needed a brand promise of a higher order because it wanted each of its new product entries to represent something unique, albeit under the rubric of the Dove name. In effect, Unilever knew it had to go up the ladder to establish a point of view that would be appropriate to the entire Dove brand product line.

In the course of its research on perceptions of beauty, in the quest for insights about the category, the Dove brand managers discovered that the beauty industry (of which Unilever is a respected part) was guilty of setting unrealistic standards of beauty that generations of women were expected to meet, if not exceed. Women felt dejected by the photos of young, thin blond models, if not downright depressed. In the numerous surveys undertaken by Unilever as part of their search for a higher-level benefit to define its brand, one stated that only 2 percent of women questioned worldwide considered them-selves beautiful. Driven by its research and fueled by this amazing in-sight, Unilever made the bold decision to differentiate its Dove brand by redefining the very definition of beauty. The Campaign for Real Beauty was the result.

Even before it had considered how to go about branding the new Dove brand promise, Unilever went well beyond below skin deep to ar-rive at a meaningfully differentiated idea on which to build its brand. The insight it took from its research was the starting point. The Cam-paign for Real Beauty was the brilliant, but simple, articulation of this insight after it had been taken up the ladder. Dove had started its life as a "beauty bar." The functional to emotional connection was quite ob-vious. But the actual work of branding didn't begin until the brand managers had clearly established this compelling and sustainable idea. In doing research for this book it was clear that Unilever had tapped into something truly amazing. At least half of the people I interviewed mentioned Dove as an example of a brand that had figured out how to use the Internet to build its brand. But more than that, they understood why the Dove branding lent itself to the digital space so perfectly. Rory Sutherland, Executive Creative Director and Vice Chairman of the Ogilvy Group, UK, put it this way. "Dove is based on a big ideal, not simply an idea. In essence, it's that Dove believes the world would be a better place if women were judged by a broader perception of beauty. Ideals endure far beyond functional benefits. More than that, they're media neutral and, in fact, in Dove's case, leave 'space' for consumers to make their own contributions to support the ideal. An ideal can be-come a shared endeavor between advertiser and consumer."

Unilever's Dove "Campaign for Real Beauty" continues to successfully connect with its core audience by finding new ways to focus on the "real" definition of beauty, in this case, as seen through the eyes of this little girl in a video titled "Onslaught."

I also talked to Kathy O'Brien, Dove's Marketing Director, about the company's evolutionary, if not revolutionary, brand idea. "We wanted to change the way society views and represents beauty," she told me. "We wanted to debunk the stereotypes about beauty. But we wanted to do it in a way that was authentic to the Dove brand. Authenticity was integral to the program. If the product had not been built on functional superiority to begin with we'd have no authority when speaking to women about beauty. We may be selling products that define beauty, but we're delivering a functional benefit. Women intuitively connect Dove and 'beauty.' However, as we moved forward, we didn't just want to express our own thoughts about what beauty means: we wanted to provoke discussion and debate about the topic among women on a global basis."

Among the first branding elements of the campaign were print ads and billboards that featured ordinary women who were not super-model thin, who did not represent the unattainable standards for beauty that the Unilever research indicated was at the heart of matter. The ads and billboards featured toll-free numbers, and viewers were asked to vote on whether they considered the woman in the photograph to be "outsized" or "outstanding." The votes were counted in real time on the billboards. The discussion about beauty had begun, and Unilever was delighted by the response the interactive nature of the creative work generated. The company was able to use its findings, whether it was what it had hoped to hear or not, as it moved the branding forward.

Going fast forward, in 2006, the brand team at the Toronto office of Ogilvy and Mather created a video to help drive traffic to self-esteem workshops it was running as part of its ongoing research for Dove. The video, which came to be known as "Evolution," showed the time-lapsed face of a young woman as she was transformed from nice looking, but ordinary, to drop-dead gorgeous through the use of cosmetics, hairstyling—and lots and lots of Photoshop editing. While the video had not originally been intended for public viewing, but rather for in-house use, the brand team realized that if Unilever wanted to provoke discussion and debate, the Internet presented an incredible opportunity. The video was posted on YouTube and became an instant hit, actually a multi-million hit, as millions of people clicked to view it. Unilever was another smart brand organization that recognized the magnifying power of the Internet to get a message across and to prompt engagement around a brand idea.

According to Kathy O'Brien, the Evolution viral video topped YouTube's "Most Viewed this Month" for the month of October

2006, and was the subject of talk shows from coast to coast. Women could relate. People could relate. And although the video was spoofed online by creative do-it-yourselfers, that was fine with the Unilever folks. It was provoking the conversations about the subject they wanted to provoke. "You can't buy the kind of exposure our branding has generated," said Kathy. She added:

> Oprah Winfrey has had programs related to self-esteem; Jay Leno parodied our advertising; Katie Couric devoted sixteen minutes to the brand and to "Evolution" on the *Today* show. We had spent so much time speaking to women around the world during our research that this, in a way, didn't surprise me. Our insight about society's definition of beauty had struck a nerve. It resonated with people everywhere, and the digital space is a natural place to keep the conversation going. The key, at the beginning, was to clearly define our point of view so that the conversations would be relevant. We want to make women feel beautiful everyday by widening the stereotypical definition of beauty. We continue to do this by providing them with products they can use to take care of themselves.

The steps on the ladder between functional and emotional benefit are easy for Dove consumers to see. They understand the brand idea and can make the connection between the branding and the product functionality. While digital technology has played a huge role in getting the messages across and provoking engagement with the brand, Kathy commented that the company is media neutral. It, like other companies who embrace digital, recognizes that the idea drives the branding; the technology doesn't drive the branding. When you have a clearly defined brand idea, a strong point of view, the branding opportunities become intuitive. "You can become overwhelmed by the power of the Internet," Kathy said. "It can be a challenge, especially when you become concerned about losing control of your brand idea to the masses. People will take the idea and run with it. That's the reality of the medium. But, if you're clear about what your brand stands for, you won't lose control." Dove has made use of digital tools the way they should be used: To get people engaged around something they have in common. And, to listen and take part in the ongoing dialogues in order to sustain and build on its brand's relevantly differentiated meaning. Dove's newest website, dove.com, combines the content of the original site along with the content and context of the brand's "Campaign for Real Beauty" site. The objective was to merge the brand philosophy with product content to make it more convenient for users as well as more relevant. The technology further differentiates the brand and enhances the conversations women are having about what real beauty is. Dove.com, as a digital brand channel, is a natural progression of the brand's global presence and its community for women.

Defining your brand in a way that transcends its functional benefit is hard when it comes to consumer packed goods. Commodities abound. But it's equally hard when it comes to commodity services, including financial management and insurance. There are hundreds of branded pages on the Internet dedicated to money management, banking, and insurance, as well as independent websites that allow you to compare and contrast rates, plans, and programs in an instant. It's becoming increasingly more difficult to distinguish one brand from another based on anything more than price and online functionality. It's difficult enough to ladder up from a functional benefit expressed as bigger or stronger. It becomes exponentially more difficult when the claim is "cheaper" or "faster."

Steve Sullivan is the Chief Marketing Officer of Liberty Mutual, a leader within the insurance industry category. He has been asked to speak at a great many advertising and marketing conferences because of his innovative approach to his business. I asked him about how a company in the business of selling insurance goes about defining itself in a meaningfully different way, especially in a digital world where everything is magnified. He said:

Selling based on price and the ability to shop many insurers online has tended to commoditize the consumer insurance market. We struggled with how to differentiate ourselves and swim against the commodity tide. On the one side we had our heritage as a workers' compensation company with ninety-five years of experience and a global reputation for safety expertise. On the other side we had consumers who weren't necessarily looking for safety expertise when they bought insurance for their homes and cars. So if we wanted to grow our consumer business without dismissing the safety heritage, which is still important to our business-to-business customers, we had to find a bridge. The bridge turned out to be right under our nose in the mission statement that has defined our company for decades. When consumers were exposed to the statement they said, "A company like that would be responsible. They'd do the right thing. And that appeals to me because I'm a responsible person, myself." It was from this insight that we developed our brand positioning, "To celebrate our customers' responsibility and relentlessly prove our own." This forms a very solid roof under which we can communicate all our brand offerings. The idea of responsibility works for our products, our service, our salespeople, and, yes, on the commercial side, fits with our historical roots in the creation of safe work environments.

Liberty Mutual did not ladder up so high in its effort to identify a meaningful difference for its brand that it was disconnected from a functional benefit. While behaving in a responsible manner is not directly about safety or even about the cost of insurance, it relates wonderfully to the idea of making the world a better place, a topic as engaging as it is inspiring. The centerpiece for the branding campaign is a series of television ads that show people "doing the right thing" as they go about their daily lives: a man who picks up a toy that has dropped from a baby carriage onto the sidewalk unbeknownst to the mother and runs after her to return it; the same young mother doing a good deed for the next person she encounters; an older woman helping a younger man across the street (yes—that's correct). The voice over: "When it's people who do the right thing, they call it being responsible. When it's an insurance company, they call it Liberty Mutual. Responsibility. What's your policy?"

"We have three primary audiences," Steve said. "The first is our employees. Our salespeople and our customer service representatives are our front-line brand advocates. They understand what it means to be responsible, and they incorporate it into everything they do. The second audience is our existing clients. Our objective in our branding is to make them feel good about their decision to buy insurance from Liberty. Our third audience is prospective clients. Our online and offline branding initiatives are created with the hope that they'll think of us when they think about insurance."

Go to Libertymutual.com, and you'll be able to see for yourself how Steve and his team have integrated the idea of responsibility into all aspects of the site. There are applications that provide basic, factual information and applications that allow dialogue, real-time dialogue, with customer representatives twenty-four hours a day. If you want insurance for your new home or a new car, you can either discuss it with a representative via e-mail or click a button and talk to someone on the phone. Steve and I talked a bit about the common misperceptions concerning the process of differentiating a brand in the digital age. He agreed completely that it's not about the ability to shout louder, but the ability to use the tools offered by the Internet to connect in a more relevant way about a relevant topic. As almost everyone I spoke with stated, technology is not the answer, it's the enabler. We talked about Liberty Mutual's search optimization initiatives, and he told me that one of the most important factors was not impeding users' access to the information they wanted in any way, but using the right vocabulary and the right programming that would get them exactly what they wanted when they wanted it.

I could sum up this chapter on how the importance of relevantly differentiating a brand in the digital arena has been magnified. But I think I'll do the responsible thing and let Steve sum it up for me:

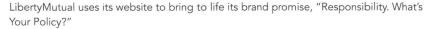

LibertyMutual uses its website to bring to life its brand promise, "Responsibility. What's Your Policy?"

I've been doing this for thirty years, and this is the most exciting era of my marketing career. For the first time, marketers have a real opportunity to create a relationship with someone before they become a customer, and they can enhance the relationship in a meaningful way as the prospects become customers. The idea of responsibility as a relationship builder and a brand builder seemed natural given our history. As a result of the Web we can engage both customers and prospects in a conversation and give them all sorts of different ways for them to engage with us. We can invite people to our website and learn about their needs before we try to sell them anything. This is what good marketing is all about. Digital tools let us do this better than we've ever been able to do it before.

3

The Importance of Delivering on Your Brand Promise

I want to go back to a member of the Landor family or, more specifi-cally, a member of Charles Wrench's family. "My mother came out to see me recently," our chairman and president wrote in one of his com-pany-wide blogs. "I suggested she fly Virgin, and I used my air miles to upgrade her to Upper Class on the way home so she could sleep. Since then, that's all we've talked about, and, it seems, all she's talked about with the ladies at the Piltdown Golf club, the neighbors, the postman, my sister, my brother, and the girls who work at Tesco. She can't say enough about the duvet, the pajamas, the head massage, the popcorn, about some aspect of every second of that flight home. She was smitten with the experience of flying on Virgin, and by now, I would suspect that all of Sussex knows why."

The point Charlie was making in his blog is something of which everyone involved with brands is aware, be they members of the Pilt-down Golf Club or not. The most successful brands become famous by making their customers brand evangelists. If a brand organization meets the obligations of its promise to consumers, if it delivers as expected, that's all well and good. But if an organization goes beyond expectations in its delivery of the brand experience and gets people talking in the way Mrs. Wrench was talking, that's even better. Whether she is aware of it or not, she has become an evangelist for Richard Branson's innovative brand of airline. Any company that generates voluntary viral communication by turning an ordinary experience into an extraordinary experience creates a brand evangelist.

In my last book, *BrandSimple,* I wrote about power signals, branding tactics that have a greater ability than others to influence consumer opinion about a brand. Every organization has one or two branding applications that reinforce more than others what the brand stands for—what makes it relevant to the customer's needs, different, and better. For some, a power signal might be a television ad; for some it's the experience of its retail environment; for others, it's the way the product performs. Then again, it might be the totality of the in-flight experience (head massage, anyone?), or it might be customer service, or perhaps even its association with a social issue. As effective as any one of these signals may be on its own, in this day and age, it is the power of talk that not only supersedes them all, but highlights the credibility of the brand promise. Word of mouth has become the *ubiquitous* power signal.

Digital communication, by itself, can influence how people think about brands in a way no other branding signal can. But digital communication, magnifying glass that it is, allows the world to see whether an organization is practicing what it preaches. Word of mouth, a time-honored marketing tactic, now acts like a megaphone on steroids. If your brand is delivering on its promise in some wonderfully extraordinary way, be it creative execution, product performance, or if your brand of airline hands out pajamas at 34,000 feet, the world will know about it in an instant. If your brand is delivering on its promise in some extraordinarily unsatisfactory way, the world will know that, too. There is no getting around or away from it. It's a branding truth that to be successful your brand and your brand organization must perform, behave, and satisfy the customers' needs in the way that the customers expect them to be. The promise your brand makes must be the promise it delivers. This truth has only been magnified in the digital space.

Fred Reichheld is a Harvard professor and founder of Bain & Company's loyalty practice, the study of how companies successfully mitigate customer attrition. In his book, *The Ultimate Question,* he argues that customer satisfaction is the number one driver of "good profits." What's more, he states that even with the preponderance of sophisticated tools and strategies designed to measure customer satisfaction, the most accurate measurement of whether or not a customer is happy can answered by asking one radically simple question: "Would you recommend this business to a friend?" The author shows that "net promoter scores"—which measure the difference between the percentage of "promoters," those who give high responses to the question, and "detractors," those who give lower scores—align closely with a company's revenue growth. Reichheld defines a promoter as a customer who gives the company a rating of nine or ten out of a possible ten. Detractors rate the company zero through six. Customers who rate the company either seven or eight are defined as "passively satisfied," and are not calculated in the final score. The concept of net promoter scores has generated both ardent advocates—including GE, American Express, and Intuit, Inc.—and those who are not quite so convinced of its efficacy. The fact is, however, there is more than a kernel of truth in the premise that people who would put their own reputations at stake to recommend a brand, a movie, a book, a restaurant, a charge card, or a mobile phone calling plan, have to be ardent believers in their favorites' superiority to do so. Obviously, there are a lot of believers out there. Millions and millions of consumers are recommending brands, and millions more are listening to them, seeking them out, in fact. A study by Edelman Public Relations revealed that 68 percent of consumers are more likely to believe other consumers than to believe traditional media sources. As opinions are blogged through the digital universe and review sites increase in number and credibility, it's not hard to understand how new communication tools have raised the value of word of mouth as a branding tool. And it's not hard to see why keeping your brand promise is paramount to success.

Whether a brand organization has formally incorporated the net promoter score discipline into its operations, as GE and American Express have, or has subscribed to the basic principle in general, all organizations are fast recognizing the power of Internet-based promoters and detractors to affect business outcome. The reality is that, as the digital world continues to grow in scope and scale, the voice of public opinion grows in scope and scale. We the people can almost instantly send a product's popularity through the roof and cause it to crash just as quickly. If an organization slips or slides in meeting consumer expectations, the news will actually slip and slide from one digital device to another, picking up speed and volume along the way. As a result of this dynamic, a brand organization must now be able to ensure that there are no slips in how its products, its customer service, its sales representatives, its store personnel, even its advertising claims, line up with consumer expectations. To ensure all is going as well as promised, those doing the branding must vigilantly monitor what's being said about the brand online. Smart organizations invest well-spent time and money on people whose responsibility it is to participate in online chats, read blogs and message boards, visit social networking sites like MySpace and Facebook, and scour product review sites for mentions of their brand's name. These folks do not do this anonymously (or shouldn't, as the chief executive of Whole Foods discovered when he was excoriated for both his undercover surveillance and for bashing rival Wild Oats), but rather identify themselves as corporate participants in the conversations. They know it's a two-way mirror. As they watch, they're being watched. But the price of being watched is worth it. Online hall monitors can stop a rumor in its tracks, make a good situation great, or help organizations understand how to fix what needs fixing. Their role is to look for anything that's being said about the brands they represent—the good, the bad, and the downright ugly. If it's good, it should be seen as a PR opportunity, as Unilever discovered relative to the Dove "Evolution" video. If the news is less than good, the objective should be to get whatever it is that's got consumers in a tizzy remedied ASAP. Time waits for no one, or no brand, online.

Brand organizations are still getting up to speed on what it means to operate in a society in which consumers can track and monitor corporate behavior with the same speed and fluidity that corporations can track consumer behavior. As a brand organization, you can see where I shop, if I return something, how and where I do my comparison shopping, and what stage of the buying cycle I'm in. As a consumer, I can see whether your brand of cell phone won't drop calls (as promised), if your tech support will support my tech devices (as promised), if the skies I'm flying are friendly (as promised), or if I'll find a live operator ready to take my call 24/7 (as promised). While some companies see the transparent, talkative marketplace as a threat to their assumed long-standing control over consumers, the smartest organizations recognize this transparency as the positive dynamic it is: the ability to monitor consumer feedback to deliver a consistently better brand experience. Astute companies make consumers de facto collaborators in the brand-building process. They use digital technology to take advantage of what's being said and passed along as the incredible opportunity it is.

I had a great conversation with Lenovo's Chief Marketing Officer, David Churbuck, on this topic. Among his first words were "talk openly." "When I joined Lenovo in 2006," he told me, "I had several years of experience designing and launching blogs. I know how the online world works, and I know how quickly talk spreads. I've seen lots of situations where topics are taken out of context, the erroneous news hits the blogs, and the company comes in with a fire extinguisher a day too late. I've seen companies not paying attention at all to what's being said about them on the Internet only to be blindsided, and I've seen situations where corporations simply didn't think trolling the Web for input mattered. It matters. Monitoring what's being said about you, especially the negative, and responding in real time and with absolute honesty and transparency is critical to maintaining credibility." David went on to say how important it is for a company to have a formal process for monitoring online chatter. Not just an ad hoc committee that uses a lunch break to surf reviews but a defined group of people whose sole responsibility it is to actively listen, assess the situation, and report back with recommended actions. Many firms hire outside resources to take on this role. However it's done, it's a new cost of doing business. Relative to Tom Friedman's reference to "judgment algorithms," David said:

> While you can't and shouldn't react to everything and everyone, once you get into a formal process of monitoring, you begin to identify the most influential bloggers or review sites relative to your brand category. You'll be able to identify the prominent bloggers in the category who know what they're talking about and have authority among consumers. At Lenovo, we actively engage these bloggers in conversation, clearly identifying ourselves as Lenovo employees. We also state, without waffling or defensive language, that we understand the problem or question on the table and that

we will address it. You cannot talk the talk and not deliver. That's an almost worse problem than the problem the online griper griped about to begin with. If someone tells you they didn't receive an order as requested, or that a computer wasn't repaired as promised, we act quickly. The way a company responds to customers has always been a critical success factor. Today it's more critical. Time is not on your side.

It used to be said that a brand was what people said about you when you weren't in the room. These days a brand is what's said when you're not online. David's point is that it's essential that your organization is the first to know about any online brand banter and that you act quickly and responsibly before being criticized for high crimes and misdemeanors relating to non-delivery of the brand promise. Stories of bloggers gone wild have become urban cyber-legend. In 2005, for instance, Jeff Jarvis, the respected author of the blog BuzzMachine, got pretty ticked off at the Dell computer company. The incident has become known, not coincidently, as Dell Hell. As David Churbuck told the story to me, Jarvis bought a laptop and it didn't work as specified. That was the first level of Hell. The second was with the way in which Dell handled or, more accurately, didn't handle the complaint. After many failed attempts by phone and email to get their attention, let alone the service he needed and deserved as a Dell customer, Jarvis got fed up and created a post on his blog headlined, "Dell Lies, Dell Sucks." When asked how he came up with the title he said it was a matter of "search-engine optimization." It seemed the word "sucks" applied to a lot of Dell-related searches. In any case, the story hit and the hits on the BuzzMachine blog began in earnest. Jarvis's experience with Dell had struck a chord and generated unprecedented response from equally frustrated customers who blogged back support. Dell eventually made good on Jarvis's service requests. More than that, the company used this as the learning experience it was. The voice of public opinion will not and cannot be denied in a digital world. The

Dell brand has been on an upswing since, but its initial delayed reaction cost the company dearly in stock price and public trust. Those who love Dell, and there are millions, are happy it's in recovery mode.

Two other incidents that have made it to the annals of cyber–urban legend involve Kryptonite, a bike lock manufacturer in Massachusetts, and Comcast, the giant cable company. Kryptonite, whose brand promise was based on the indestructible quality of its lock, was taken to task when a San Francisco bicyclist posted a video online demonstrating how the lock could be opened by cramming the empty barrel of a ball point pen into the keyhole. Kryptonite, although it had a website, paid little attention to what was happening online until this incident occurred in 2004. Lesson learned, and customer brand experience made better: After creating a lock exchange program and replacing forty thousand locks in twenty-one countries free of charge, Kryptonite invested heavily in time and money redesigning its bicycle lock. It also hired Technorati, a firm that, according to its founder, Peter Hirshberg, tracks over one hundred million blogs for clients who want to monitor brand-related chatter.

Comcast's storied problem with online whistle-blowers began when *Advertising Age* columnist Bob Garfield tried to get the company to pay attention to his requests for service. Less than happy with the treatment he received from Comcast, he created a blog named ComcastMustDie.com. The content of the blog is self-explanatory. Within hours of posting the blog, the feedback started rolling in, all responses supporting Garfield's contention that the company needed a wake-up call. One response to his blog was in the form of a video of a Comcast repairman who had fallen asleep on a customer's couch while on hold with his own customer service department. The video posted to YouTube received over a million hits. In a *USA Today* article following the launch of his blog, Garfield explained that his intent was "to get the scales to fall off [Comcast CEO] Brian Roberts' eyes.

If Comcast were to provide excellent customer service, the rewards would far exceed the cost." Comcast got the message and reacted quickly, immediatcly citing changes it would make to improve its service. It now uses Nielsen Buzzmetrics to check ongoing online chatter. Hopefully any new buzz will be better buzz.

One of the most fertile Petri dishes for word of mouth are online social networks, be it Facebook, MySpace, or any of the dozens of others. These sites are like virtual civilizations, with spoken and unspoken rules for commerce and community. The proximity the residents have to one another, along with the technical applications that make quick work of opinion sharing, make these online spaces contemporary equivalents to Wisteria Lane, home of those *Desperate Housewives,* or Mayberry RFD, home until the end of time to Sheriff Andy and little Opie. When someone whispers, it has the potential to turn into a verbal tsunami. International banking firm HSBC learned the power that social networks have as agents of change when it tried to change one of its student loan policies. Nigel Hollis of research firm Millward Brown related the story.

> Like most high street banks in the UK, HSBC used to allow university graduates a year's grace to pay off their student debt without paying interest. Then HSBC decided to roll back the offer and sent out a notification stating that the free ride was over. The rumblings started in Facebook, a community highly saturated with college-age kids. To be honest, there weren't that many students directly affected by HSBC's revised policy, but because of a few disgruntled residents of Facebook and the viral conditions that exist in social sites, the rumblings turned into a roar of protest. The mass media picked it up, which magnified the situation even more, and HSBC was forced to put the original program back in place for those who had initially signed up.

Nigel's story confirmed yet another truth about how branding is magnified in the digital space: Consumers may be in control, but brand organizations have the power to control the volume. Had HSBC been more aware of the dynamics at play in social networks, it might have dealt with the situation in a different manner. Live, listen, and learn.

Just as the Internet and all things digital magnify the scale of the wailing about an experience that doesn't deliver on a brand's promise—hopefully prompting the organization to right its wrong— they also magnify the scale of praise from those who believe the brand is living up to its promise. These are the people who use digital devices, from blogs to social networks to text messaging, as the inherent evangelizing tools they are. Teachers, for instance, were so delighted with an initiative created by GE that they told other teachers, all of whom used this GE branding tactic as part of their classroom curriculum. In this case, the branding that was used to define GE's brand promise also exemplified its promise; meta-branding, as it were.

The story begins pre-digital—or at the very least, pre-digital evangelism. As the world turned the calendar page from one century to the next, GE's senior management recognized that to be relevant in the twenty-first century it had to reposition its brand promise. Long associated with its ability to "bring good things to life," this idea was generally connected to making life better with better quality appliances and light bulbs. In a speech given by Beth Comstock, GE's Chief Marketing Officer, she told her audience, "Our employees told us they had enormous pride in the company. They also told us how much they liked being part of a winning culture—one that passionately believes in getting things done. But they also wanted more of the culture that embodies the Thomas Edison spirit of innovation. This is heritage that carries through to today, rooted deep within our cultural DNA. Which should we be, they asked, 'innovators or executors?' We all agreed we needed to be both."

After doing its research, the challenge became clear to GE's management. How would it build a bridge from GE's roots to the future?

What's more, with the increasing flattening of the world, how could it position itself in a way that would resonate around the globe? The insight that led to the new position came from inside the company, from the people who told stories about using imagination to get to solutions that would profoundly change everything from the quality of health care to the quality of the air. "Imagination at Work" was what they did, and it became the idea that the company would use to move its brand forward. This new promise has been at the heart of everything associated with the GE brand, from low-noise jet engines to energy-saving wind turbines to medical technology capable of detecting the onset of Alzheimer's disease.

While the product innovations themselves were branding signals that brilliantly delivered on the promise of "Imagination at Work," there were many other branding executions that did the same. Among them were GE's remarkable television advertising created by BBDO, GE's advertising agency for eighty years, and the equally remarkable online branding campaigns created by BBDO's interactive unit, BBDO @tmosphere. One of @tmosphere's first assignments was to virtually take the "Imagination at Work" idea around the globe. The objective was to use the Internet as it should be used—using the GE promise as glue to promote community and to connect people from one corner of the planet to another.

I spoke to Arturo Aranda, Creative Director and partner at @mosphere BBDO. Aranda said: "The 'Imagination at Work' online initiative had to achieve a number of things. First, obviously, it had to brand GE. It had to reflect what we wanted users to associate with the brand. Then, it had to engage users. The Internet is an interactive space. When you can get people to voluntarily engage with anything they can better understand it. This builds brand credibility and brand equity. Third, our endeavor had to have pass-along value. The beauty of digital is that it's inherently viral. If you give people something to play with, something that's fun and entertaining, something that has a 'Wow' factor, as GE CEO Jeffrey Immelt, calls it, they'll take advantage of their digital tools to pass it along."

The resultant branding initiative was known as "Pen." In essence, it was an interactive online pen that worked sort of like an Etch-a-Sketch®, using white space and interactive graphic tools to inspire imaginative thinking. It derives from the brilliantly simple insight that great inventions often start with a quick sketch, a few jottings on a piece of scrap paper, or perhaps on the back of a napkin. "Pen," much like an inventor's initial sketch, allowed the initiator to work collaboratively with others to more fully develop and enhance the idea. In this case, the "scrap paper" was an empty, online whiteboard in banner-ad format on which participants could use a computer mouse to manipulate the "pen" icon and draw using a variety of colors and type styles. After using their imaginations to create the art, participants could digitally forward it to friends and family who could then watch the image unfold. Launched in 2003, the Pen generated nearly fifty million impressions from users in over 140 countries, even Vatican City. A community of repeat users returned to ge.com to play again and again.

"The project was such a simple, pure expression of GE's promise," Arturo said. "It was amazing to see the ways people would embrace it. They'd share their drawings in their blogs, and on their social network pages, in effect saying, 'Hey look what I did.' One of the most exciting examples of the viral dynamic at work is that teachers used the Pen to promote the value of collaborative imagination: 'Look what happens when you get together and share ideas.' It became part of the curriculum in many elementary schools. Innovation is all about collaboration. We used this online branding vehicle to dimensionalize the GE promise. There was no way we could have done this in any other medium."

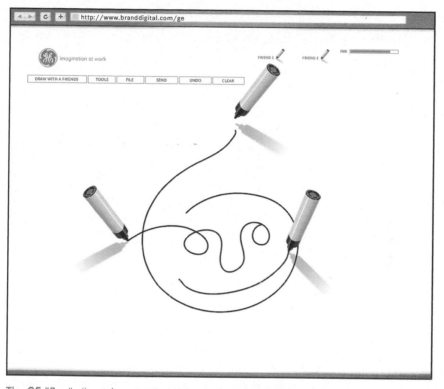

The GE "Pen" allowed users to experience "imagination at work."

When I spoke to Jen Walsh, GE's Digital Media Director, she told me that "everything we undertake must embody 'Imagination at Work.' This idea is what GE is all about. It's what differentiates our brand. The ultimate goal for the GE Pen was to get people to directly experience the brand, to build their awareness of what 'Imagination at Work' means, and to increase the relevance of the brand. The campaign was scheduled to be up for three months. We've kept it going for five years."

When teachers become evangelists for a corporate brand, you know you must be doing something right. More than just right, the Pen was awarded the Gold Pencil at the One Show Interactive Awards in 2003 for its achievement in taking users "beyond the usual banner experiences" within the interactive space. The branding extended GE's notion that "Every great idea begins with a sketch," an idea that came from watching its scientists, engineers, and other product development teams at work. It delivered the promise of the brand and gave consumers the tools to carry the message forward.

A similar story came out of my conversation with David Roman, the Director of Interactive Marketing for the Hewlett-Packard Personal Systems Group. David said:

> Consumers have always had a high awareness of HP personal computers, but mostly with regard to our technology, and mostly the result of tactical or promotional initiatives. We recognized that with PCs becoming more and more of a commodity, we had to strengthen our relevance to users. People were buying on the basis of price and standard functions. Quite frankly, we needed to be able to convey, 'This is what we stand for.' More than this, as a technology company, it was critical to the credibility of any promise we made to be able to tangibly demonstrate why the HP experience was different and better. HP products are phenomenal products, but we had to prove it, not just say it. In the course of our research, we went back to the way people felt about their computers when computers first came out. In the beginning people thought about the magical aspects of the machine. They then moved on to seeing it as an investment. We wanted to bring back the magic of the personal relationships people have with their computers. Our lives are on computers: the photos of our families, our mail, our conversations with friends, our address books, our schedules, our financial records, the movies we like to watch over and over. We take this life with us wherever we go. Computers and specifically PCs are like digital autobiographies. As a company, HP wanted to show that we understood this and that our products would deliver. That's what 'The Computer Is Personal Again' initiative is all about.

David and his team, which includes advertising agency Goodby, Silverstein & Partners, began working on the initiative the way all good marketing teams begin. They looked for insights about consumers;

who were their primary targets, how they spent their lives, what's relevant to them, and how could digital tools help make life more efficient, more convenient, and more fun? While the team found that an older market scored best in terms of understating the "Personal" concept, they decided to skew their branding efforts to what they called the "Net generation," a group that grew up conditioned by the Web. It was a deliberate choice. If you're going to sell a promise based on technological magic, you go to the people who know best how to make magic and spread magic. The Goodby Silverstein folks created a campaign that focused on people and the relationships they had with their PCs. Not celebrities, per se, and not ordinary people, but people you wouldn't normally associate with HP—among them professional snowboarder Shaun White, tennis star Serena Williams, fashion designer Vera Wang, rap star Jay-Z, and, oh, yes, Princess Fiona, friend of that gentle ogre, Shrek. Given that the branding was intended to address the Net generation, most of the campaign was created to take advantage of digital technology. It was designed to be engaged with, to be shared with others, and to tangibly deliver on the promise of the brand. The purpose was to show that everything about the computer has been developed with the way customers live their lives in mind.

"These online videos and the TV ads created to support them are a logical extension of the brand idea. Jay-Z is a rapper, but he's also a PC user," said David, continuing:

> The video we made with him includes music he's composed, which fans can download and send to their friends. This particular video generated lots of online attention, including a battle of the rappers on YouTube. There were twenty-three user-generated videos uploaded to YouTube, some spoofs, some people doing their own deliberate versions of our Jay-Z campaign. Spoofs are great. If people are taking the time to generate some brand-related interaction, even if it's less than positive, it should be taken as an opportunity. Fortunately, most of the videos we saw were well-intended.

http://www.branddigital.com/hp

Serena Williams' interactive tennis game is one of the many interactive branding initiatives that get consumers personally involved in HP's "The Computer Is Personal Again" campaign.

Another campaign was created to coincide with the U.S. Open. We did a spot featuring Serena Williams called "Belle of the Ball." She talks about how she uses her HP PC for everything from keeping in touch with friends, to tracking the competition, to playing UNO against her computer (the computer always wins), to designing her clothing line Aneres. The range of applications built into the "The Computer Is Personal Again" site to allow users to personally experience the brand idea is incredible. Our developers even captured Serena's famous on-court "grunts" that users can download, as cell phone ringtones.

That HP took advantage of its technology to prove *how* its technology is better and different and relevant to users is wholly evident. I had the opportunity to speak to Hashem Bajwa, Digital Strategy Director at Goodby Silverstein. Hashem said:

People have turned from passive recipients of branding into active users with the power to view or take part in whatever they like. In our work with

HP, the objective was to create an experience that was informative, fun, addictive, and that had pass-along value. No one, especially those in the target group, is going to call someone up and say, "Hey watch this ad, or go to the website," but they will forward it to someone. Telling a story has always been a good way for brands to connect with consumers. The digital space facilitates the sharing of stories, which facilitates information transmission, which facilitates sales. When we look at how to use digital in our campaigns, we ask ourselves what a particular product or service can do for consumers, how it can make life easier or more entertaining. How can we turn it into a story? The old marketing model is "Let's go to where the media is." On the Web, it's "How can we get people to come to us?" If the right people find you and you give them something engaging, something worth passing along, you can spend less money and have a far greater impact. Content that is shared voluntarily is of incredible value.

I have personally shared many of the videos from HP's "The Computer Is Personal Again" Web pages. I've discovered that Princess Fiona stores her favorite recipes on her HP PC, and that Jerry Seinfeld invites viewers to share videos of them doing something funny, which he'll personally rate for funniness. I'm not sure whether Jerry would agree, but some of these people should stick to their day jobs. In any event, HP has proven that it understands the dynamics of the digital space, including the fact that digital tools enable consumers to scrutinize more closely whether brands are delivering as promised. An interesting anecdote that Hashem shared with me was about a venture capitalist he heard speak at a conference on digital media. "When I look at a technology company to determine whether it's a good investment opportunity, I look at its marketing budget," this fellow said. "If the company has a huge budget set aside for marketing, I assume it's in failure mode and needs the money to build awareness. If it has a relatively small marketing budget I tend to become more interested. If you have superior product functionality and know you can take advantage of the digital space to sell your promise, it's a good sign."

Not that HP had a relatively small budget. The production value of its branding work is spectacular, equal to its product performance. In "The Computer Is Personal Again," the brand promise is delivered not simply via the outstanding functional applications, but through amazing special effects and graphic elements. It is, as Hashem indicated, addictive. You can't watch anything on this site just once. But, the venture capitalist did have a good point. To extrapolate a bit, if your organization is clear about the idea it wants to deliver, if it's clear about the brand promise, and if it's very clear about the power of digital, it doesn't need a massive budget. Just give people something to talk about, give them the tools to spread the word, and you're a good part of the way there.

4

The Importance of a Simple Idea

Every December around the holidays, I set up my old Lionel trains for my kids. Each year, I add a few more cars and accessories, making it more elaborate than the year before. Suffice it to say, it now takes hours to assemble. For those of you who don't know about Lionel trains, they are as captivating for the adults in the family—the male adults, anyway—as for the kids. During my most recent set-up endeavor, I decided to spend some time testing (okay, playing with) the trains so that I'd know they'd work when my kids came into the playroom the next morning. As I watched the Union Pacific locomotive pull the freight cars along the track, it occurred to me that that the engine pulling all the other cars round and round was sort of akin to marketing in the pre-digital world of brand building. In those days, which seem eons ago, it was traditional advertising, mostly in the form of thirty- or sixty-second television spots, that was the locomotive responsible for getting all the other cars to their destination. A talented group of people would identify a relevantly different idea on which to build a brand. Then, they'd hand this idea to equally talented groups of people in both the creative and media departments of an agency. The creative folks would come up with a storyline—an entertaining narrative complete with talking tigers, cars doing hairpin turns on mountain roads, or some guy squeezing toilet paper, to help consumers understand this relevantly different idea. The media folks would then buy time on television shows to broadcast these advertisements. It was a culture of the masses, and this was the way mass media worked. Like different cars on the Lionel train, any other branding elements were sort of anchor-bolted on—the direct marketing, the events and promotions, the hangtags in the store. It was up to the talented, creative folks in departments not involved in television or print advertising, or "below-the line" marketing, to which it is often referred (sounds, pejorative, doesn't it?) to figure out how to align their branding communications with the engine driving the train.

Those of us who grew up watching network television got most of our notions and information about brands from television commercials. Those of us who grew up working in branding and advertising during those days came to accept this linear form of branding as gospel. You waited until the TV storyboards were given the green light by the client, and then you got the marching orders for everything else. This was the way it was.

Well, in the digital world, there is no train. The marketing paradigm has shifted from linear to very nonlinear, and digital technology has done the shifting. While traditional media still plays an important part in the branding equation, it no longer drives everything else. That's because consumers are no longer sitting en masse in front of their television sets, being told why one brand of cereal is better than another. For starters, there's no "en masse" anymore. Like no other time in marketing history, consumer segments are fragmented. Television is neither the most obvious game, nor is it the surefire answer it once was. Companies are now reevaluating how they spend their branding dollars. More than this, the way consumers pick up information has become fragmented. It is harder than at any other moment in the history of branding to break through marketplace clutter, to get people to pay attention, and to focus on any one thing for very long. I witness my nieces and nephews simultaneously texting on their mobile phones, playing video games, watching television, and still being able to jabber with each other. I see people at the gym talking on their Blackberries, flipping through a *Wall Street Journal,* and glancing up at CNN headline news while they work out on treadmills. I am as guilty as anyone of checking e-mails while I chat on the phone and peering up now and again to check the Yankees score on ESPN. Personal, portable technology is can be an incredible drain on time, it numbs the mind, and it's one of the chief culprits of our multitasking, attention-impaired world. It's not just a matter of brand attention deficit disorder (or BADD, as I call it); it is the inability of any one of us to focus on one task without being distracted by another.

Every day, if not every hour, the tug of digital distraction gets stronger and stronger. Someone is always telling us to check out one website or another. If we're doing research, there are pages upon pages of data. If we're shopping, there are pages upon pages of products and price points to compare. If we want to be entertained, there are videos and television shows to download and watch, and music to download and upload, there are Facebook profiles to check out, games to play, and consumer-generated content to be generated, and content that just has to be passed along. There are chat rooms and news sites, gossip to read and gossip to spread, hotels to discover, airline tickets to book, restaurants to review, restaurants to find, and directions to restaurants to be printed out. Add this to the hundreds of cable channels, and the branding that appears on the sides of buses, in the back seats of taxis, the floors of supermarkets, the cubicle doors in restrooms, on the mini-TVs in elevators, on the backs of charge receipts, etcetera, etcetera, etcetera—and it becomes clear that the only "mass" in media is the mass options people have.

Based on any number of branded interactions, people learn and form their opinions about brands, and there is no rhyme or rhythm to the way or the order in which they do this. Consumers are in control, and they are channel neutral. They get their branding where they want it, and only if they want it. Being able to click off is as easy, if not easier, than clicking on. From the consumer's perspective, branding—in form and content—is on a self-select, need-to-know basis. This means that if you're still relying on traditional advertising as the steam engine to get your relevantly different brand idea across, you might just be going round in circles.

The current paradigm shift has created a huge mental change in the way organizations are beginning to think about branding. Smart companies are beginning to realize that the way to play the branding game in the digital marketplace is to be as channel neutral as the consumers. Instead of assuming that traditional advertising should be the branding tactic of choice, smart companies begin by establishing the key idea they want to convey about their brand and let the idea drive the branding strategy. They determine which branding channels can be used to best reinforce to consumers what makes the brand different, and which branding channels will convey why this difference is relevant and better. Just as the importance of establishing a relevantly different idea on which to build a brand has been magnified, so too has the importance of making this idea simple to understand.

Because organizations can no longer think about branding in terms of specific media or tactics, everybody and anybody responsible for branding in any of its guises must be able to understand the brand idea and be able to embed it into the branding for which they are responsible. If someone is instrumental in delivering on the brand promise in any way, shape, or form, this person must be able to comprehend instantly what the brand stands for and what is their role in conveying it to consumers. There may be no branding train, but there is an engine, and this engine is the simple idea. For obvious reasons it's what we at Landor call the brand driver—a word, a phrase, or notion that captures the essence of a brand's relevantly different promise to consumers. As the driver of all branding, it must have the clarity of meaning to intuitively stimulate every brand-related activity and behavior, from advertising to product design to customer service.

With so many different brand touch-points on so many dimensions, with so many different groups of people touching brands, the importance of making the idea that drives the branding as simple as possible and as "sticky," or memorable, as possible has been magnified. In a marketing arena chock full of branding options, a brand driver must be articulated in a way that ensures that no matter how a consumer engages with the product or buys into a brand, the experiences created by the organization will reinforce why the brand is meaningfully better and different. The brand driver must be able to intuitively promote pertinent brand associations. When people experience any aspect of the brand, they must get it.

The beauty of a simple and memorable brand driver is that it has greater potential to drive inspired branding. When those responsible for creating the branding understand exactly what the brand stands for, they can implement it with greater precision and creativity. Freed from having to ponder their objective, they can use their time to brainstorm brilliant ways to express the brand idea. A clear, concise brand driver will generate branding that's not only innovative and provocative, but relevant to the consumers branders want to reach. It's branding with the power to break through all the other branding in the marketplace and to break through the muddle of brand claims consumers carry around in their heads. A brand driver that accurately reflects the meaning of a brand can actually help an organization minimize branding expenses. Ambiguity can be very expensive.

As a result of this new branding paradigm, brand organizations are uncoupling the anchor bolts between departments, between agencies, and between every other entity involved in their branding. Instead of looking at branding as a linear exercise, they're circling the wagons and putting the brand idea smack in the middle. They are not thinking about how media should drive the branding but how the brand idea should drive media and every other form of brand expression. Michael Mendenhall, Chief Marketing Officer of Hewlett-Packard, was one of the folks I spoke with about this new paradigm. He explained how his organization looks at its brand building. "Many companies continue to look at marketing in conventional ways—from a mass market point of view. Branding today is not about the media; it's about the idea," he said as we began our conversation. "You need to dismiss the conventional way of thinking and start with an understanding of the value of each communication channel and how—or whether—it will engage people. The idea should be the organizing principle, and it should inform everything you do to help consumers grasp your brand promise in whatever channel you're reaching them: the television, the blogs, the banner ads, or the word of mouth."

The simple idea that drives HP's newest initiatives takes advantage of the reality of the digital space itself—that people now look at their digital tools as personal extensions of their lives. "The Computer Is Personal Again," HP's branding effort for its PCs, draws on the brilliant but simple insight that, for all intents and purposes, we carry our lives around with us on our laptops. We take our laptops everywhere. If my house was on fire—after making sure my family and the dog were safe and sound—I'd grab my laptop. It's got all our most precious photographs, our home movies, our critical financial information, and the e-mail addresses of everyone important to us. The HP brand idea demonstrates that the company understands this about me and everyone else you see clicking away at coffee houses, in airports, and on park benches. It's one of those ideas based on the observation of the obvious. Its brilliance is in its simplicity. The equally simple brand idea for HP copiers follows the same line of thinking. "What do you have to say" makes clear that HP understands that technology is about "me." It's what we use to express ourselves and shape our identities. Consumers use technology to take charge and make choices that are personally relevant. "We see personalization as a major trend in marketing. And we think that a centralized data warehouse complemented by a robust CRM program can bring the customer insight necessary to offer truly personal, customized products and services," said Michael. "It's not about any specific long-form or short-form media tactic, interactive or otherwise. Rather it's about what will get people engaged."

Mass media has dominated the branding landscape for so long that it may be hard for some marketers to make the shift from a media-specific approach to a brand-idea–driven one. However, as consumers continue to adopt technology at the current speed, the pressure to make the shift will only become more intense. HP recognizes that a brand idea will only take hold if consumers take hold of it where it's personally meaningful to them. Just as technology is about "me," so is the way we choose to become aware of brands. The fact that that the HP has "uncoupled the anchor bolts" between branding constituencies is a critical element of its success. Another of the key points that Michael made was about a brand idea needing to be in complete alignment with a company's business goals. Suffice it to say, if the brand driver isn't in sync with your business strategy—how your company makes money—it isn't going to drive you very far. In fact, it may just drive you into the ground.

Burger King is another company that was among the first to recognize the channel neutral nature of the current marketing culture and the technology-driven nature of branding. In 1974, Burger King established "Have It Your Way" as a tagline and also as its simple brand driver. The promise was that unlike the experiences at other fast food retailers, you could go into Burger King and order your burgers, fish, or chicken prepared to your liking. You controlled the experience. The simple idea that you could "hold the pickle, hold the relish, special orders don't upset us," enabled the brand to clearly and meaningfully set itself apart from its chief competitor, McDonald's. It used this idea as its simple brand driver with great success for many years. After a bumpy hiatus, the brand driver has been brought back and is apparently more germane now than it was over thirty years ago. Having it "your way" applies to the brand's product and the brand's branding. Russ Klein, President of Global Marketing, Strategy, Innovation at Burger King, explained his company's take on the shift in the marketing paradigm. "The premium on both relevant differentiation and entertainment value has been heightened in the digital space," Russ began. "Content has become more important than ever, and the user is more actively in charge in how they access the content they want. Consumer empowerment has been brought to life by the technology. What all of this means is that to have impact an organization must knowingly create a brand platform that enables people to become engaged in its brand in a relevant way. Ironically enough, the simple idea of 'having it your way' was ahead of its time. We brought it back to drive our business and our branding."

"We never contemplated how relevant this simple idea would become in the customized world of technology," Russ told me. He continued:

It was developed over thirty years ago, but it's perfect for the times in which we live. We realized there were lots of meaningful ways we could convey the idea of "having it your way" from both a technological standpoint—people controlling our media content—and from a product benefit standpoint—guests controlling the way their food is prepared. Our core target customers, people we call "super fans," are eighteen- to thirty-four-year-olds, skewing slightly younger and male, who are time-starved and embrace out-of-home eating as part of their lifestyles. The digital environment is a virtual playground for this group. They spend an incredible amount of time online. They also visit restaurants in the hamburger category an average of sixteen times a month. We know that a brand can't be all things to all people, so we made the decision to focus our efforts on this audience and to use the digital space the way it should be used—for the pass-along value. The objective was to come up with some really clever online content to get our brand idea across and let the word-of-mouth dynamic do its job.

Clever is an understatement. In 2004, Burger King launched a viral branding campaign called "The Subservient Chicken," which became an instant YouTube favorite. As quick back story: Burger King had learned from prior experience that developing marketing plans to deliver against specific business opportunities was a smart way to operate in the fast-changing fast-food category. After extensive research, the organization concluded that there was a sizable opportunity to offer a better fried chicken sandwich to its core audience than could be found at category competitors. The new Tender Crisp Chicken Sandwich was developed to be chicken "your way." The challenge was to introduce chicken "your way" through branding that was relevant to the way the core audience would most likely eat. The Subservient Chicken achieved both objectives. The branding campaign was launched on a website that featured a person in a chicken costume. Based on the viewer's command, the chicken could be asked to do wild and weird things—including doing a headstand or cartwheel, singing, walking like an Egyptian, reciting Shakespeare, doing the YMCA dance, playing golf, "moonwalking" like Michael Jackson, or doing the Electric Slide. If asked to do anything offensive, the chicken would walk up to the camera and shake a scolding finger. The creative execution, developed by the advertising agency Crispin, Porter + Bogusky, was a huge hit with the audience and, as hoped, the viewers passed along the content via YouTube and social network pages. It was also a huge hit with those in search of a great fried chicken sandwich. The brand driver drove the chefs in the Burger King kitchens to deliver the simple idea that you could "get chicken just the way you like it." It also drove the company's ad partners to deliver branding just the way its core audience liked it: entertaining, engaging, and worth sharing.

In addition to talking to Russ Klein about the company's return to one of its most successful brand drivers, I spoke to Brian Gies, Burger King's Vice President of Marketing. "Among the many things we've been receiving credit for from our audience," Brian told me,

> is that we "get it." We show that we clearly understand where they consume media, where they hang out. Burger King as a company "gets" the digital space and we get high marks for authenticity, for being as cool as our target market. Sure, we could have come out with ads that said, "We have this really tasty new chicken sandwich," but the media channel or the content wouldn't have been relevant to the customer or the brand persona we've trying to establish. All of our branding communication is done with a slight wink, as if to say, "Hey we know what's on your mind." We like to think of our brand's voice as the voice of the cool uncle, the guy who's old enough to have street smarts, but not so old that he can't remember what it was like to be young. The Subservient Chicken was like lightning in a bottle. The way we communicated our message was meaningful to this audience. They appreciated that we got who they are and how they spend their time. This was as much a part of being true to the brand idea as giving our customers chicken just the way they like it. We weren't *communicating* our way, but their way.

Burger King's focus on its super fan target, its focus on doing everything *their* way, has been a key factor in the company's financial

Burger King launched successful and entertaining branding initiatives like the viral hit "Subservient Chicken," which supported their brand driver of "Have It Your Way."

uptick. Same store sales were up year over year, 2006 to 2007, and its stock increased 32 percent during the same time period. After Subservient Chicken danced its way across the digital tools used by this core audience, Burger King had another branding win with its "Whopper Freakout" promotion. Driven by the same simple "Have It Your Way" brand driver, it was created to demonstrate what would happen if the hungry hoards *couldn't* have it their way—a time-honored deprivation tactic given a twenty-first-century media twist. In a *Candid Camera*-like venture customers were videotaped being told by the Burger King staffers that the much-loved Whopper sandwich was off the menu—permanently. The videos, intended to be used as the foundation for both online and television campaigns, almost immediately made their way to YouTube's list of the top-five most watched videos, and viewer responses appeared on YouTube complete with shrieks of outrage, pounding fists, and less than civil commentary. When I went to the Burger King website to do research on the company, I was amazed to learn that there are over 221,184 possible ways to order a Whopper. Talk about having it your way. No wonder the viewers were outraged. To further support its simple brand idea, Burger King has arranged sponsorships with the National Football League and NASCAR, and tie-ins with one of its super fans' favorite television shows, *The Simpsons.* Burger King also partnered with Microsoft on an Xbox gaming promotion, which led to 3.2 million sales of the game created for the event. Burger King clearly has a bead on its audience—on their likes and their dislikes, on how they like their food served up, and on how they like their media served up. These super fans like to have it *their* way, and this simple idea is the driver behind Burger King's recaptured success.

While we're in the neighborhood, Microsoft's insight about *its* tech-centric audience is, not surprisingly, at the core of the Xbox brand driver and everything having to do with the brand. As the fastest-selling gaming console in history, the popularity of Xbox, manufactured by Microsoft, is driven by the millions of users who love the social gaming experience. Its success as a brand is driven by brand managers who know that human beings like to have fun. The driving idea behind all things Xbox is to literally "make life fun through Xbox." "To be a great marketer you have to have a passion for your brand," remarked Jeff Bell, Vice President of Marketing at Xbox. "Everyone who works here has a natural passion and interest in gaming. We recognize that our audience uses gaming technology as a way to relax and to forge communities and relationships by playing games with others. The Xbox brand is like the guy in high school who got along with everyone. The guy who never put anyone down, but, instead, looked to find a common bond between people to bring them together. That's the basic idea that drives everything associated with the Xbox brand. If you don't have a lucid brand idea, you're reduced to competing on price and other commodity factors. You find the passion and bring people together around it."

It was clear from the start that Microsoft knew what Xbox stood for, and what it wanted its users to associate with its brand. From a basic product standpoint, with "make life fun through Xbox" as the inspiration, the Xbox engineers created hardware that's as fun as it is easy to use. The graphical user interface of the latest Xbox, the 360, is intuitive (even I can figure out how to use it), it's clean, and it's customizable. The real action starts with the Games panel, which displays the user's Gamer Card containing the player's reputation, Gamer Score, and the Zone that defines his or her style of game play. There's one-click access to already downloaded content—such as arcade games, game demos, trailers, TV shows and movies, along with listings of games played, and accomplishments. The console also makes it simple to access friends and messages through easy applications, and, when it is not being used as a gaming device, users can download a media panel to view slideshows or listen to music. The Xbox LIVE Marketplace feature enhances the fun by enabling users to buy virtual in-game merchandise, interface themes, and game add-ons.

Then there are the games themselves, driven to the core by the idea that you can "make life fun with Xbox." Depending on your idea of fun, you can virtually shift your gears with *Forza Motorsport2,* play *UNO* with Serena Williams, hang with the *Simpsons,* battle the universe with *Gears of War,* or save the universe with *Halo 3.* The special effect graphics are extraordinary. Even if you don't play, it's fun to just stand over someone's shoulder and watch.

As might be expected, the branding beyond the product's functionality is meta-branding at its best. It uses the magic of Xbox technology to sell the technology. From the very beginning, the ad agencies who worked with Xbox have created campaigns that lend themselves to viral marketing. Tom Bedecarre, CEO of AKQA, a digital strategy and creative firm that does extensive work with Xbox, said:

> Interactive media can give consumers a much richer experience with a brand. We create websites and mobile campaigns that people *want* to interact with. We've created immersive brand experiences that people will spend twenty, even sixty minutes with. We just launched a campaign for *Halo 3,* which was the largest entertainment property ever launched. We created an online experience for core Halo fans based on the three-dimensional diorama created for the game itself. You could see inside the game's environment, explore all the features of the game: the vehicles, the weapons, the enemies. Viewers watch it and can then attach a message and send it along to others. For *Forza Motorsport2,* we created a site that expressed the depth and complexity of the engineering customization that went into the game. It gets your adrenaline racing just to interact with the brand campaign. It's a crowded space. We're forced to continuously raise our own bar in terms of innovation.

Jeff Bell and his team work hard to demonstrate how play is an integral part of a balanced life. The Xbox hardware, software, and the advertising initiatives are all branding vehicles that reinforce its powerful brand associations with its core users who, like Burger King's, are males in the eighteen- to thirty-four-year-old age range. The viral exposure, the PR buzz, and word of mouth are certainly one reason for the brand's success, but the overarching reason is the brand organization's commitment to its simple brand driver.

"We need to keep being true to who we are," Jeff said as he ended our conversation. "Any brand must have a clear idea of what it does, its unique point of view, how it can meet an unmet need. Whatever it is, you need to stick with it. This idea should play into every decision you make as a brand organization. It's not that we have a page on My-Space, it's that our brand page on MySpace enables people to have fun. Our inspiration is that people like to have fun. We're inspired every day to *make* life fun through Xbox."

That the clarity of a brand idea is critical cannot be overstated. If you can't get your brand idea across within an organization, you'll have enormous difficulty getting it across effectively outside. In the digital environment, in a world of global, matrixed organizations with multiple marketing teams, multiple divisions, multiple agencies, and multiple distribution and licensing partners, the challenge to stay "true to who you are" has become more of a challenge than it ever was. The chance that some rogue brand experience will slip outside the lines of the brand promise is more than possible. With competition for ears and eyeballs so fierce, with time seeming to move so much more quickly than before, the chances of slipping are great. Great brands take care to ensure they don't. And they take care to see that, as the experiences of the brand evolve over time, they don't take their eyeballs off what drives their brand's success. For example, in *BrandSimple,* I used HBO as an example of a brand that established a brand idea that stayed different and relevant to television viewers, season after season. "It's not TV, it's HBO" clearly defined that this was no ordinary television network; it was the network where you'd find things to watch you couldn't find on any ordinary television network. This simple, bold statement continues to work as the brand's tagline, and its brand driver.

Courteney Monroe, Executive Vice President, Consumer Marketing for HBO, said, "'It's not TV, it's HBO' is still inherent in everything we do," as we began our interview. "Whether it's the programming we develop, the marketing campaigns, the technology we use, or our digital strategy, they all have to reinforce who we are. The challenge is that the space is getting more competitive, not less. We're competing with both content and format. People have lots of new choices for entertainment, including where and how they view it, their television sets, their computers, their cell phones. We're all about telling the best stories on television. It's the lens we use for everything we do. We're competing with other lenses. We have to keep proving we're worth paying for."

One of the examples Courteney gave me that proves her point is about HBO's blockbuster show, *The Sopranos.* Between seasons six and seven of *The Sopranos,* there was a longer lapse of time than between prior seasons. HBO was looking for a way to get consumers caught up with all the action in a manner befitting the idea that it was HBO, and not TV, its viewers were dealing with. What they did was definitely not ordinary, and it was definitely in line with HBO's brand driver. The network partnered with Google Maps to highlight several of the locations in New Jersey where events from the most recent season had taken place. Viewers were directed to a website, uplinked from HBO.com, on which they could zoom in and out of the Google Map and watch video updates of the season. It was the first time Google had partnered with another entity to undertake this sort of initiative. "It was as ground-breaking and innovative an initiative as viewers expect from HBO," Courteney said. "Because we were HBO we couldn't have just done the basic fifteen-minute, pre-show 'here's what you missed' type of thing. We had to do something that would generate as much talk as possible. Our programming always gets people talking. We wanted to capture the word-of-mouth dynamic. We knew we had to create something consumers could engage in, something that was immersive, and that was reflective of our brand. We used online and on-air promotions, but like a lot of our programming, it was propelled by the talk value."

While HBO's most powerful branding signal is its programming, everything it undertakes is driven by the simple idea that "It's not TV, it's HBO." Its advertising campaigns have been shot by world-

HBO partnered with Google Maps in its typically innovative way to bring viewers up to date between one season of the Sopranos and the next.

renowned photographer Annie Leibovitz. Another special branding campaign, titled Voyeur.com, was a video shot by Jake Scott, son of director Ridley Scott. The objective was to showcase the genius of the storytelling that viewers would enjoy by subscribing to HBO. In individual vignettes, it portrayed the lives of the occupants of a single apartment building in New York City. The site sparked immediate interest and generated over two million visits. Equally impressive was that visitors to the branded site were spending an average of ten minutes, an eternity in the digital age.

Season after season, year after year, HBO's business success has been driven by the incredibly simple idea that's "It's not TV, it's

HBO." Its adherence to this mantra informs everything—including its relevantly different programming, its promotions, its merchandising, its partnerships, and anything else it wants viewers to associate with its brand. Like many other smart marketers today, HBO recognizes that, in the digital world, it's not any one branding tactic that drives the train, but a powerfully simple brand idea. The marketing paradigm has shifted, and it requires a huge mind shift. With so many different constituencies responsible for branding efforts, with the many new ways for consumers to pick up branding signals, it's critical that organizations understand that it's the power of the idea that drives success, not the power of an individual touch point. Consumers are channel indifferent. They choose when and how they want to interact with a brand. Companies don't orchestrate the order in which consumers interact with their branding. Consumers do. To ensure that the relevantly different idea that defines the brand comes through wherever consumers interact with it, it's essential that the idea that drives the brand experience is understood by everyone responsible for the branding. While this has always been true, this truth has been magnified in the digital market. If your branding is still being pulled round and round the track with a traditional sort of engine, it's time to get off the train.

5

The Importance of a Clear Brand Voice

In 1958, "the man in the chair," a print advertisement for McGraw-Hill, made its first appearance. While the original man was replaced three times over the years (once with a woman), and the chair was changed twice, the copy in the ad remained exactly the same for over four decades: "I don't know who you are. I don't know your company. I don't know your company's product. I don't know what your company stands for. I don't know your company's customers. I don't know your company's record. I don't know your company's reputation. Now—what was it you wanted to sell me?"

There is no mention in the ad of McGraw Hill's publications or its corporate point of view, nor is there any self-congratulatory verbiage. The objective of this award-winning business-to-business ad is simply to emphasize that, in order to build a relationship with its customers, it is vital for a company to have a credible persona, a presence beyond what it produces. It spells out in stark terms that a company jeopardizes its ability to sell anything to anyone until it establishes an emotional connection. The ad lasted as long as it did because the relevance of its message.

Companies are, for the most part, rational places. They are fact-driven institutions, often led by people who have risen through the ranks of finance or operations. Numbers drive key decisions. Even in theoretically touchy-feely environments—like Hollywood studios, Madison Avenue firms, and non-profit organizations—when push comes to shove, the tendency is to gravitate toward the rational end of the spectrum. The "what" of the organization often trumps the "who." By this, I mean that *what* the company produces and *what* the company promises are given precedence over *who* is doing the producing and the promising. Far too often, the company either forgets there is an emotional end of the spectrum, or it doesn't come close to reaching it. What the man in the chair was sternly conveying is that overlooking the "who" can be detrimental to an organization's health.

"*What*" is a transaction. "*Who*" is a relationship. The most powerful brands are built on relationships. They appeal to consumers on some emotional level beyond just the straightforward details of the transaction. Much like political candidates, for whom charisma plays a decisive role in a voter's ultimate decision at the polling booth, personality traits play an equal role at the cash register. (I would argue that more elections are won on charisma than are won on hard facts, no matter what the pollsters say.) When I interviewed Thomas Friedman for my last book, he said "People listen with their gut. If you connect with them on a gut level, they'll say, 'Don't bother me with the details.' If you don't connect with them on a gut level, you can't offer them enough details to bring them around." I couldn't agree with him more. People listen to the enticements of politicians, potential spouses, and of brand organizations with their gut. If it doesn't get them at this level, it's not going to get them.

The most successful brand companies know that to build a relationship with a consumer, it's essential to define and develop the "who." I don't mean in conventional terms, as in, "Hey, we're the easy-to-deal-with-friendly-professional company," but as a discernable personality. This is yet another of the important truths of building brands that has been magnified in the digital arena. Because people are exposed to more news, noise, and information, having a distinguishable and definite character can help a brand stand out and differentiate itself in a cluttered environment. Second, and equally important, digital devices foster communication. We use these tools to interact—person to person, brand to person, person to brand. These devices are, by nature, relationship-builders. In this day and age, more so than in any other, consumers have a genuine opportunity to engage with brands and to actively participate in the building of brands. They are not merely passive recipients of information about diapers, beer, dishwashers, or soap; they can engage in "conversations" with the organizations that represent these things and, in some cases, the products themselves. Digital tools create social experiences. It is critical that an organization thinks about its brand with this mindset. As a result of the online relationship model, brands have become more real to people. Their virtual reality affects the way people talk to each other about brands and the way they talk to and interact with brands. As such, organizations must imbue their brands with more human attributes.

To build strong relationships with its customers in the digital marketplace, an organization must define and fully develop a palpable brand personality. More than this, it must clearly define the voice of this personality—the voice of the brand. With so many different points at which a consumer can interact with a brand and with so many people involved in creating branding signals, it's important that everyone knows intuitively how to assume the brand's personality and its voice.

If there are several people within the company responsible for blogging to consumers, they must all talk the same talk. If the brand has product review sites, MySpace pages, and chat rooms, the voice must be uniform from venue to venue. Advertising, customer support, and retail environments must all reinforce the attitude and spirit of the brand voice. Within the cacophony of branding signals, a distinct brand voice will help differentiate the brand. In a world as disorderly as ours, multiple personality disorder is not the order of the day.

Apple is a terrific example of a brand that has had a clearly defined personality and voice from day one. Apple is so sure of its brand's voice and personality that it could go out and do a casting call for it. In a branding campaign called "Get a Mac," which began in 2006, Apple was able to capture its "who" in the real persona of actor Justin Long. This "Mac Guy" pleasantly and with great assurance took on an inept "PC Guy" to point out the differences between Apple technology and its users and PC technology and its users. The campaign included over forty creative variations and generated scores of takeoffs on YouTube. According to *Advertising Age,* this campaign has been a significant factor in the increase in Apple's market share.

While any one of us could list a few adjectives that describe the Apple personality and voice, Apple brand managers, in particular its uber-manager Steve Jobs, have gone deeper in their psychological assessment of the brand in order to ensure there are no missteps in its branding. While we might define the Apple brand as cool, innovative, and friendly, the reason the "Get a Mac" campaign did so well is that Apple has a greater recognition of its brand's persona than can be summed up in just four or five words. As a brand, its self-awareness is first-rate. In a study done by the interactive research firm Mindset Media that appeared in *Advertising Age,* it was demonstrated that in its casting for the "Get a Mac" campaign the brand team knew just what to look for in a Mac look-alike, the guy who would represent the Mac and the Mac user. According to the study, this had to be a person who showed openness to new ideas and new ways of doing things. These are people who "Think Differently," as an Apple campaign illustrated in the 1980s. Apple customers are people who are intellectually curious and more comfortable with emotions than the average person. Apple people are more likely to drive hybrids and buy organic food. They have great concern about environmental issues, are perfectionists, and probably replace sneakers more often than other people do. In the same *Advertising Age* article, it was noted that data collected by ChangeWave Research showed that, compared with 59 percent of people who bought a Dell PC, 79 percent of people who have purchased an Apple computer were very satisfied. The people who reflect the persona of Apple are very self-assured.

Every organization has tone and manner guidelines for its brand personality. Most have a set of graphic standards—colors, terminology to be used in copy, and typefaces that reflect the brand. This all helps, but unless an organization can elucidate what makes up the "ness" of its brand, it's very difficult for those doing the branding to infuse branded touch points with the brand's personality traits. This makes it more difficult to differentiate the brand in the marketplace, and, in turn, more difficult for consumers to get a sense of "who" it is they're dealing with. Peter Friedman, currently CEO of LiveWorld, a social network marketing agency that has partnered with WPP agencies on multiple brand initiatives, talked about this topic relative to his time working at Apple. "Apple understood the critical nature of brand voice early on," he said. He added,

> I was there from 1984 until 1996, and the company knew that its products and everything associated with its products had to personify its brand. Steve Jobs not only created a very strong vision for the company, he established the voice. "Apple-ness" is intuitive in the organization. I can best describe it as a cultural sensibility of emotional engagement and creativity. Everyone

at Apple thinks about its brand in terms of human relationships. You have a relationship with your Mac or your iPod. They're not just machines. You go to the Apple store, and you feel you're interacting with a distinct personality. Go online and you experience its personality. The organization and its customers are emotionally bound to this brand. It's funny. Sometimes in my work now, a client will say to me relative to something they've seen written about their brand online, "That's not *my* brand they're talking about." I say, "Well, that's how people are talking about your brand which means it's how they perceive your brand, which means it *is* your brand."

It is sometimes the case that the founder of a brand will drive its voice. These are folks with intense passion and a very clear idea of how they want their brands to be perceived in the marketplace. It might be that it is *their* personality that the brand takes on. As Peter said, Steve Jobs of Apple is, and continues to be, instrumental in establishing the character of the Apple brand. Herb Kelleher is the good-humored, easygoing man behind the good-humored, easygoing personality of Southwest Airlines. Richard Branson's hip and "yeah, baby" demeanor can be felt in every Virgin experience. And it's Ben and Jerry, the originators of Ben and Jerry's Ice Cream, we think about when indulging in their outrageously delicious confections. But, in most of the other millions of instances, it's up to the organization and its management to establish the brand personality and voice. Identifying something that is meaningfully different to represent in the minds of consumers is hard enough. Defining the "who" of this relevant differentiation can be even harder.

Julie Roehm is a marketing consultant who has held senior management positions with some of the largest brand organizations in the country. I spoke to her about her work with Chrysler, where she was a director of marketing. Specifically, we talked about how the brand teams created separate personalities for Chrysler, Jeep, and Dodge. "I always begin any initiative by trying to create some sort of visual representation of the brand," she told me. "It's very hard to stand up in front of an agency team and just verbalize the character of a brand. I use a visual to portray the brand as a real person. Generally, this representation takes on some of the traits of the core customer, but if your intent is to interact with this customer on a personal level, your brand should be on the same wave length. The most important element of this exercise is not to introduce the concept of the brand itself—in this case, the car."

Julie asked me if I was old enough to remember *Charlie's Angels*. Not the recent movie series, but the television show that starred Kate Jackson, Farrah Fawcett, and Jacqueline Smith. I told her I was definitely old enough. She said, "Okay, let's say we used the characters in this show to help us clearly define the characters of the Chrysler, Dodge and Jeep brands." She continued:

> If we did it right, you'd be able to tell us precisely which character defined which individual brand of car. For example, in the show, Kate Jackson's character was a little rugged around the edges. She was very direct, very no-nonsense. She liked to wear clothing that was a bit masculine in nature. She was very sure of herself. She listened to music that had a heavy bass beat, lots of energy. She preferred beer nuts to any other type of nut. Then, there's Jacqueline Smith's character. She's suave, sophisticated. She probably wore designer clothing and listened to classical music, or classic jazz. She liked cashews. Farrah was sort of New Age. She was a free spirit. She wanted to experience the world on her own terms. Breezy music, blue jeans, and trail mix were her things.

My reputation as a brand professional was at stake. I told Julie that Kate Jackson represented Dodge; Jacqueline Smith, Chrysler; and Farrah Fawcett, Jeep. Julie told me I was right, and my reputation was preserved. This example of the type of exercises she uses with her management teams to fully define a brand's character is representative of the type of exercise any brand organization should use. The deeper one is able to get into characterizing a brand's persona, the more "in character" the branding will be, and the better an organization's chances of ensuring that its brand is on the same wave length across all points of touch. With so many people responsible for so many different aspects of the branding process, it's essential that the brand character hold up to any sort of branding tactic, and equally important that the brand speak with one voice. As stated on the home page of its website, this is the deliberate intention of the publication *The Economist:* "Many hands write *The Economist,* but it speaks with one voice." The inference is to the many editors and writers who contribute content and shape the magazine's character. What's interesting is that, as a result of speaking with one definitive voice, the dynamics of the online world are playing a part in honing its character even more.

I had a fascinating discussion with Ben Edwards, Publisher of Economist.com. It was particularly interesting to me because I wanted to learn more about how the dynamics of the digital space affect a brand's personality. "Our readers are actually helping us develop a more distinct personality," remarked Ben. He continued:

Our business objective is to help make sense of the world for our readers. We go deep into a subject, say Japanese politics or Zimbabwe or wine manufacturing and then report on it with wit and acuity. We also help readers make the connection between a particular issue and global economics or politics or science. What's been happening online with respect to brand's personality is that we seem to have captured the essence of an Oxford-style debate. One reader or group of readers takes on one expert position and another group, the opposing position. One or another of our editors acts like the moderator or the "floor," as it's called. It's more than just a blog; it's layers of conversations. We've been using the power of digital tools to create branded experiences that reinforce what makes our publication different. More and more, *The Economist* is being perceived as not just the purveyor of intelligent content, but the moderator of intelligent discussion. We've taken on a dimensional persona. People respond as if they're writing to a distinct person. Some people have written one-thousand-word essays and posted them, which you don't often see. We connect people to each other and encourage conversation and debate.

It is unequivocal that the Internet and other digital technology enable dialogue and interaction. As this environment evolves, what is fascinating to observe as the environment evolves is how these dialogues and interactions work on so many levels. They work to reinforce a brand's identity just as they work to poke holes in it. One of the reasons people enjoy Facebook and MySpace so much is that they can use them to create identities for themselves and control other peoples' perceptions of them. Marketers like Ben Edwards are learning that the ability of consumers to help shape a brand's identity is both a huge opportunity and a challenge. He and the editorial staff keep a steady hand on the controls to ensure that the perception of the magazine stays within the guardrails they've established. *The Economist* is taking advantage of reader interaction with its brand to help sharpen its personality in a way that benefits everybody.

Some brand categories lend themselves to personalization more easily than others. Media vehicles, like *The Economist,* are tough. The recognition that it could genuinely be perceived as the moderator of intelligent discussion was smart on the part of *The Economist*'s marketing team. As a result of being a good judge of its own character, the organization has been able to more clearly differentiate itself in the media marketplace.

Perhaps an easier category of brand to personify is beer, although maybe not as easy as some would like to think. Rolling Rock beer, now owned by Anheuser-Busch, had a reputation as a sleepy, back-porch kind of beer. The organization wanted to refresh its image, to make it more hip, but in a manner that would clearly differentiate it

115

from behemoths like Budweiser and Miller. In late 2006, the company came to Goodby, Silverstein & Partners for help with this challenge. I spoke to Harold Sogard, Vice Chairman and a partner at the agency, about its work for the Rolling Rock brand. "Among the first things we needed to do was get clarity of voice," he said, adding:

> We had to get everybody in the room to say, "This is the voice. This is the personality. This is the brand." One of the things we discovered about the audience was that they thought of themselves as independent thinkers who didn't need or want the big splashy beers, like Bud or Miller, with their over-the-top advertising. They didn't want to be associated with big corporations or humorless middle-aged guys. We took advantage of this insight and created a voice, a personality for the brand that played on the image of the independent thinker. We liked the sense of mystery, the offbeat, the unconventional mentality afforded by this type of persona. We also recognized that we had in the Rolling Rock demographic an extremely net-savvy group of guys who, if we played our creative hand right, would use word of mouth to pass along the Rolling Rock brand idea to others.

To say the Goodby team played its creative hand right would be an incredible understatement. What they did was create a series of branded videos, most of which aired exclusively on the Internet. The first featured a gorilla, wearing a green Speedo with a cooler of Rolling Rock strapped to his back, parachuting from the sky toward a group of visibly bored people at a pool party. One exceptionally nerdy guy looks up and cries with delight, "Hey, everyone, it's the Rolling Rock beer ape, and he's here to save the day!" Upon landing, the ape begins tossing out cans of the beer to the astonished guests while a rockin' Rolling Rock anthem plays in the background. The gorilla struts his stuff with the ladies, and, at the end of the video, plunges into the pool with his green and white electric guitar—an obvious parody of big, splashy beer commercials. In another video that did appear on television after Anheuser-Busch bought Rolling Rock, we meet Ron Stablehorn, the fictional new director of marketing for Rolling Rock, who is nothing less than a bumbling idiot. It seems his primary responsibility is to keep apologizing for his brand's tasteless commercials, including the Rolling Rock beer ape advertisement. This meta-parody of a typical beer advertising campaign has been effective because it's exactly what the independent drinkers of Rolling Rock would expect from their beer of choice.

The other hand Goodby played right was in knowing that, if it convincingly expressed the brand's personality to a core audience that shared the same character traits, this particular audience would pass along the content to like-minded folks. With this in mind the agency did not use television at all in its initial launch, but instead posted the "beer ape" spot on YouTube, an unconventional but perfectly apt communication strategy. As the Goodby team hoped, these independent, offbeat beer drinkers took to the strategy and passed it along to others. The video was viewed more than 1.2 million times. In November 2006, it became the YouTube's most-watched video. The brand's sales, which had been in decline, rose 15 percent.

"People loved that this unconventional beer was taking on the bigwigs," Harold said. "We could have spent millions of dollars building a brand campaign, but because we pegged the brand and the audience, we ended up spending pennies, relatively speaking. We created a personality for the beer that was out of the ordinary and connected it to an audience that liked to think of itself as out of the ordinary." As a final note on this out-of-the-ordinary story, if you go to YouTube and take a look at these very clever spots, you'll find that each one is preceded with the notice that "This ad is not running on TV due to an overwhelming number of complaints. However, we think it is one of the best commercials of all time, and we will continue to air it on the Internet." Goodby had the Rolling Rock personality pegged from every angle.

Rolling Rock is a new personality on the block, created from scratch. Another brand personality was created from scratch ninety years ago. The challenge, in this case, has been to keep the character and voice up-to-date given the digital conditions.

In 1921, the Washburn Crosby milling company held a competition asking housewives from across America to send in their favorite recipes. The response to the contest was enormous. Equally enormous was the number of women who wrote in with specific questions about cooking and baking. As a way of giving a personalized response to these inquiries the company created a fictitious character named Betty Crocker. Crocker was the last name of a retired company executive, and the name Betty was chosen because it exuded warmth and friendliness. The company decided it would add intimacy to the character's relationship with her audience if she personally signed her responses. Washburn Crosby chose someone from within the company who had good handwriting to sign these letters. In 1924, Betty Crocker acquired a "real" voice as star of the radio program "Betty Crocker School of the Air." By 1936, Washburn Crosby was now part of General Mills, and the lovely lady's face appeared on packaging for the company's products. General Mills was more than successful in creating a personality for the brand, as indicated by the fact that Betty Crocker came in second only to Eleanor Roosevelt in a 1945 *Fortune* magazine poll of the most popular women in America. This fictional kitchen expert had become very real indeed to women in search of advice on food and families.

Jim Cuene is the Director of Interactive Marketing for General Mills. We had a conversation about the growing importance of differentiating a brand within the digital environment—specifically, how the organization has used the space to reinforce a brand's personality with its target users. "Our team focuses on three areas," he told me, continuing:

> The first is to look for ways to strategically weave interactive tactics into the consumer communication plan. Second, we look at creating best-in-class campaigns with interactive and website content at their core. Third, we focus

on database management—delivering relevant value to our customers on a one-to-one basis. The key to success at the intersection of these efforts is to talk to consumers in the way they would expect to be spoken to from a brand standpoint. This is where alignment with a brand personality plays a vital role. There is such clarity of what "Betty Crocker-ness" is that our team members ask themselves before committing to any initiative, "Would Betty do this?" People talk about Betty as though she's a real person. "Oh, that's just not Betty," or "this needs a little more Betty-ness." The clear brand voice facilitates a better creation of the execution.

As I mentioned earlier in the book, the ability to consistently express "brand-ness" from one experience with the brand to the next is a critical success factor. If you have a guiding light in the personification of the brand, it helps direct all those who play a part in the branding efforts. If the character of the brand is so well defined that it becomes real to people, it brings the branding to life. This is as true, if not more true, for online experiences as for traditional branding experiences. Because of the growing fragmentation of the marketplace, integrating branding experiences is taking on greater importance. Because of the growing importance of online experiences and the personal nature of the Internet, organizations are being pressed to fine-tune the personalities of their brands. Jim and his team recognize this and use their online presence to further differentiate their brand's promise. In the face of competition, not just from specific packaged goods brands, but from cooking sites, recipe sites, kitchen appliance sites, and other sites that offer advice on food and families, BettyCrocker.com is reinforcing its differentiation by honing a character close to ninety years old.

Way back when, Betty Crocker was a trusted authority in the kitchen. She was trusted to help customers sort through recipes and find tasty meals that could be prepared with the family budget in mind, or recipes that would work beautifully on specific occasions. The idea of helping people find recipes faster and recipes that fit the occasion is central to Bettycrocker.com. "If you were visiting Betty in her kitchen," Jim said,

> she'd most likely flip through an index card file and say, "Here's what you need. Here's a sprinkled Christmas cookie your family will love." We've taken search technology to create a similar experience. People come to the site for this purpose; to get personal advice on cooking and baking. It's not about the technology: it's about how people get information these days. In 1932, they'd go the Betty Crocker cookbook. Today, they come to our website. The obvious advantage is that now our customers can interact with us and they can interact with other people like themselves. Our research, part of which we do in the field visiting people in their kitchens, showed us how women evaluate recipes, how they share them, where they get them, how they customize them. We used insight from this research to design a website that replicated these activities. We took the consumer's actual experience in her kitchen and aligned it with how "Betty" would deliver the experience online. The site which reflects the presence of Betty Crocker, has kept the brand differentiated and sustained the community of women who love and trust Betty Crocker.

As the McGraw-Hill "man in the chair" admonished, it is critical for a brand to take on a recognizable and credible presence beyond its rational benefits if it expects to succeed at building a strong and trusting relationship with consumers. As digital tools enable consumers to get closer to brands and to interact with them; as technology, and branded applications enable consumers to interact with each other and with brand organizations, the truth of this admonishment has taken on greater importance. As Harold Sogaard said, clearly defining your brand's personality and its voice are among the critical steps in any branding initiative. In an environment where dialogue, conversation, and engagement rule, they become even more critical. To succeed in the digital world much more attention must be placed on creating the "who." Consumers want to know who they will be having conversations with, and with whom they'll be building relationships.

6

The Importance of Following the Customer's Journey

At one point in my life, I wanted to be in the movies. Not as an actor (anyone who has played poker with me will tell you this is not my forte), but as a director. As a communications major in college, I had taken my share of filmmaking courses, but recognized soon after graduating college and getting an MBA that establishing a career in marketing made better use of the talent cards I had been dealt. However, during the time I spent as a brand manager at Lever Brothers, I did have the opportunity to experience what I can only assume a film director experiences. A principal part of my responsibility was to ensure that any department within the company with a direct impact on the brands I was assigned knew what role they played in delivering on the brand's promise. I had to make certain that they knew whether something was going to contribute to the final outcome in a way that supported what Lever wanted the brand to represent in the minds of consumers. I might say: "No, we can't use a less expensive printing for the packaging, because we want the graphics to feel more like cosmetics than soap," or, "Yes, using cheerleaders does make sense as a public relations tie-in for Caress." Basically, my job was to ensure that the brand held together. I made the judgment calls about where we could nip and tuck and where we needed to hold the line.

Next to establishing a unified voice for a brand, getting everyone in an organization to understand how their role affects the totality of the brand experience is the most difficult, yet critical, branding activity. And it's getting more difficult. Given the accelerated speed of business, the old command and control management approach is simply not fast or flexible enough to keep the organization competitive. As a result, more and more companies are empowering their employees to make more decisions at the operational level. This is both a good and necessary thing. But, as the digital marketplace continues to evolve, it's not just the brand organization's employees, or even its manufacturing partners, who are involved in the branding process. Digital technology continues to spawn new and innovative ways for brands to touch consumers and for consumers to touch brands: website applications, search applications, text messages, blogs, reviews, chat rooms, banner ads, viral videos, and pages on social networks, to name a few. This requires the addition of a motley crew of constituencies to the branding team: multiple agency partners, technology and media partners, blog writers, search specialists, and courters of brand evangelists. The challenge to represent a brand as the sum of its parts is now a job that requires more than just one person making judgment calls.

Digital technology has put a powerful magnifying glass on just how many ways there are for consumers to come into contact with a brand and whether each delivers on enhancing the experience of the brand. It has also magnified the importance of helping those responsible for the branding to see how their roles influence the totality of the brand experience. While almost all organizations have some sort of formal written guidelines for branding, these documents are relatively narrow in focus. They produce cookie-cutter outcomes for branding tactics that demand cookie-cutter outcomes, like signage, logo placement, print ads, and website formats. They help maintain consistency across graphic elements and in fundamental brand aesthetics, but these guidelines don't address how the myriad other brand-related initiatives should reflect the brand promise. Where, for example, in a set of branding guidelines, could you find out how the Snuggle bear should look and behave? Or whether a video intended for contagion on YouTube won't spread the wrong message?

The added challenge is that, while it's never been easy to assess which of the consumer's interactions with a brand has had the greatest impact on their buying behavior, it's now harder than ever for an organization to make this assessment. Consumers may see an ad on television (if they haven't used technology to skip it); they may visit a corporate website; they may be on the receiving end of brand evangelism; they may get caught up in the contagion of a viral branding experience; they may see reviews of a product on a category site; they may get an e-mail, or they may do all of the above within the same timeframe. Consumers have become "media multi-taskers." According to Lee Doyle, North America Chief Executive for Mediaedge:cia, an agency that buys media space, over 60 percent of adults report that they are engaged in some other activity while watching television. Over two-thirds of those people say they are online while they watch television. "It's more challenging than before to determine the power of one channel of branding communication over another," he told me during our conversation, adding:

> Word of mouth, recommendations from friends, viral campaigns, even the circulars in Sunday editions of newspapers take on new meaning as influencers in the digital economy. It's necessary for marketing organizations to determine not just where branding engagement is taking place, but where *active* branding engagement is taking place. You have to take into consideration a target

audience's likely state of attention when exposed to a particular brand touch point. You have to consider their motivation for initiating a brand interaction. Are they in a buying mode, a consideration mode, or just passively watching what someone told them was a cool YouTube video? What's more, in a study we did, we found that there can be a huge difference in the influence one branding channel has over another relative to the specific category of a brand. For example, word of mouth plays a huge role in categories where the consumer is making a considered purchase, like a car or an appliance, but not nearly as much influence in lower interest categories. Among the other interesting phenomena is that marketing is becoming more of a public relations function. Organizations are recognizing the need to not just insert themselves into virtual dialogues, but to shape these dialogues. On the flip side, the relevance of their participation can be scrutinized more easily. People don't necessarily hate advertising; they hate anything irrelevant. The opportunity for marketers is to do a better job of identifying the right audience and addressing the right branding at the right time. The whole notion of the customer journey has changed.

The whole notion of a customer's journey with a brand *has* changed. And focus on the journey a customer takes across the fast multiplying brand touch points has become integral to helping drive an understanding of "brand-ness" into the organization and beyond. In my last book, *BrandSimple,* I wrote about the importance of mapping out the journey a customer takes with a brand; literally illustrating where a consumer interacts with the brand. Of course, the route a customer took from initial awareness of brand choices, to purchase consideration, and finally, to activation used to be relatively linear. Even a company's after-purchase branding initiatives could be viewed as a pretty straight line of loyalty programs and follow-up communications to remind its customers of warranty expirations or to introduce product extensions. However, the journey consumers take with a brand today is anything but linear. It's circuitous. While a map of today's customer journey is more akin to an onboard navigation system, it's still one of the best ways to enable those responsible for the branding to see where and when consumers interact with a brand. Equally important, it will help them envision their roles in bringing the brand experience to life in a manner appropriate to the specific branding interaction. Given the side roads and U-turns that digital tools add to the customer's journey, this exercise is actually more critical now than during life before digital. It's hard enough to get a single organization focused on the same goal. With so many different constituencies involved, a map of the customer journey is a practical way to demonstrate how all the parts of the journey must hold together to meet consumers' expectations across the board. When communicating and teaching, I've found that, as the world gets more complicated, simple tools work even better. If I tried to take a hundred-page deck into an organization to demonstrate the same concept I'd bore people to tears.

Another reason a map of the customer journey is so important in today's environment is that, as the market changes, it can help an organization evaluate, and reevaluate which branding signals best reinforce a brand's relevant differentiation. This becomes even more significant in a marketplace where digital tools may tempt some to play without thinking of whether a whiz-bang initiative will differentiate the brand from its competitors. It's a fact of brand-building that not all branding signals are created equal. Some have far more influence than others in getting consumers to think about a brand in the way the organization wants them to. It's at these points of contact that the organization should make its greatest branding investments. For example, for entertainment companies—such as Pixar, Sesame Street, or HBO—it's the quality of the content that is the most powerful branding signal and where these organizations *do* make their greatest investments. When Fred Smith founded Federal Express in 1971, he invested in a business model that delivered on the idea of reliability, both literally and figuratively: "On-time delivery by 10:30 a.m." There is no ambiguity in this simple promise. FedEx makes its greatest branding investments in processes and services that best reinforce this relevant difference. The Gatorade brand is known for improving an athlete's performance on the field of play, whether it's a Little League or a major league field. The company makes its greatest branding investments in the research and development of hydrating beverages and in keeping its brand's name clearly visible on the sidelines of athletic events worldwide. While the Ralph Lauren website can certainly play a beautiful supporting role, as a lifestyle brand the company is smart enough to know that its greatest branding investments must be made in the retail arena, in its clothing and home furnishing designs.

A cell phone manufacturer might spend part of its branding budget on television or take advantage of its website to provide information about its pricing and calling programs, but the substantial portion of its branding investment is (or should be) in the area of product performance. This is where it can most critically differentiate itself from the competition. The topic of dropped calls carries far more weight as a topic of blog conversations about mobile carriers than the variety of calling plans offered. The company should definitely invest in online applications that enable brand evangelists to pass along word of its brand's stellar performance, but it should give top priority to what it wants the buzz to be about. On the other hand, if a company sells books online, the greatest branding investment should be in sophisticated digital applications that enable people to virtually browse through their selections and get through the checkout process quickly and efficiently.

A map of the customer journey is not the only step, but it's the first step in getting a branding team to see where consumers engage with the brand and which interactions are most likely to cement strong relationships. There are many other means a company can and should use to assess where and when consumers engage with a brand. But, as a starting point, a map is a wonderful way to initially spec out all the points at which customers touch the brand and to also identify which engagements matter most, to both the consumers and to the company's bottom line. A map allows the organization to get a sense of the operational requirements necessary to deliver on the brand promise and enables it to assess which branding initiatives are simply cost of entry and which will genuinely differentiate the brand in the marketplace. Digital tactics, in and of themselves, matter in the branding investment equation only when they enable a company to deliver on the brand idea better than any other branding initiative can. Pages in social networks, blogs, banners, and YouTube videos are certainly nifty branding tools to play with. But, if it's digital for digital's sake, it's as gratuitous as any form of branding that's created for the sizzle and not the steak. The importance of knowing where you should play and knowing where you can win is another of the truths of branding that has been magnified in the digital world. Or, as Esther Dyson, a WPP Board member and an early guru of all things digital, told me when I asked her about how the new technology changes the rules of branding: "It's not the equipment in the kitchen, it's can you run the restaurant right."

One brand that knows how to run the restaurant right, or at least the beverage list, is Pepsi-Cola. Long thought of as the "choice of a new generation," Pepsi has clearly differentiated its brand of soft drink by driving home the simple idea that its brand is a little younger and a little hipper than other cola products. While the Pepsi brand has a long history of fantastic branding initiatives that have successfully gotten this message across, one of its most recent initiatives has been an investment in a rather traditional touch point: the design of its cans. Pepsi has changed the look of its cans only ten times in its 109-year history. Why, in the digital age, did it decide to make such a sizable branding investment in its packaging? The company took a look at the map of its customer's journey, assessed the competitive environment, and realized that the good, old-fashioned supermarket aisle in concert with new word of mouth was where it could play to win at enhancing its brand difference in the minds of consumers. The following provides a bit of context to further explain the company's decision.

If you stroll down the aisle of any supermarket, drugstore, or discount retailer, you'll notice that the number of well-known brands taking on package redesigns over the past couple of years has grown exponentially. While the standard operating procedure for most consumer brands has been to keep the package design status quo for six years or so, brand name bottles, bags, boxes, and cartons are now undergoing major renovations with greater frequency. Why this incredible shift? From my branding purist's perspective, I'd say there are two key dynamics driving marketers to take a second look at their packaging to see if it's working as well as it should be to differentiate the brand. The first is the media multi-tasking Lee Doyle referenced. It's never been more difficult for a company to determine if it is reaching, let alone connecting with, the audience it wants to reach. As media is sliced and diced into a thousand points of awareness, so, too, is consumer attention. The second dynamic at play is the value of packaging relative to other branding activities. The last things consumers see before they make a purchase also happens to be among the last pure branding spaces available. Before a consumer even opens it, the package can tell a clear and simple story about what the brand stands for. With so many brands vying for attention across such a broad spectrum of branding options, the package can be a branding winner.

When it comes to the package, people can't ad-skip as they move down a supermarket aisle. If you don't have luck connecting with the audience you want as they sit in front of the television or laptop, sooner or later they're going to show up in front of the retail shelf. Packaging is one of the only consumer touch points at which a brand can literally reinforce the core difference between itself and the brand sitting next to it. And that's what the brand managers at Pepsi had in mind when they developed the "Design Our Pepsi Can" branding initiative. Taking advantage of its packaging and the techno-centric nature of its core audience, Pepsi designed a branding initiative that wowed consumers in the aisles. "We looked at the media landscape and the consumers we wanted to reach and decided to change the playing field," said John Vail, Director of Interactive Marketing at Pepsi. "Given the interactive nature of the marketplace, we decided to make the consumer the CMO, the chief marketing officer. It was an opportunity to get the consumer engaged with the brand in a genuinely relevant way. It was an opportunity to use digital tools in a relevant way."

The branding campaign, promoted online, in general media, and on the cans themselves, directed consumers to the designourpepsican. com website. Once registered on the site, participants had the option of using their own design applications or the applications provided by Pepsi. Designs were posted on the website, where viewers voted for the winners. In the initial endeavor, the winner took home a $10,000 prize and the winning artwork was featured on 500 million Pepsi cans across the country. Pepsi made even better use of its youthful brand spirit by asking some of the world's top musicians to contribute their artistic talents. The All-American Rejects, Big & Rich, and Pharrell Williams created special designs. The cans which they created feature a unique URL that directs their fans to exclusive footage of the artists and their new projects. "It was actually not surprising to us that a majority of the submissions reflected Pepsi 'brand-ness,'" John said. He continued:

Consumers get what Pepsi stands for. There were few, if any, inappropriate design submissions. About 90 percent of the participants used the graphics applications we provided on our site with the other 10 percent using their own applications. We had about one hundred thousand submissions. It was extraordinary. In 2008, all of the Pepsi cans will feature user-generated designs. This initiative was farther reaching and had far more impact than any traditional promotion would have allowed. We got people literally engaged with the brand. We know our audience is highly adept with digital technology. We know it's where they get information and where they hang out. We know what type of music they listen to and how culturally savvy they are. We used the Internet as a springboard to consumer engagement with the brand. It's working just the way we hoped it would.

The branding initiative continues to work the way Pepsi wants to because the brand managers know how to get and keep the consumer connected to the brand in this crazy media world. The packaging is often a forgotten branding channel for many marketers, but lots of others, like Pepsi, took one of the most fundamental points of touch and looked at it in a new way—as a "springboard" for getting the consumer involved in the entirety of the brand experience. Andy Horrow, Global Marketing Director, for Pepsi, also spoke to me about the company's new foray into old branding territory:

The store environment is really critical to us around the world. We asked ourselves whether we were making the most compelling case to our customers when they see our brand in the store. For us, it was looking at traditional branding vehicles like in-store and sampling in conjunction with newer marketing tactics like digital media. The question is: How can we use packaging to help consumers connect the marketing pieces so they can get the most out of the brand experience? For example, the Pepsi can designed by the Black-Eyed Peas is just one part of the consumer experience. We use the can to pull that consumer through a range of experiences, to pull someone through the Pepsi story. We sponsored a global tour for the band, which we advertised on TV, on our Pepsi sites, and on our packaging. You can win tickets to a concert. You can download the band's music. You can download special coupons for Pepsi prod-

Pepsi looked at its packaging, often a forgotten branding channel, and made it the springboard for active consumer engagement in the brand experience.

ucts and related merchandise. You can send things to your mobile phone and pass information and music along to others. And we play it all up at point of sale. Branding is 3-D. It's not a matter of abandoning one point of touch for another. Consumers have more opportunities to connect, but brands have more responsibility to connect the message in the right way at the right points.

The right way is dependent, first and foremost, on the insights you form about your core consumer: what's relevant to them, and where they are most likely to interact with a brand. Then, as Lee Doyle said, it's dependent on the category in which your brand plays, and on your overall branding objectives. Where should you be making your greatest branding investments at a given point in the consumer's relationship with the brand? Which branding investment will have the greatest influence on how consumers think about a brand? The management and marketers of BMW, for example, can express through television and print ads that its brand is all about "the joy of driving," but if the car isn't ultimately a joy to drive, the words would ring hollow very quickly. BMW's engineers understand the simple idea driving the brand, and they make sure it hits home with every BMW test drive and beyond. The company makes its most substantial investments in the performance of its automobiles, spending an enormous amount of time on engine design, down to the smallest details, and on the mechanics of every other component in its cars—not to mention the operations necessary to support all of the inner workings of its cars. I had an interesting discussion with Joe Torpey, Internet Manager for BMW of North America, about the BMW customer life cycle, about what the company considers the "ideal brand journey," and about how the promise of the brand is expressed during this journey. He told me:

> Our goal is to deliver joy to the customer, the joy of driving. This is the backbone of the brand idea. The ultimate promise of the brand is in the driving, but we need to get consumers to this point. We look at all the places users may cross our path and determine how to connect the dots for them in terms of the total experience. Everything has to represent the brand well, both our values and our product. As we researched how our current customers and our prospects start their journey, we found it's more often than not on the Internet. Knowing that there are many sources they could go to for information—third-party and even competitors' sites—we realized that we had to make a major investment in this branding experience. We wanted to make the BMW site enjoyable, because that's what our brand is all about, but we also knew we had to provide a robust online experience in terms of communicating the strength of the brand and why it's different. One of the things that makes the BMW unique is the ability to customize the vehicle and order it specifically to your liking. Not just the exterior colors or interior trims and leathers, but certain technological features you'd like added. One of the best branding investments we've made relative to this stage of the buying process is the "build-your-own" section of the site.

Of course, as part of my research for this book, I had to spend some time building my own BMW—on the company's site, that is. One of the first things I discovered was that it *was* enjoyable, really enjoyable. I started by choosing the basic BMW Series model I wanted, and then I went to work adding and subtracting. First things first, I played with variations on the interior and exterior color op-

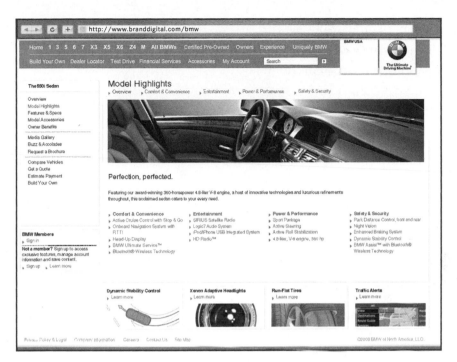

The BMW site enables users to design their own vehicles, virtually demonstrating exactly why the BMW is "a joy to drive."

tions. Then, I went to work on the entertainment options, the types of seats, and the weather options. Did I want all seats to have individual heat and cooling control units or just the front seats? I went to the safety option section and learned more about one of the many reasons BMW owners experience the "joy of driving": they feel so safe behind the wheel. (As a former BMW owner, I can attest to this.) There are numerous ways to make this safe car even safer, and the choices are the owners' to make. As I added and subtracted features, I could see at a glance how the price of the car had changed. This allowed me to prioritize options: which ones I absolutely had to have and those that were not as important to me. I liked how this put me in control of the car-buying experience before I made a decision to schedule a visit to a local dealer, or even schedule a test drive, both of which were also things I could request on the site. During our interview, Joe also mentioned:

> Many customers perceive an auto dealer's showroom to be a confrontational environment. People can be intimidated by car salesmen. Our goal has been to change that. We wanted to give consumers as much information as possible before they committed to visiting a showroom or to purchasing a vehicle. There are 130 million different combinations of BMW that can be built. We wanted our customers to have the same information our client advisors have so that once they get to the showroom they feel more in command of the buying process. The site was structured to be fun and educational. Consumers learn about the safety features and the entertainment features as they progress through the build-your-own process. The site is comparable to the experience someone might have in a showroom. The client advisor would take the time to carefully explain all the options and use it as a way of educating the consumer about the car, component by component. It reinforces the unique nature of the car as machine. The buying curriculum online is much like the curriculum we use to train our own people.

Talking to Joe further about the company, I learned that all of BMW's manufacturing processes operate in such a highly efficient, yet flexible, manner that customers have the ability to make changes to their customized orders very late in the process, down to a few days before the cars are actually constructed. What makes BMW great, as a car and as a brand, is how it operates as a company. "We say, 'Here's our user. Here's their lifestyle. Here's the experience they expect from us. How do we deliver on the experience at every touch point?'" Joe told me. "Our website reflects the quality of our cars and of our company. People get engaged with it. Most of the applications on other automotive sites are pretty straightforward. There's text, there are beautiful photographs, there's basic pricing information. But you have no idea why you should pay extra for, say, a special navigation package. We've tried to dimensionalize the experience, provide a greater depth of information, and allow people to see what makes the BMW a different kind car. They roll up their sleeves and want to play with it. Everything is about the joy of driving."

The objective of any branding initiative should be to enable consumers to instantly understand what differentiates a particular brand from its competition. It's clear that everyone associated with BMW knows how to "be the brand." It's clear that the company knows how to use its branding to define its brand. And it's clear that it knows how to use digital branding to bring its promise to life in a way that's not only meaningful to its customers, but has transformed the buyer's relationship with the brand.

Nike is another brand using its branding to transform the relationship it has with its customers. In this case the customers are runners, nor drivers. Not many people remember that Nike started out as a running company. It was founded by Bill Bowerman, a coach at the University of Oregon, who partnered with Phil Knight, Nike's current chairman, to create a running shoe. The company had a run of fabulous successes with its superior brand of shoe until it started to branch out into other sports and sporting apparel. At the same time that Nike's market share was declining, brands like Adidas and New Balance, jumped into the gap created by Nike's distraction. Dedicated runners started to abandon the Nike brand in favor of brands that focused on the needs of runners. The people at Nike realized that they needed to find a way to get back in the running game, and consequently, its recent branding has transformed the field on which it plays. Michael Tchao, General Manager of Nike+, Nike brand's incredibly successful initiative for runners, talked to me about the nontraditional branding effort that both redefined the way the brand connects with its customers and reestablished its meaningful difference in the marketplace. "Today's youth consumer spends a lot of time online, said Michael.

> It's where they live and breathe so it was important for us to connect with them in this space. But while we knew technology can create great things and was the vehicle for Nike to make the critical connection, the initial step and the key to the success of Nike+ was stepping back from the technology and focusing first on what motivates runners. Once we understood what was important to them, we could determine how best to use technology to enhance and amplify what they were already doing. Nike+ was developed as the result of three primary insights. First, runners are motivated by information about "the run." They want to know how far they've gone, how fast they've run, how many calories they've burned. Second, more and more runners—especially younger runners—use music as motivation during their run. Many even tell us they won't run without music. The third insight used in the development of Nike+ was that while running is often seen as a solo activity, what's really driving growth in running is the power of the community. More and more people see running as a social activity—even those who primarily run with music. Whether they're running in major marathon events, running for good causes, or simply running for fun and exercise with their friends or running clubs, people like running together. Nike+ lets runners connect with other runners around the block or around the world to share and compete in a way that builds on the community aspect of running. Nike has always been about using innovation to serve the needs of athletes. Nike+ is a perfect example of how we can use digital technology to enhance the running experience. Nike+ combines information about "the run," music, and community to make running not just a better experience, but a surprising, more delightful, more rewarding and more motivating experience. In building tools to create the world's largest running club, it's less about Nike's view of what running should be and more about creating an indispensable service for runners that makes it easier and more enjoyable to do things that are motivating for them.

Nike recognized, as do all good brands, that success starts with smart insights. It also recognized that it wasn't just a matter of using these insights to produce a better feature or benefit, but using the insights gained to weave together an entire experience. The company started by identifying something that consumers were already doing and developed something around this behavior that would make it a better, or, as Michael said, a "more surprising and delightful" experience.

I spoke to a number of Nike+ users who supported this contention wholeheartedly. Among them was Robin Kietlinski, who ran with a team in college and was looking for a way to keep up with her running after graduating, especially once she moved to Japan to conduct research in graduate school. She told me,

> I started running with Nike+ after I moved to Japan. When I ran in college, the members of the team gave each other motivation and we had someone tracking our speed and distance. It wasn't just that I needed motivation to run after college, but I also wanted to know how far I was running. I knew how long my routes were in the United States. When you're not running on familiar routes, this is information you'd like to have. I had an iPod so I decided to try Nike+ and I loved it. I'm not very technologically savvy but it was really easy to upload my information online and keep track of my runs. Oddly enough, what's really incredible is hearing the voice of Lance Armstrong or world-class marathoner, Paula Radcliffe, tell me when I've reached a new personal best. "Congratulations, you've just run 500 miles, or congratulations, you've just run your fastest mile." It's unexpected. I'm always surprised.

To Robin's point, it's not just that Nike used its insights to create a better experience for runners, but that it serves it up in a fresh, surprising way. It is incredible to hear Lance Armstrong tell you "you've had your best run yet." It's a super simple, but very compelling way to differentiate the brand and the experience; a touch point that uniquely expresses what the Nike brand is all about.

If you go to the Nike+ website you'll see very little product sell. There is a lot more emphasis on the community it's created. Among the things you will find is information about Nike Run Clubs, which are clubs for runners that have been created in certain Nike retail establishments. The Run Clubs sponsor events, organize informal groups of runners within local neighborhoods, and offer the service of pacers, or running coaches. There's no fee for any of this. You just show up and hook up with a group of runners with similar abilities. It's an easy way to build relationships with runners and, at the same time, build your appreciation for the Nike brand.

The ingenuity of this very powerful branding initiative is at the intersection of digital applications and the real-time experience Nike affords runners. It's a community on two dimensions, but a community that comes together in a way that differentiates the Nike brand of running shoe in a way no traditional media possibly could. In fact, there's probably no TV commercial that could convince runners to come back to Nike. No actor or athlete could drive trial or prove that Nike understands the mentality of the dedicated runner the way this initiative is doing. The interactive nature of it has helped turn running into a social activity, a massively social sport.

This Nike branding initiative was one of the most successful product launches in the company's history. According to an October 2007 article in *Time* magazine, Nike's market share went from 47 percent to almost 57 percent after the website launched. And, according to *Advertising Age,* in 2007 Nike spent just 33 percent of its $678 million marketing budget on television ads and other traditional media. As I said earlier in the book, many companies are beginning to reevaluate their branding dollars, using more funds to engage with consumers in the consumers' worlds as a way of building brand loyalty. When you consider the multitasking nature of our society, it's apparent that Nike is very aware that it's difficult to get someone's attention while they're doing something else, like running. By creating a community of runners, Nike changed the branding field in its category. Its most significant branding initiatives continue to be in nurturing and adding value to this community. It has transformed the way its customers think about the Nike brand, and why they perceive the brand as being meaningfully different in its category.

Nike created a branded community for runners, a community that crosses from online to offline and back again. This community is relevant to the brand's core audience and is also a branding tool totally appropriate to the brand's promise. The inherent interactive nature of digital technology has given rise to many other communities, some branded, and some not; some appropriate as branding tools for a particular brand, and some not. The acceptance of social networking sites as places to meet and greet and share is a given. The acceptance of these sites as communities in which all brand organizations should have some degree of presence is open to debate. The position taken by smart marketers relative to participation in a social network community is to take part only if it's a good brand fit. Kevin Lane Keller, Professor of Marketing at Dartmouth's Tuck School of Business, gave me his first rule for marketers who are considering participation in a social networking site as part a branding strategy. "I liken social networks to frat parties," he said. "There's a lot of talk and sharing of experiences by like-minded people. There's camaraderie and an innate sense of belonging. Let's say you're a professor, even a really cool professor, who hears about a frat party and decides to make an appearance. You put on your coolest duds and waltz over to the frat house. You open the door, casually stroll in and are stricken when all conversation comes to a standstill. It occurs to you that as cool as you may think you are, you're still the professor and they're still the frat boys." Kevin's point is obviously that as cool as a brand might think it is, it's still the brand, and they're still the consumers. You can't crash the party assuming you'll fit in simply if you put on cool duds and learn to speak the vernacular.

If you think that making a branding investment in a social network is something your organization must do to succeed in the digital age, think about the nature of your brand and then reconsider. As Nike proved, a community is created for specific reasons. The people who belong have common interests, vocations, passions, or needs. It might be dance, or as it is on Flickr, about photography. It could be running or mothering or political activity. In the two most well-known online communities, MySpace and Facebook, it's fraternizing. While originally intended for high-school and college-age kids, the doors to these sites have since been opened to people of all ages. In any event, users on these sites collect "friends" based on shared interests. For an organization to make a branding entrance at any of these online communities, it must understand that it's only a guest and must act accordingly. To be trusted, brands must prove they have something relevant to add to the conversation.

Jon Cook, President of VML, a leading interactive unit within WPP, talked to me about companies considering making a significant branding investment in the online social scene: "A brand's job within a social media venue is to listen before engaging. Identify who's there, what they're talking about, and determine if your brand can contribute anything of relevance. Your branding objective should be to demonstrate to participants on the site that your brand brings something relevant to the table, something valuable and something worth talking about. Oh, and brands don't make the rules, they follow them."

Lots of brand organizations pay to have profile pages on Facebook and MySpace. Those that succeed in these branding initiatives do so because they follow both Kevin's and Jon's rules. They don't pretend to be something they're not, and they make sure that they have something of relevance to offer to those who visit these pages. They also make sure that the branding initiative serves to differentiate the brand from other branded participants. Noah Kerner, Founder of the agency

Noise, talked to me about his firm's work with JP Morgan Chase, the venerable banking institution. Noise was tapped to launch a new Chase credit card program called "Chase +1." The core audience was college students, a group not prone to having faith in, letting alone doing business with, venerable banking institutions. The agency made the decision to stage its primary branding initiative on Facebook. "It's obvious. If you look at where these kids hang out, where they pick up news and information, it's on social networks," said Noah. He then talked about the possibilities of entering Facebook:

> This is precisely where the audience was congregating at the time. The marketing model in any space, and especially the Internet space, is "right message, right time, right place." Facebook was definitely the right place. We figured, why try to pull the audience away from a media venue it's already engaged in? The key was to find a way to get them to look up from what they were engaged in and pay attention to our message. The first thing we knew we had to do was enter their space as Chase. Just because the brand was stepping into the students' domain didn't mean it should behave like a student. One of the tenets of marketing is that if you try to behave as something you're not, you'll fail. This is even more important in an environment where everything is transparent. We recognized that for Chase to succeed with this population we had to determine what a venerable banking institution would say to a group of college students, a group not necessarily known as being financially savvy.

The branding initiative that Noah and his team launched was designed to serve up financial information in a non-condescending way, but without the use of generational colloquialisms that would have sounded phony coming from Chase. What's more, the details about the program, information about the +1 credit card, the rewards one could earn, how to share points with friends, were utterly simple, given the multitasking nature of the audience. The subject matter was relevant to these kids. The bottom line was that after the launch of the program Chase shot up in the rankings of financial brands among students. "Consumers are in control," Noah told me, "but they're happy to be led if you have something meaningful to offer. Chase never pretended to be something it wasn't, and the content it brought to the party was useful and compelling."

A social networking site is just one more of the many new places a brand can play. As the number of branding opportunities continues to proliferate, the importance of knowing where consumers are engaging with brands is even more important. The market is moving too fast for someone at the top of an organization to control all branding decisions. And, with so many disparate groups contributing to the branding efforts, it's too complicated a task for a single person at brand management level to ensure all branding initiatives hold together. A map of the customer journey is a valuable and practical way to help those who have responsibility for branding to envision the results of their efforts. As I mentioned earlier, this map should not be seen as a static document, created once and then left as is. Rather, it should be reevaluated on an ongoing basis to keep pace with the changing ways consumers pick up information. Think of it more as an onboard navigation system—updated as market conditions change, as consumers change the way they get information or make purchases, and as a way of dealing with competitive roadblocks. Some of the points at which a consumer interacts with a brand will remain the same, and, given the evolution of digital technology, some will most definitely change. Managing the customer's experience with a brand has always been essential to maintaining a brand's credibility and to ensuring it keeps its promise across all points of touch. The ability to keep track of where and how consumers interact with a brand is a competitive advantage that has only been magnified in the digital space.

PART TWO

Building Brands in a Digital World

7

Stop, Look, and Listen
Get Insights about
Your Digital Audience

Digital tools have magnified what people talk about when they talk about life, love, and material goods. They've magnified what people talk about when they talk about their families, their careers, their political leanings, the charities they support, and their financial aspirations. More than this, digital tools have magnified not just what people talk about, but what they do. As marketers, or just as mere mortals, we can monitor what cars people drive and where they drive them, the food they serve their dogs for dinner and where they get their dogs groomed, whom they vote for and what social causes they espouse, where they get their appliances repaired, where they get their hair done, which fast food restaurants they frequent, where they buy airline tickets, which hotels they visit, and what they order from room service.

Digital tools magnify human thought and behavior. And people are perfectly willing, if not genuinely excited, to share the most personal details of their lives; to document their lives online through words and pictures, moving and otherwise. This digital ethnography gives marketers the unprecedented opportunity to watch, to listen, and to learn. Brand organizations can monitor chatter and follow streams of conversations from a global perspective. They can track a consumer's journey from purchase consideration to final purchase, and can determine what one consumer tells others about the whole experience. Web 2.0, or 3.0, if that's what it is now, is a perpetually ticking meter of people's lives. At no time in the history of trying to sell the right thing to the right person at the right time have marketers had so much fuel for their fire. Given that the primary objective of any brand organization should be to get a better understanding of human thought and behavior in order to serve peoples' unmet needs, the magnifying power of digital is a very good thing, *if* it is used in this manner. It is a good thing *if* an organization uses it as it should be used to gain meaningful insights about its core audiences and its primary competitors and to then use these insights to deliver great brand experiences. The best brands embrace digital to get a clear understanding of what their customers want and need. It has always been critical for a brand organization to get customer insights. Today, though easier than ever before, it's necessary to understand how to go about it in a way that benefits both customer and organization.

It used to be pretty difficult to gauge what was going on in a consumer's mind. This wasn't just because the woman to whom you wanted to sell dishwashing detergent lived in Cleveland while you were on Madison Avenue. It was because, even if you brought this woman to a focus group in Cleveland or on Madison Avenue to get her opinion, she might tell you what she thought you wanted to hear. She might just echo what the nine other women around her were saying at the focus group table. Or, she just might not be able to articulate her feelings well. She might also very well tell you one thing and then go off and do another once she got back home. A number of marketers, myself included, used to do in-home research. We'd sit at kitchen tables from Cleveland to Fargo and observe women as they washed dishes. Now, this was a terrific way to get great insight. As I mentioned earlier in the book, you could hear these ladies sigh with exasperation as the grease from the pots and pans stuck to their fine china. It was one of my responsibilities to take these insights back to the office and get the appropriate people working on a solution. The problem with this type of research was that it was relatively expensive and would allow marketers to get input from only a relatively small segment of the target audience. Today, we are awash in data that enable us to derive insights about consumers. We are flooded with real-time information and real-time dialogs between customer and customer, and customer and organization. The challenge for marketers today is to identify the most valuable sources of online conversation and information and to know what to do with it once they've mined it.

I had a long discussion with Peter Hirshberg, Chairman of Technorati, an Internet firm that monitors over a hundred million blogs. One of the most popular uses of the service is by brands and their agencies to find out what's being said about them as well as to identify who's doing the most talking and whose talk is the most credible. "Most marketers still hinge their research efforts on the old, passive model. You hire a research company, and you watch people behind the glass, so to speak. You assemble reports and surveys and spend huge amounts of time making assumptions, taking educated guesses about what consumers want, and then you produce things to meet these assumptions," he told me. He continued:

The tremendous opportunity for marketers today is the ability to actively listen to consumers within days, hours, even minutes of a brand interaction and then to make these consumers stakeholders in the process of making the products and services even better. There are amazing online tools and technologies for doing this. I've seen companies develop their own internal processes for doing this. I've seen them use readily available tools, like Google Blog Search, sign up for any of the free watch lists that are out there, or partner with firms like Technorati, Buzz Logic, or Biz 360. It doesn't matter how an organization listens in and watches how consumers behave. It's just important *that* they do it. You're not going to get valuable insights about your customers if you don't transform the way you get information. I've discovered that as much as they know they should, companies are reluctant to get their hands dirty. While they have beautiful websites they don't go deeper online than that. You've got to avail yourself of all the amazing online tools to hear what people are saying and to act on what they're saying.

It's been my observation that, more than not availing themselves of online tools to see what their customers are up to, many companies see research as a one-time event. They start a research effort at the beginning of the fiscal year or right before a major initiative. In the past, this was driven both financially and by the traditional once-a-year strategy and media-planning business model. In a digital marketplace, where things change with such frequency and consumers can torpedo even the best-laid plans in an instant, research can no longer be looked at as a one-time event. Nor can one-time media planning sessions. Both research and planning must be considered ongoing activities. Even the major television networks are recognizing this, eliminating their once yearly announcement of new programming in favor of ongoing new programming. This means the traditional "up-front" media buying spree has been eliminated, as well. The ability to learn and evolve plans as you go is essential to staying ahead of the competition and on good terms with your customers. Peter Hirshberg put it this way: "You don't think about what your wife thinks or feels about things on a once-a-year basis. You listen as you go, as the relationship evolves. The same should be true for brand organizations; listen and evolve as you go."

In addition to not being a one-time-only event, listening and observing customer behavior should be something in which everyone in the organization gets involved. For example, Jonathan Schwartz at Sun Microsystems encourages his product managers to listen to what consumers are saying about the company in blogs and on industry sites, and to engage in conversation with these bloggers, clearly identifying themselves and their roles in the company. The objective is to hear what Sun customers are saying about the products in real-time so that the right people in the company can get to work on something that needs fixing before the situation gets out of hand. If enough people are blogging about a specific Sun server not being up to snuff, it's critical to get the engineers to look into it immediately. These days, research a year after the fact is 364 days too late. The development team at Lego, the well-known build-it-yourself toy company, is another brand that uses ongoing online dialogue with its customers (or the parents of its customers) to make changes to its products or marketing plans as it goes. While engaging in a blog discussion about a new line of Lego construction toys, for instance, its research and development folks discovered that it wasn't just kids who were using their imaginations to build their own versions of robots, rockets, and skyscrapers, but that there was an audience of grown-up men who enjoyed plying their own do-it-yourself resourcefulness. (Check out the Lego MindStorms NXT website, and you'll understand why.) It isn't just the Lego brand inspiring the customers; it's more a matter of the customers inspiring the folks at the Lego brand.

Johnson & Johnson is a company now taking advantage of an array of online monitoring tools to better respond to consumer needs—not merely to maintain a positive status quo, but to get insight for new product development. Landor is currently working with a company within Johnson & Johnson that deals in surgical devices. One of the areas this well-respected healthcare product company is becoming involved with is cosmetic surgery. As the company started doing its research on a specific surgical device, it held numerous focus groups with women across the country to hear them talk about their experiences with cosmetic surgery. I spoke to Susan Can from Ethicon Endo-Surgery, an operating company of Johnson & Johnson, about what happened *after* the focus groups, which is what led the organization to reassess its research processes. "We conducted over 16 focus groups with women in our primary target audience," she said during our discussion.

> The biggest insight for us actually came from what happened after the focus groups. After each session, the women gathered in the lobby to continue talking about their surgical experiences. These conversations, completely without the facilitation of a moderator, were much more natural and relevant to our research needs than what we'd heard from the women while they were in the groups. It became very obvious that these women were hungry for connection and that there was no available forum in which they could talk freely about the topic with anonymity. We worked with a company called Communispace to develop an online, private community for our market research purposes. The advantage to Ethicon Endo-Surgery was that it allowed us to be in touch with our target consumer twenty-four hours a day, seven days a week through facilitated, monitored conversations. More than 450 women were recruited based on the market segments we wanted to reach, to interact on a site called beautyconnection.com. In essence, we built a social community for women with a shared life experience. We've never been able to get such deep consumer insights.

The women who participate in the social community beautyconnection.com know that it's a market research site, and they know it's sponsored by Johnson & Johnson. Total transparency is a must-have in the digital environment. But, because of the anonymity of the participants, they feel free to talk. And they talk, not just about plastic surgery, but about the idea of beauty, about aging, and about society's perception of cosmetic surgery. I like to think of social networks as Petri dishes for word of mouth. This Ethicon Endo-Surgery network is like a turbo-powered Petri dish that produces new insights and revelations around the clock. By listening in on the conversations you can sense how passionate the participants are about their views and also what an emotional subject cosmetic surgery is. As the Landor and Johnson & Johnson teams work together, they continue to find new ways to engage the participants. They have the moderators pose different questions or solicit opinions about potential brand campaign ideas. Rather than looking at research as an external brand-to-consumer activity, developing first and testing after, Ethicon Endo-Surgery is using this innovative digital tool to engage the consumer in the actual brand building in real time. The brand is living with its core audience segment 24/7 and testing ideas as it goes along. Ethicon Endo-Surgery is virtually leveraging the audience to help it create a product that will be of greater benefit to the audience.

While Ethicon Endo-Surgery currently uses this digital application as a research and development tool, it anticipates making the site a public forum once it launches its new product. Another company that used a similar activity in the development of its product is GlaxoSmithKline, which manufactures Alli, an over-the-counter diet pharmaceutical. After it launched the drug, it made its research site public as a way of opening up the conversation to all customers and prospective customers. This has allowed the company to continuously monitor what's being said and to address user concerns or questions before they become problematic. The ability to monitor online chatter and preempt potential problems is a tremendously efficient public relations opportunity. More than that, when you take advantage of a branded online community to help in the development of products and marketing, you establish a homegrown group of brand evangelists. "What you get when you solicit consumer involvement from the very

151

beginning is true advocacy," Susan said. "The women who partici-pate in our community are emotionally invested; it's a completely ground-up way to build a brand. You form the community, listen to what the participants say, and leverage this learning in brand devel-opment. When you're ready to launch, you know who you're talking to, know how to speak their language, and how to fully engage them."

Among the many things that Peter Hirshberg talked about was how interesting it is that so many companies are afraid to interact on-line with their customers. They shy away from soliciting response and input and even getting engaged in public debate because they're afraid of what they might hear. This is extremely shortsighted. "Brands need to harness the collective intelligence of consumers," Peter told me dur-ing our conversation. "If negative stuff gets said, that's okay. It's more than okay. Don't you think it lends more credibility to your brand if you can respond and fix things? If someone's taking the time to write about your brand, it means they have some degree of interest in it. It's in your best interest to look at the interaction as the positive oppor-tunity it is." With all the talk, past and present, about customer-centric organizations, I think that all companies will come to the realization that they don't have all the answers, and that customers can give them incredible input on their products because they use them on a day-to-day basis. If I'm a product engineer sitting at a computer or a drafting table all day, I'm not spending all the time I could be or should be lis-tening to what consumers are saying about what I'm designing. Active, ongoing listening, as a required job responsibility, is a benefit to every-one. It instills a greater degree of accountability in those responsible for design and manufacturing processes. What's more, by monitoring how people feel on a regular basis it's easier for a company to pick the products and product features that will be winners. Listening and learning from consumers is a culture changer, but it's a culture changer for all the right reasons.

As I discussed earlier in the book, the best brands *do* look at negative online discourse as the positive opportunity it is. If you look at the companies that have been burned by the power of the people, you'll find that most saw it as a chance to transform the organization. After the "Dell Hell" incident precipitated by Jeff Jarvis' blog entitled "Dell Sucks," Michael Dell jumped in with both feet and ensured that the company he had worked so hard to build didn't succumb to the rabble-rousing. Rather, he used what he heard his customers saying about his brand as constructive insight to bring back the brand in a way that would serve consumers better than it had before. He got very involved in the Dell website and saw how useful it would be to the company to have more robust customer feedback applications like blogs, message boards, and support forums. It used to be there was almost no way to interact with Dell other than the ineffective customer service channels. Now, there are a dozen or more very gratifying ways to engage in real-time dialog with the company. After Wal-Mart's infamous fake blog about a couple RV-ing their way across America, the company offered a genuine mea culpa by establishing a totally transparent blog site and inviting all who had something to say to say it—slings, arrows, outrageous fortune, and all. Among the smart things smart companies do to become better at listening and learning is to study brand organizations that have risen from the online ashes to learn from their mistakes. Along with the other digital tools they use to get insight, they also study how the competition monitors consumer online chat and activity along with the other digital tools they use to get insight.

Online ratings and reviews are among the most valuable tools for obtaining insight about consumers and their feelings about your brand, and they are also the easiest to establish. This simple application will not only yield a treasure trove of information, but, just by virtue of its presence, it will add to a brand's credibility. Brett Hurt is

Founder and CEO of Bazaarvoice, a technology firm that helps companies leverage what people are saying online to strengthen their products and services. "Bazaarvoice" is all about the voice of the marketplace," said Brett. He then went on to say:

> It's a centuries-old concept made current. The whole premise of our business is based on the fact that your customers can be your best source of information. We live in an age where word of mouth is digitally archived. It's the first time that companies can see directly what consumers are saying about them to other consumers. What we do is create platforms for *creating* word of mouth in an environment where people are most likely to talk: on the brand sites where they shop. My wife and I have a fourteen-year-old miniature Pincher. She's a big part of our lives. My wife and I talk about her a lot. PETCO is a place we know we can connect with people and share this part of our identity. We're pet lovers. If you write a product review on PETCO, you know that other pet lovers are going to see it. This is more valuable to the product's manufacturer than having someone say something on a generic blog because the PETCO site attracts like-minded people. PETCO has been a client of ours since 2005. We've been able to document that those consumers who visited pages on the PETCO site with top-rated products converted to sales at a 50 percent higher rate. You can't spend enough marketing money to get results like this.

Bazaarvoice works with brand giants like Macy's, Home Depot, QVC, and Sears. More and more of the biggest brand organizations in the world are recognizing that online word of mouth via product reviews is among the most powerful forms of marketing since the dawn of well, the bazaar. As much as we try to derive insight from focus groups and the like, there is nothing like being able to watch what people do, and hear what they say, in real time. People are beginning to live more of their lives online. It would only make sense that this is one of the reasons people feel so comfortable sharing with others online. Sam Decker, the Chief Marketing Officer of Bazaarvoice, also talked to me about the enhanced ability of marketers to get customer insight as a result of digital technology:

One way to think about social commerce is to determine what type of activity or application you can create for the 15 percent of customers who will interact with a brand online that will help the other 85 percent. Foster communication between the customers you want to attract. Reviews are an obvious answer. Consumer reviews are seen as more credible and more useful by other consumers than are brand-initiated activities. Another online application that works is something we call "Ask and Answer." Consumers can ask questions of other consumers, like, "Is *300* an appropriate movie for my thirteen-year-old? Is there lots of blood and head-chopping?" One mother of a thirteen-year-old is more likely to believe another mother more than she'll believe the entertainment company's commentary. It's getting more and more possible for consumers to search online for very specific review information. The key to successfully connecting with the consumers you want as customers is to give them good reasons to come to your website for advice from consumers just like them—rather than have them visit a competitor's site or a category-general site.

While still somewhat experimental, 3D virtual worlds like Second Life are being brought into play more and more as research tools by certain companies. Users, or "Residents," of Second Life create avatars of themselves in order to socialize with each other and to interact with representatives of any brands that happen to make an appearance. Launched in June 2003 by Linden Research, Inc, or Linden Lab, as it's more commonly called, Second Life is creating the opportunity for companies to test and research in extraordinary new ways. I spoke to Robin Harper, Vice President of Marketing and Community Development at Linden Lab, about how companies are using the website to gain better insight about both their customers and their products. She said, "Second Life is a great space in which to begin a conversation with consumers."

It's not a research vehicle in the traditional sense, but an excellent way for companies to watch consumers virtually use or interact with products. For example, Starwood Hotels was planning to introduce a new hotel concept and wanted to get feedback about the lobby and guestroom designs. It created a virtual rendition of these spaces on Second Life and was able to see how people moved through the spaces, where they sat, what traffic patterns they followed. There were fountains and fireplaces in the proposed lobby, and the Starwood folks were able to [learn] whether these design features were placed appropriately in the space and how people reacted to them. The company also set up virtual blog terminals in the concept lobby, at which users could post their reactions to the new designs in real time. It was 2D and 3D combined and a sensational way to evaluate an idea before putting it into market.

As Robin said, Second Life may not be right for every type of brand. You obviously have to determine if the consumers you want to attract hang out in these virtual spaces. But, for those companies who deal with early adopters of this type of digital technology and want to see how consumers physically interact with a product, it's a great way to gain insight. Scion and Pontiac, for example, were able to learn a lot about their hoped-for buyers by testing automotive designs and specific features on the site. Apparel manufacturers like Adidas and Reebok give Second Life avatars a chance to design their own shoes. They also watch to see what kind of clothing these avatars wear with these shoes, a great opportunity to test an idea before committing substantial amounts of money to product development or marketing.

Marketing is not one to many anymore. It's a global dialogue. The whole notion of marketing has changed from being a one-way street to being a major intersection of voices. Messages are not just pushed from brand to consumer, but from consumer to consumer to consumer and back again. The reactions these messages generate actually become part of the greater message. Consumers want to be heard and, for all the right reasons, they want to help companies to listen. It is incumbent upon companies to follow the intertwining trail of online talk and action, to watch it evolve, and to determine which points of conversational entry yield the most constructive feedback and insight. It's also incumbent

Starwood Hotels took advantage of the research opportunities offered by Second Life to see how consumers would "virtually" interact with its new lobby design. Courtesy Linden Research, Inc. and Starwood Hotels.

upon companies to identify which voices within the chorus of online voices are most influential. Of the five thousand or so bloggers on one subject or another, which ones can actually effect the brand's perception in the marketplace? Some online opinion-givers carry significant weight, while others are a lot of hot air. It's critical to be able to pinpoint which voices to heed and engage with for their potential as brand advocates. Companies like The Conversation Group and Cymfony are well known in the consumer discussion industry for being able to identify what consumers are talking about online and which voices are the most influential as change agents. In one fascinating initiative, Cymfony was able to report back to brand organizations that paid a fortune for advertising time on Bowl XLII which ads were responsible for the greatest degree of online chatter and for what reasons. I spoke to Jim Nail, Chief Strategy and Marketing Officer at Cymfony about how to approach online opinion monitoring. "It's obviously very difficult to differentiate a brand on product performance anymore," he said.

> Monitoring online conversations allows you to pick up the nuances about what's being said about a brand. It's insight that goes deeper than what you hear in focus groups where participants have an unconscious desire to please the moderator. However, it's not enough to monitor simply *what* people are saying, it's important to be able to get to the "so what." Computers work with numbers. They can't pick up emotional nuances. After using technology to track online dialogues around a brand you still need someone whose head is in the game to interpret it for you. What people write about on blogs, discussion boards, review sites, and social network pages is totally spontaneous. It comes directly from their experience and feelings. Brand organizations can use the dynamics of online monitoring to help them in more than advertising, but in everything that consumers associate with their organizations.

Jim's point is that the power and beauty of the very visible online activity to marketers is how valuable it can be in helping organizations understand the impact of everything they do, from advertising, to product design, to customer care. It's in observing and reading through the words and activities of consumers that these organizations can uncover emerging trends, unmet needs in the marketplace, and simply unmet brand promises.

I spoke to Ian Wood, a brand strategist at Landor in London, about how brand organizations should take advantage of the very visible online activity to gain insight about consumers. "Consumers are self-publishing," he said,

> They share anything and everything. The trick is to determine which conversations to listen to and which activities to take seriously when evaluating what changes to make to products or services or to marketing plans. How can companies make good use of the clatter of life online? One of my favorite examples of great media planning may provide a clue. A research firm sat down to brainstorm the best places to advertise a specific product. They

came up with a list of the usual suspects: print, television, online. The firm then asked a group of consumers to do the same thing. The consumers came up with the same predictable list. Then, the firm gave these consumers mobile phones and asked them to carry them around for a week and text to a special number every time they came across the to-be-advertised product being used in daily life. It was when these people saw the product in use that they were able to better think about which brand experiences would best break through the fabric of life. When marketers look at life online—at which brands are breaking through the fabric of life online—these are the conversations and activities to take seriously as you look for insight about your customers. These are the things that you should take into consideration as you evaluate how to use this insight to provide better brand experiences.

Digital tools magnify what we know to be true about branding, and gaining great consumer insight is the first step to building a powerful brand. Digital tools also magnify and amplify human thought and behavior. The best brands embrace these digital tools to get a clear understanding of what consumers are saying and doing and what they want and need. They use these tools to gain insight. Here's the insight they'd share with all brand organizations:

1. **Learn as much as you can about the digital tools.** Make good use of those tools that will allow you to look at and listen to what's happening online. Avail your organization of any and all that make sense. Currently, there are two basic types of tools: tracking and analysis. Tracking tools are automated keyword-based tools that search news, blogs, websites, user groups, reviews, complaint sites, and forums. Keywords should include both positive and negative descriptors of your brand, company, and competitors. Google and Yahoo Alerts, along with industry-oriented RSS feeds, can be delivered to your mailbox or desktop in real time as they appear online or at a frequency of your choice. Analytic tools,

on the other hand, are natural language processing, text analytics, and sentiment analysis that can help you decipher the overall feelings or sentiments of a consumer's comments.

2. **Create a listening culture.** In fact, share the listening and learning responsibilities with those in the company who can benefit most. It won't do any good to have a cloistered team of people monitoring the blogs, chat rooms, and message boards if what they see and hear stays in their cloistered offices. Marketing, finance, operations, product development, and customer service departments can all benefit from seeing and hearing directly what's going on online and being given the opportunity to exchange ideas with others in the company and with consumers. When individual departments within an organization have direct knowledge of a customer's experiences and insights, it will make it easier to address any issues before they get out of hand.

3. **Invite consumer input.** While monitoring consumer conversations is vital, take the next step and ask for feedback. This allows you to take control and provide context, parameters, and a venue for conversation. For example, consumer beta testing is a mainstay of most new Google applications. Getting consumer involvement in the creation of advertising is another vehicle to entice consumer participation, as are contests that entice consumers to share their stories relative to the brand. One of the easiest and most valuable ways to get feedback is to feature a "ratings and review" section on your brand website, a feature that is becoming increasingly more popular and expected. Although it sounds counterintuitive, don't be afraid of losing control. The more you clamp down, the less you'll learn and the less power you'll actually have to quell negative online behavior.

The more you open up, and the greater level of engagement your organization has, the better it will be for your brand.

4. **Determine who your most influential online influencers are.** Take the time to monitor all the online voices closely and separate the wisdom of the few from the nonsense of the masses. You'll find there are a few key online sources that matter most. Take the added step of investigating their backgrounds and other online activity to verify their impartiality (that is, that they're not being paid by the competition). Create blogger outreach programs. Take the time to engage those who have the greatest impact on consumer opinion in meaningful discussion. Invite them to be beta testers or reviewers of your new products. Keep them in the loop with public relations kits, news alerts, and invitations to events. Court them as the brand evangelists they want to be and should be. Your objective is to listen in order to make things better.

8

Call Attention to What Makes Your Brand Relevantly Different

While there are many variations of the definition of "*brand,*" there is one definition on which everyone in the business will agree: A brand is a promise. It's a promise between a company and a consumer that a product or service will perform exactly the way consumers expects it will. It might be a promise based on a functional benefit: what's inside the box; what the product does; how it smells; how it tastes; I expect my clothes to be whiter, my teeth to be whiter, or my car to get more miles to the gallon. It might be a promise based on an emotional benefit, something outside the box. When I use this product I'll feel more confident; I'll feel healthier; or I'll be perceived as a better parent. Or, the promise might be based on the expectation of the total experience of the brand—everything inside, outside, and all around the box. In other words, when I fly on this airline, stay in this hotel, or buy this MP3 player, all aspects will come together as one fabulous experience.

The agreed-upon definition of *"branding,"* on the other hand, refers to the expressions of the brand that consumers associate with its promise. Branding is how the brand's promise is conveyed. It's the packaging that describes specific ingredients that perform the wash-day miracles, and signals that the detergent inside will get clothes whiter. It's advertising that features confident-looking people doing things I'd like to picture myself doing. It's white earbuds that identify me as part of a specific MP3 community. It's a customer service representative who has my room preferences at hand when I make a hotel reservation and sends me an e-mail within minutes of my transaction. Virgin stood out as a different kind of airline brand experience for Mrs. Wrench, the mother of Landor's chairman—not simply because she was given pajamas, but because everything about her flight from San Francisco to London was memorable, and, to this day, worth sharing with her friends and family. Branding is what consumers remember about a brand. It's what triggers a customer's preference for one brand over another.

It's a common misconception that if a company spends lots of time and money making consumers aware of a product or service they'll buy it. Sort of along the lines of "advertise it and they will come." The most successful companies know *why* this is a misconception. They know that to succeed, a brand has to stand for something that is different from its competitors and that this difference must be relevant to consumers. A company can create all the noise it wants to about its brand. If the brand is no different than any other product in its category, or it's irrelevant to its audience in any way, all the noise and awareness won't matter a bit.

One of the most proprietary tools in the industry proves this point. Named BrandAsset Valuator® (BAV), it was created by Young and Rubicam, an agency that is part of the same communications family as Landor. Unlike other brand valuation tools, BAV goes beyond placing a value on a brand. It gauges the future health of a brand and offers up prescriptive actions should a brand's future appear none too healthy. BAV demonstrates that the two factors that contribute most to a brand's strength are the way it differentiates itself from the competition and whether this difference is meaningful to consumers. The BAV study shows that relevant differentiation not only drives top-line growth, but it is a strong factor in delivering superior financial results.

The strongest brands have high degrees of both differentiation and relevance. Consumers can immediately understand what sets these brands apart from the competition and why they will make life better in some meaningful way. When the brand has a higher degree of relevance than differentiation, it becomes a commodity. In this case, the only recourse it has is to compete on price. BAV is both predictive and prescriptive. It can indicate when a brand's differentiation is starting to fall off, and it can point out when people are beginning to find other brands more relevant to their needs. The key to continued brand success is to establish something that meaningfully differentiates your brand from others and to ensure that you stay on top of whatever this is.

It's by differentiating itself in a way that people care about and expressing this difference in a consistent and compelling way through its branding that an organization makes it easier for consumers to see why its brand is better than any other brand in the category. The reason brands and branding have always been critical to consumers (and to brand organizations) is that they work as shortcuts. Brands and branding help people make purchase decisions. They serve as visual and verbal and emotional cues that help consumers distinguish between brands they want to invite into their lives and those they don't. Having a strong, well-defined brand idea, along with branding that consistently delivers on this promise from touch point to touch point, is the most effective way to help consumers in their endeavor to make personally relevant choices. It's also the most effective way of getting their attention and keeping it.

The dynamics of the digital age have magnified the importance of this basic principle. Beyond being confronted with an infinite number of product choices on store shelves, beyond seeing ads for financial service or insurance companies in the newspaper or on television, consumers are confronted with an overwhelming number of choices on the Internet. Search functionality presents hundreds of product options and opportunities, not just on a local or even a national level, but on a global level. We can buy clothing, music, books, cosmetics, electronics, and household goods from every corner of the world. There are so many things are available—so many more ways to see and hear about them, and so many ways to compare them to similar products—that organizations are beginning to realize that they've got to look deep inside the box, way outside the box, and, in many cases, across multiple dimensions to find something that will differentiate their brands in some meaningful and memorable way. Once they've done this, they then have the added challenge of creating branding that will cut through the clutter in an equally differentiating manner.

But even when consumers think they've found something different that suits their needs, the Internet gives them the tools to slice and dice through comparable brand promises with ease. There's a whole new category of digital entrepreneurs whose online tools let us compare and contrast one product or service to another in a flash. There are hundreds of branded and independent websites that offer product reviews and customer ratings. Consumers can immediately determine, at least on the basis of price and performance, what makes one brand more appropriate to their needs than another. By navigating through a site, a consumer can experience just as quickly what it might be like to deal with the brand on a long-term basis. What's more, because digital technology makes it impossible for a brand to hide from any disingenuous behavior, we can learn from others like us whether the brand really delivers as expected on its promise. We can determine quickly and easily whether the organization is credible and actually trustworthy. Just as a search will serve up a long list of product options, it will also serve up a list of blogs and YouTube videos discrediting any one of these options. A customer whose expectation of a brand's promise is sorely under-delivered will make it very clear, and with no holds barred.

Brand organizations have always understood the need to identify something that makes their offer both relevant and different, to make a promise to consumers and deliver on it as expected. Now under the gaze of digital, companies are recognizing the need to do this with a greater degree of acuity and diligence than ever before. This is because, amidst the noise and clamor for their attention, and amidst the barrage of promises, consumers are assessing their choices with greater acuity than ever before and doing so with greater due diligence. Consumers still want and need shortcuts, and, in fact, they will reward companies whose branding helps them navigate through this virtual territory (without sending them down the wrong track). Companies today must do a better job than in the previous decades to make sure that they define something that makes their brand genuinely, and meaningfully different—and that they express this difference in a way that allows the product or service to deliver on the expectations of its branding's inherent promise.

The challenge is how, in a world run amok with products and promises, does an organization go about determining something to stand for that's meaningfully different? I'm sorry to say there is no magic formula. There are no ABCs, no 123s, no models, or no paradigms. The most critical task for marketers is also the most difficult. It is to know as much as you possibly can about your customers. Lest you be concerned, there are specific activities an organization can undertake to make this task more rewarding. The first thing is not only the most obvious, but in part, what was discussed in the previous chapter. It's vital to know as much as you possibly can about your customers. You have to find out what's on your customers' minds and what unmet needs your brand can meet. This is not to say they will tell you directly even if you engage them directly in online communities and forums to help you crack the code of their unmet needs. In all my years of experience, I have yet to come across a consumer who will say directly, "I want a dishwashing liquid that will eliminate grease from dishwater," or, "I want a very tiny device on which I can download thousands of my favorite songs." Parsing through digital research, and poring over traditional research, you'll see what frustrates consumers, and you'll hear them talk about it. They'll tell you how they live their lives, what annoys them about shampoos, and what worries them about children's products. You can track them as they investigate car insurance, see where they set up college funds, or what they hate about credit card loyalty programs. They'll tell you what makes them feel happy and what makes them feel secure, but they won't give you the ultimate answer. The "Eureka!" is up to your organization. It's your job to read through the lines of online and offline consumer words and behaviors to uncover the nugget of truthful insight that can set your brand apart.

As I wrote about in *BrandSimple,* it's surprising how often a brand benefit that proves to be different and relevant to a particular target is hiding in plain sight. It's an inspiration that springs from an observation of the obvious. "Ever wonder why they give you those teeny, tiny headphones and expect you to hear the movie over the roar of Rolls-Royce engines?" "Ever wonder why a hand-operated can opener makes your hand hurt?" As a result of asking the first question, Bose came up with a brilliantly different and relevant idea for its brand. Its line of Quiet Comfort headphones have made listening to in-flight movies and music a joy. The fact that they block out the shrieks of the two-year-old sitting behind you is also a joy. OXO Good Grips came up with a unique and practical line of kitchen products in response to looking at something that now seems pretty obvious. The meaningful difference of its products can be experienced in the way they feel and function as well as in the inventiveness of its packaging and retail presence.

A number of other well-known companies have also found that the way to reveal a different and relevant brand idea is to look for a universally accepted truth that's hiding in plain sight. Among the most recent is a company founded by a couple of perceptive young men who came across an idea hiding in plain sight under their kitchen sinks. In 1999, Eric Ryan and Adam Lowry asked the question, "Ever wonder why products which are supposed to get your home fresh and clean are toxic?" With a small amount of seed money from family and friends, they launched Method, a company that makes cleaning products that are not only environmentally smart and green, but whose packaging looks aesthetically smart enough to grace even the toniest kitchen counters. Recognizing that peoples' homes are not only a reflection of their design tastes, but also a reflection of their awareness of environmental issues, Eric and Ryan took a simple insight and turned it into a very big business. They gave panache to mundane products like soaps and cleaners. In 2007, Method's sales clocked in at a $40 million annual run rate.

Stewart Owen, of mcgarry bowen, talked to me about how Method was able to identify an unmet consumer need and parlay it into such a big success so quickly:

> We're living in a world where people are involved in more media but less passively. It used to be that there were mass media, mass culture, and mass brands.

Everyone was part of the same mass culture. You either liked Folgers or you liked Maxwell House. That was as big as the battle got. The cycle is now reversed. It's very easy for marketers, if they're smart, to be able to connect with people based on a more narrowly cast set of needs. Media is more intimate. There are more ways to reach people and multiple ways to get into personally relevant conversations about the same product. It's becoming increasingly important to look at the emotional component of brands and determine how consumers are using brands more as a means of self-identification. What's brilliant about Method is that its point of relevant differentiation tapped into the needs of multiple consumer groups simultaneously. The promise taps into people who want to be identified as socially aware users of "green" products, people who see the product packaging as reflective of their style of home décor, and people who are interested in the price-value equation. The products are formulated so that you use less than you'd use with traditional cleaning products. The founders of Method recognized these were all consumer issues that had been underserved. The key to their success, however, was creating a single brand that addressed multiple needs at the same time.

Eric Ryan and Adam Lowry recognized how important it is in the digital age to connect with people based on who they are and not just on the functional benefit of the brand product. They also recognized that the Internet enables multiple conversation entry points. They've embedded this recognition into their brand building. The Method website is a beautiful reflection of their credo as well as a tribute to how well their products perform. There are several "green" blog sites and community forums filled with very dedicated brand evangelists who don't have to be prompted to spread the word of their love of Method products. What's more, many design magazines have written about the brand in their editorial content. One look at any of the Method bottles and packaging, and you'll see why the home décor elite don't hide these products under the sink. Among the things that are great about Method is that its founders took a product traditionally very low on emotional involvement and connected to consumers in both an "in the box" and an "out of the box" way. There are tangible components to the brand promise; the design of the packaging and the cleaning ingredients inside. And there are very clear emotional components to the brand promise: what having them on your kitchen counter says about you as a person. The real beauty is how entwined these components are in delivering on the ultimate promise. The products get your house clean.

Given that the Internet is giving consumers the ability to compare and contrast the functional differences between one product and another with such virtual ease, more and more companies are looking to combine elements inside and outside the box as a way to establish their brands' uniqueness. This is due in no small part to the rapid pace of technology, which has made staking a claim on functional superiority for a product or service shortsighted. The speed at which one company can catch up with another in terms of a product attribute is lightning, if not frighteningly, fast. When Apple came out with its iPod, it knew enough not to stake its success on how many songs the little device held. This was certainly a difference it could own, but only for a while. Instead, it concentrated on what the iPod would communicate about its users' identity as individuals. How they'd feel seeing other like-minded folks with the same sleek and slim devices. How they'd feel opening up the classic but minimal packaging and maneuvering the Click Wheel with a gentle turn of the thumb. Creating a total iPod experience was smart. It continues to be more robust than any functional promise could possibly be in this category. And by weaving together a total experience, the iPod promise becomes harder for the competition to attack. Because the tangible qualities of a product can be so quickly imitated, if not eclipsed, by the competition, staking a claim that's above and beyond a functional benefit is much more sustainable and much more defensible. There is a phenomenal amount of energy driving digital means of communication. As a result, organizations are recognizing the need to spend equal amounts of energy to define something about their brands that can stand up to the digital forces.

Albert Cheng, Executive Vice President of Digital Media at ABC/Disney, told me that it was a rather unusual insight about consumers that led the company to its inside- and out-of-the-box differentiating factor. "It's important to start with ABC TV pre-digital," he told me.

> Historically, broadcast networks didn't have any presence as brands. Consumers were more aware of our *shows*, but they didn't think about the networks in any differentiated way. Then cable came along. The cable networks were much better than traditional networks at building brands primarily because they targeted niche audiences with unique programming for these groups; news, weather, old movies, independent movies, women's movies. There was a focused product offering on which to build a differentiated brand idea. Around 2005, it started to become very obvious to all networks that consumers were beginning to take control over how they wanted to consume content and when they wanted to consume it, whether it was downloading it from the Internet, another digital device, or recording it on a DVR. We recognized it was important for ABC to embrace this new technology in a way that would enable it to reach consumers in every way it possibly could. Oddly enough, as we began doing research, we realized that access and convenience was such a driving compulsion for consumers that they were pirating content. There was nothing that was going to stop them from getting entertainment on their terms. It was this insight that led us to change the way we thought about our business. We had to create an experience and product offering that would surpass what consumers would get through piracy. This meant creating a world-class consumer viewing experience that delivered on access and convenience. We needed to create a product that was not like any other online video platform at the time, as well as treat our content in a way that communicated its premium value and our progressive outlook as a company. Our objective was to change the way consumers thought about online content by delivering it in the most compelling way possible. As part of the Disney family we had to *over-deliver* on

customer expectations. Disney never just delivers as expected. We wanted to deliver on what consumers expected from the Disney innovation and magic. We wanted the ABC online presence to over-deliver. We wanted our online presence to be perceived as easier, more enjoyable, more accessible, and of a higher quality than any other network content provider. We didn't want to be NBC or Fox. We wanted our brand's experience to be unique. Our abc.go.com is a paradigm shifter.

If you go to abc.go.com, you'll immediately notice that it comes across as a unique online network experience. And it begins with the "player" format, which *is* a paradigm shifter. The quality of the site is not Internet-like in any way, but more like a high-definition television network or video player. In fact, the whole viewing experience was created to be theatrical. Viewing the programming is like sitting in a high-end movie theater. The clarity of the video is incredible. In fact, the entire site is beautifully designed—very slick, clean, and striking. More than this, the navigation is a cinch to use and content downloads quickly. There's a neat icon system that makes it simple to catch up on *Ugly Betty, Grey's Anatomy,* or *Desperate Housewives,* or to see new programming in its entirety. It's definitely not tool-centric, but user-centric. The only way to do a side-by-side comparison with other online network sites is to *experience* the difference. It's not a single feature or benefit, but the whole gestalt.

Another thing that differentiates the ABC brand presence online from its competitors is a critical factor in cementing the relationship ABC has with its viewers. When you want to download an NBC or Fox program, there's an aggravating step that separates brand from user. In 2007, NBC and Fox teamed up with AOL, MSN, and Comcast to create Hulu, an aggregator of online content. In order to watch any NBC or Fox content, viewers must first go to Hulu and then figure out how to get the NBC or Fox shows they want. ABC made a very wise branding choice to reinforce its relationship with viewers

ABC.com provides its viewers with a movie theater–like experience on its website to give them an easy way to access the programming they want.

by making it intuitive for them to download their favorite ABC shows. Want ABC? Go to abc.go.com.

The insight that ABC had about needing to make it easier for viewers to get what they wanted when they wanted it, not harder, has become a huge differentiating factor in its online presence. More than this, in its search for some meaningful way to set the brand apart from its competition, the company knew it had to go beyond the functional benefit of simply being able to download a show. Every network does that. With the clutter of options for online viewing, ABC sought to create a totally differentiated experience outside the expected Internet box. They did. "We had to stand for something different, something that consumers would expect from a Disney brand," Albert said. "The ABC tagline is 'Start here.' We want viewers to think about us first."

As a brand, you do want people to think about you first. The objective is to become a useful shortcut to give people a clear-cut way to differentiate your brand from every other brand. As I said earlier, in a marketplace where there are so many products and so many ways to compare them, many brands are "laddering up"—taking a functional attribute, like taste or shape or performance, and looking for a way to present it from an emotional perspective. Oddly enough, the newest challenge is that many brand promises are crowding the same rung of the ladder. One way to deal with this is to differentiate your promise through your branding execution. For example, if you're selling an analgesic that helps relieve the pain of arthritis, you'd want to find some other way to express relief than with pictures of the same spry couple dancing or bowling or gardening. If you're in a commodity service category, like insurance or financial planning, and want to promise peace of mind, you don't want the branding to compete with companies expressing the same thing with photos of couples walking hand-in-hand down the beach or playing checkers with the grandkids.

Another way to compete with all the other brands on your ladder is to find another ladder. This is exactly what Ameriprise did. Ameriprise, a leader in financial and retirement planning, changed the emotional end benefit. As they should, all financial firms that deal in retirement planning begin with the functional benefit. They'll help you manage money. Most take this functional benefit up the ladder to a promise that their money management skills will ensure you'll have enough money to pay your rent, travel a little, play checkers with your kids, and mitigate the chance that you'll end up having to eat cat food. They ensure a soft landing. Ameriprise, on the other hand, said, "Wait a sec. We're not dealing with a generation that identifies with soft landings, but with exciting take-offs." Ameriprise didn't look for a different rung of the same ladder every other brand was on, but found its

Ameriprise's brand idea demonstrates its understanding that baby boomers look at retirement in a totally different way than generations past; it's about reinvention and dream fulfillment, not rocking chairs.

own ladder. It completely transformed the emotional end benefit of what having enough money for retirement means.

It was with great interest that I spoke to Giunero Floro, former Vice President and Head of the Ameriprise brand, and Doug Pippin, currently the Executive Creative Director of Ameriprise business at ad agency Saatchi and Saatchi. They both spoke about the challenges of launching Ameriprise as a new brand after the company split with American Express in 2005. They both agreed that, in spite of the fact that it took two years to completely separate the infrastructure of the two companies, the due diligence was worth it. "We wanted to start with a completely clean slate," Giunero told me. "More than this, given that consumers are increasingly making use of the Internet for their financial dealings, we saw it as a tremendous opportunity to differentiate this new brand via the tools that would allow us to engage with our clients and prospects in meaningful conversations. We didn't want to talk at people; we wanted to talk with people. We wanted digital tools to be an intrinsic part of the idea that set our brand apart from the competition. Starting from scratch made it possible to do this, from the infrastructure of the company out to every other way we interacted with consumers. We wanted the Web as a brand-building mechanism to be integral to the brand idea."

"From our side of the table," said Doug,

when we sat down with Ameriprise for the initial business pitch, the website was among our top priorities. We knew it would take strong traditional media like TV or print to build awareness of this new brand, but we also knew the interactive space would be incredibly important. This is where so many people would have their first hands-on experience of what the brand is. The interactive nature of the space makes it possible to give consumers more information, more personally relevant information, than general media. We wanted to use the tools to set the company apart in a way that would immediately demonstrate that Ameriprise was not your father's financial management firm. We knew that, when clients and prospects engaged with the activities on the site, it would be an incredible way for them to actually experience the Ameriprise difference. Agencies talk about the digital space. We wanted to use it to establish Ameriprise.

For those on the younger end of the age spectrum, please let me tell you, if you don't already know, that after family and health, the topic that becomes top of mind as you get older is money. Will you be able to save enough for a house, for a vacation house, for college tuition for your kids, and most of all, for a stable retirement? Given the massive baby boom demographic, and given its insights about the baby boom generation, Ameriprise decided that a smart way to launch this new brand was to go after those thinking these thoughts. The financial category is for all intents and purposes a commodity category. Not in the same way tissues and laundry detergent are commodities, but one with equal potential for same-old, same-old. This is especially true in the area of retirement planning. As I said earlier, photos of pretty sunsets, pretty sailboats, couples walking hand-in-hand down country lanes and windswept beaches are common. So are branding executions that include stern warnings, facts, figures, charts, and graphs. The teams at Ameriprise and Saatchi recognized that this was not the way to go. Not because it wouldn't cut through the clutter (which it wouldn't have), but because this is not how real baby boomers think about retirement.

"There are 78 million baby boomers," Doug explained, when we talked about the planning process. "They grew up in an era during which they were crazily empowered to break down the doors of convention. They were turning the world upside down. They viewed the establishment with a somewhat jaundiced eye. If you fast forward you find this generation hasn't changed its approach to life. They feel younger than their parents did at the same age and continue to think that anything is possible. You see this in everything they do. It's only been magnified by the new channels of communication. This is a generation that is going to approach retirement much differently than its parents did. We knew we had to throw out the dictionary definition of retirement. This was the insight we used to fuel our thinking about how to position Ameriprise."

Baby boomers are about reinventing, rewiring, recharging, anything "re-" but retirement. Today's fifty-plus generation views the second half of life as a second chance to do the things they'd always wanted to do. They're more used to exciting takeoffs, not soft landings. While most other financial management firms were coming at the promise from either a numbers-driven perspective, or from the peace-of-mind rung of the ladder, Ameriprise determined that, while retirement is certainly about money, it's also about using money to accomplish all the things you've always wanted to accomplish. Start a business. Build a boat and sail it to the Caribbean. Go back to school and study something you've always wanted to study. Raise horses. Grow grapes and make wine. In other words, fulfill your dreams. This was the simple, relevantly different ladder on which Ameriprise set its brands apart. Giunero said:

> The idea of fulfilling dreams is at the core of the brand strategy, and the Dream Book is at the centerpiece of the campaign. The Dream Book was created to be emotionally driven, not numbers driven. It's a tool people can use to take stock of their lives and determine what they want to accomplish. We established different modules, one for clients and another for prospects, because one group already has a relationship with us and the other is in a learning mode. We also created different points of entry, or conversation starters, based on age. There are different triggers, different life events that drive behavior for people in their forties, versus people in their fifties or sixties. One group may be more interested in learning how to balance saving for a child's college tuition while also saving for their own retirement. It might be financing a second home or a small business. It may even be how to start over after a divorce. These are emotional events, not mathematical events, and we wanted to treat them as such. The key message is that Ameriprise can help you go beyond your dreams to live a more satisfying life, recognizing that everyone's dreams are different.

The simple brand idea, which is captured in the words "Dream. Plan. Track," conveys the customization inherent in fulfilling lifelong ambitions and financial objectives simultaneously. The Dream Book, a great interactive tool, takes the user along a personally relevant path, addressing questions and offering up relevant next steps along the way. Information is provided quickly and intuitively, something key to a target wanting to get on with things without a lot of hunting and pecking. Ameriprise recognizes it's dealing with an impatient culture and an equally impatient audience. While the Dream Book engages the user in the actual experience of the brand, the television spots, which star Dennis Hopper, support the online branding in genuine spirit. Dennis Hopper is a strong icon to baby boomers, a man who lives his life, both on- and off-screen, in an authentically independent way. All of the branding initiatives are carefully integrated to add credibility to the brand idea, however and wherever it is executed. The meaningful Ameriprise difference can be easily understood and appreciated.

"We're not dealing with a boxed product," Doug told me at one point in our conversation. "We are dealing with life issues. There was no way we could go about differentiating the brand without elevating its meaning above number-crunching, and without expressing the idea in a way that would ring true with the audience. We're talking about what people are going to do with the time they have left. It's an emotional topic. It's not a rational topic."

It is an emotional topic, but the Ameriprise brand team did an excellent job of making sure that consumers could easily make the rational connection from dream fulfillment to smart financial planning. They didn't go so far up its ladder that consumers couldn't make the connection to its functional benefit. Most important, taking its brand promise up a totally different ladder from other brands in the category, completely changing the end benefit, has insulated Ameriprise from competitive efforts. For retirees looking for exciting take-offs, not soft landings, the Ameriprise promise is hard to beat.

Given how many new products and services pop up on search engines and the variety of ways in which consumers can determine why one brand is different or better than another, establishing a relevantly different promise that *is* hard to beat is a hard act to follow in the digital marketplace. It's not only critical to define how you want your brand to be perceived, but to ensure your branding breaks through in ways that genuinely deliver on this promise. While not an easy task by any means, there are a number of tools and tactics brand organizations use to make the challenge more rewarding.

1. **Look for something obvious that other companies might have missed.** Some of the most successful brands were launched after their founders or brand teams saw a point of difference hiding in plain sight. Southwest Airlines, for example, flies people from point A to point B just like other airlines do. They just happened to wonder why the experience of flying couldn't be a lot more pleasant, and figured out a way to make it so. On the other hand, if you find something obvious that is more or less a cost of entry in the category—a table stake, so to speak—the way you execute it, your branding, can relevantly differentiate your brand. You can use the branding as a way to transcend every other brand in the category. The Liberty Mutual Group, which I wrote about earlier, looked at the idea of responsibility, which all insurance companies claim as part of their value system. But it elevated the notion to such an extent that the company is able to own the idea. What's more, it's such a simple and clear idea that the company is able to create branding expressions that seem completely natural, and intuitive to the brand. It has focused its branding efforts on bringing the idea of "responsibility" to life in a way its competitors can't.

2. **Ask your customers.** There are a wide variety of digital tools and applications that organizations can use specifically for this purpose. The Johnson & Johnson brand managers working on a new surgical device found that when they enlisted the assistance of their online community they were

rewarded with innovative ideas from people with perspectives they had never considered. Nikon went to the real community to learn more about the feelings people have about digital cameras. It took a bunch of its D40 cameras to a small town in South Carolina and filmed people using and talking about the cameras. The feedback they got—that once people actually experienced how easy it was for any photographer to take great pictures with a digital, single-lens camera—allowed the company to leverage this insight to execute its branding in a way that demonstrated it knew exactly what consumers wanted and needed. It also enabled Nikon to use the Internet to share its findings with a very broad audience in a compelling and efficient way. Many automotive brands, including Audi, have done the same thing. Before coming out with its RS 4, its super sporty sedan, it engaged with gear heads in the blogosphere to get their input and ended up with a winning sedan as a result. Other auto makers, like Scion and Pontiac, have tested designs on Second Life. What's more, while the classic marketing model used to be to innovate, test, and then tweak something before putting it into market and hoping for the best, the new marketing model enabled by digital tools turns this old one on its head. The Internet allows organizations to find the right consumers, float a bunch of ideas, try a variety of offers, and then go back and innovate based on this information. This makes it more likely that they'll hit a home run the first time at bat. While consumers won't tell you exactly what it is your brand can do to make their lives better, with enough of the right information, you can learn to read between the lines and mine the insight you're looking for.

3. **Go back to the customer journey.** Determine if you can make the *entire* brand experience more memorable than any other brand in the category. If you embed your promise in everything your company does, it makes it very hard, if not impossible, for the competition to take you on. Nike did this in its development of Nike+. More than this, it created totally new points of touch on the customer journey that serve to further reinforce the brand's promise. Nike+, the incredibly successful initiative for runners, is based on three critical insights: Runners are motivated by information about their "run"; runners use music as motivation during their runs; and people like running together. The Nike+ technology, the website, and the Nike+ community are, at once, a complete branded experience and examples of touch points that bring the Nike promise to life in a proprietary way. Not content to rest on its laurels, Nike is building on the insights used to successfully launch Nike+ by sponsoring an event called "The Human Race" in August 2008. The Human Race, the world's biggest running event ever, will offer runners around the globe the chance to compete together and share the experience physically and/or virtually. Being held in twenty-five major cities and including exclusive music concerts, this great event is being launched to reestablish Nike's ties with existing Nike+ members and to introduce potential Nike+ members to the technology and the community. By tapping into consumer insights and using digital technology in a way that is consistent with the way consumers like to run, Nike has changed the running category by both extending and enhancing the running experience in a way no differentiated product feature could ever achieve. The Nike+ community is a touch point on the

The Human Race is a worldwide event sponsored by Nike+ that will allow runners to compete with each other across the globe and share their experiences in an online community.

customer journey, and "The Human Race" an elevation of this touch point that no other brand could own.

4. **Ladder up to a more emotional promise.** In this day and age, trying to differentiate a brand based on a tangible feature or service offer is very difficult. Looking at a product feature or benefit from an emotional point of view is something that can set one brand apart from another. It's an exercise we've used with a number of clients. "There are two key components to this exercise," said Katie Ryan, who works with our Landor clients on this exercise:

> The first is getting information from people about their emotions when they interact with a brand. The second is to know what to do with this information once you've got it. For example, ask people to comment on a product's attributes or its benefits, and people will talk about the color or the taste or the shape or how

easy it is to operate. When it comes to asking them how they feel about these benefits the process begins to get harder. You've got to get people to free associate without feeling embarrassed. That's why companies often use clinical psychologists for the project. You don't want your participants to simply say, "I feel safe or happy or comfortable." You want them to go higher. "It makes me feel like I felt when I learned to read." "It makes me think of my grandfather's garage." "It reminds me of the time I met my husband." Once you've found the rung of the ladder on which you can stake an emotional promise, make sure it's not so far up that consumers can't make the connection to your functional promise. If you find other brands in the category occupying the same rung, see if there's a way you can differentiate your position by way of break-through branding.

5. **Find a different ladder.** If there are too many organizations trying to express the same emotional point of difference, change the emotional end benefit in a way that transforms the category. Ameriprise, for example, steered clear of retirement clichés. Instead of trying to compete with others in the category by promoting a serene rocking chair sort of retirement, it got into the heads of its primary audience and got real. Retirement for baby boomers is a time for reinvention—trying things they never had time for, starting new careers, learning a new language or a new skill. There are many ways of looking at the same topic. Throw out the rules, and look at your category from a different perspective. Better yet, call in people who know nothing about your category and have them talk about it. You won't hear the typical jargon or industry buzz words. In the exercises she does with clients, Katie Ryan often brings in men to talk about women's products and vice versa. Sometimes she'll get opinions about new products from kids, who often look at things without typical societal attachments.

9

Keep Your Brand's Promise

For anyone not familiar with the movie *The Wizard of Oz* (*is* there anyone?), there's a pivotal scene at the end of the film when Toto, Dorothy Gale's cheeky little terrier, literally pulls back the curtain on the great and terrible Oz to reveal him as the mere mortal he is. Dorothy is enraged. She's been duped into believing that Oz is a wizard capable of granting wishes and keeping promises. While the story eventually has a happy ending (the wizard's a great spin doctor, Dorothy forgives him, and the whole thing is just a dream, anyway), here's an ending to the story that Frank Baum, the author of this magical tale, could never have envisioned. It's not an Emerald City, but a digital world, and we're all tenacious terriers ready to bite the hand of any institution that doesn't keep its promise. None of us are going to wake up and find life has been a dream, including those hiding behind the curtain. Getting duped by any institution, corporate or otherwise, is a reality show, and as consumers, we have the tools and the motivation to expose any and all who don't deliver as expected.

In the preceding chapter, I explained that a brand is a promise between a company and a customer. It's the promise to deliver a relevantly

187

differentiated brand experience in the way the customer expects it to be delivered. In a marketplace that magnifies the number of product and service choices consumers have, it's become a huge challenge to find something your brand can stand for that's different and relevant and that no other brand has thought of. It's also become a challenge to be able to express it through branding that both breaks through the clutter and reinforces this promise. Relative to promises, there is another truth of branding that has been magnified by digital technology and the people who use it: the need to *keep* your brand's promise. We live in an age when all of the curtains have been pulled back. If a company does not deliver on any aspect of its brand promise, the only wizardry will be the technology that enables the millions of people watching to have the last laugh.

As I wrote in the first part of the book, digital technology makes everything transparent. It has given us all sales-pitch perfect hearing and peripheral vision. No, make that X-ray vision. There is no act that goes unnoticed, bad or good. While people have always had some recourse in making their feelings known about brands gone bad, it was relatively inconsequential. Sure, a letter to the CEO, a rant to the local news station, a call to the Better Business Bureau might have yielded some action. But it was an isolated and insulated event. Very few knew about the promise ill met, or the resulting action. Today, just as the transparent nature of our digital society enables people to hear and see what makes people happy about the brands they interact with, this transparency enables people to hear and see what makes them furious. This is not just true of the functional aspects of the brand organization's promise, *what* the company promises to do. This truth also trickles up, down, and all around *who* is doing the promising. The pressure on a company to deliver on every aspect of its brand's promise, whether it's inside the box or out, is intense.

Equally important, and equally intense, is the pressure on all institutions to behave in an ethical manner. There are now millions of people who can easily observe their actions, ferret out the slip-ups, and pass along their findings. Everyone knows everything, and my belief is that it's good news for everyone—the brand organizations and the consumers to whom they've made promises. In a conversation I had with Scott Osman, Managing Director of HFX, a brand strategy and communications group, he put this notion into broader perspective: "In the digital world there's no friction. There's nothing hindering the flow of news and information. Friction stops people from being able to see and hear what's going on. In a frictionless world you've got to be the brand you say you are."

There were very few, if any, people I spoke to in the course of researching this book who didn't agree that a transparent society is good for business. Ultimately, it should ensure that all organizations get better at making promises and even better at keeping them. All you have to do is go back to read Bob Garfield's account of his Comcastmustdie.com episode, and you'll quickly realize that his intention was to help the company deliver on its promise, not, despite the title of his blog, to bring about its demise. So, too, was Jeff Jarvis's intent as his Dell Hell initiative grew in strength. Dell rose from the ashes and is back on track, with Michael Dell giving Mr. Jarvis a nod for helping bring the matter to his attention. Had Dell been more aware of the activity online, it might have been able to save itself a few dollars. But in the long run, it'll be delivering on its promise better than ever. All companies today, any institution promising anything, could learn from the tagline of the *Aspen Daily News,* "If You Don't Want it Printed, Don't Let it Happen." Or, they should listen to and learn from one of the best prognosticators in the business, Faith Popcorn, who I mentioned earlier in the book as the proponent of the "goodness factor."

I spoke to Faith at length about her work with Faith Popcorn's BrainReserve, the company she founded over three decades ago. Before I share her insights, it might be helpful, first, to share *her* firm's position: "If you knew everything about tomorrow would you do things differently today?" Faith and her affiliates are respected for helping some of the biggest companies in the world get a sense of what will be happening tomorrow in order to do things differently today. She began our conversation by saying:

> The Internet is forcing companies to be transparent about their actions because it acts as both megaphone and microphone. People evaluate what you have to say; they look into your company, much more deeply than they ever did, or ever were able to. In a world of transparency, every corporate practice is knowable and watchable, and employees and consumers are voting with their wallets. They are often the same person. What we're seeing is that it's not just about Dove anymore, it's about Unilever. It's not just about Tide; it's about Procter & Gamble. It's not just about any individual brand or product, but the company with which they're affiliated. It's about the behavior of corporate management inside and outside the office—about whether the company is genuinely concerned with the environment or just paying lip service, about how a company takes care of its employees, for example childcare and the customized health-care plans. It's about something our firm refers to as "the goodness factor."

Faith continued:

> Our belief is that this goodness factor seeping into the fabric of our lives is a result of the cascading effects of 9/11. What we're seeing are behaviors that are by-products of this event. There's a mindset of distrust. A life rage, we call it. People expect the establishment to lie, to cheat, or to abuse the environment, and they're demonstrating through their words and actions that, much like the guy in the movie, *Network,* they're mad as hell. Any establishment, whether it's been guilty of less than ethical behavior or not, has to reach a higher bar, a bar set as a result of consumer expectations. All companies have to work harder to earn peoples' trust. We're seeing that

consumers are finally, en masse, reacting to what hyper-consumption is doing to our planet. They're beginning to endorse minimalism and sustainability. I don't think people think of themselves as consumers anymore, as much as citizens who have to take the responsibility for change into their own hands. The Internet is giving them the power to share the ways and means to do this with each other, and to demand it from the institutions they deal with. Don't forget, your consumer is your shareholder. They "sell" when they are privy to a company's not so great practices.

Consumers are more skeptical of what brand organizations are up to because they can see what's going on with more clarity of vision than ever before. And, even if your company delivers on all the tangible aspects of its promise, it can still be taken to task. Why? As a result of the megaphone-microscope nature of our society, consumers have become much less literal in their interpretation of a brand's promise. They hear stories about a company's health care policies for its employees, the crazily inflated salaries and bonuses of its upper management, the fact that a company's carbon-emission footprint is in direct conflict with its stated concern for the planet. It's no longer just a matter of whether the product or service performs as expected. It's whether the company as an entity performs as expected. Consumers today demand that the promises made by companies pertain, in equal part, to both product functionality and corporate integrity. This means that organizations must scrutinize all of the implications of the promises being made and assess, under their own magnifying glasses, if there any seams that are showing or frayed. It's not enough to promise a biodegradable diaper that keeps your baby's bottom drier. You've also got to promise and deliver on the fact that your company is not polluting the earth in another way. An article in the May 2007 edition of *The Economist* stated that GE was beating Silicon Valley's venture capitalists when it came to delivering on investments in cleaner energy. While this is an incredible accomplishment, the reason consumers keep buying GE Energy Smart light bulbs and water-saver appliances is because GE puts its money where its mouth is to ensure it meets its *own* standards for making the planet a cleaner place. As enormous a company as it is, its promise is airtight, and the delivery of its promise equally so.

As consumers we now look at the entire system of beliefs held by an institution, and we use our own judgment, along with the judgments of millions of others, to determine whether the institution's behavior is genuine or smacks of hypocrisy. Companies must clearly understand a consumer's expectation of its brand—from the inside out and from the top down. To return to Faith Popcorn's point, a company must weave "the goodness factor" into its brand promise and ensure that there is no way it can unravel, or become unraveled, by even a single thread of Internet conversation.

If, however, it does unravel, a company must be ready to react and remedy the situation very, very quickly. If ever an era was ripe for Murphy's Law, the digital era is it. Whatever can go wrong will go wrong, at the worst possible time in the worst possible way, and it will catch on faster with the masses than you can say Murphy's Law out loud. Even the organizations with the best intentions have to be ready to troubleshoot without missing a beat. While the Kryptonite lock folks should have known before some random bicyclist figured out that their promise of a lock that couldn't be compromised was not iron-clad, the bigger problem was their delayed reaction. They took flak because their lock didn't work as promised. But they took more flak because they waited so long to acknowledge the incident and make amends. When news travels as fast it does, organizations must be at the ready to put out fires before they spread. Whether the situation is critical or not (remember, with the Internet anything can be perceived as critical), it's essential to have a team ready and empowered to act when they sense that the seams of the brand promise are about to unravel.

More than that, acknowledgments of promises not kept should start from the top, as they did in the cases of Dell and Comcast, and in the case of JetBlue Airlines' potential unraveling in February 2007, an episode that proves even the most respected brands can't take their eye off the ball, or the weather.

When winter storms hit the Midwest and the Northeast over the February 2007 holiday, weekend air travel was, to put it mildly, a mess. The weather wreaked havoc with families setting off for school break, and it wreaked monumental havoc with JetBlue's reputation, which is based on its long-standing promise to put the humanity back into flying. Due to operational breakdowns as well as not having enough planes and crew at JFK Airport, one of its biggest hubs, JetBlue cancelled 71 of 570 flights in one 24-hour period. As if that weren't bad enough, passengers on one JetBlue flight were stranded on board for almost 11 hours. Given how well regarded a brand JetBlue was, it was an almost unbelievable situation. How could an airline known for putting the humanity back into flying—be it through its personnel, its pricing, or its onboard entertainment—make life so inhumane? David Neeleman, the company's CEO, asked the same question and got on finding an answer immediately. He had to. The number of stranded and irate passengers began e-mailing, texting, and blogging their plight within minutes of being stranded and becoming irate. Bloggers picked it up. Media picked it up. David Neeleman picked it up and immediately issued an apology. "I don't blame our customers for being upset with us," he said in his interview with the press. Acknowledging that it was critical for him to quickly restore the company's good reputation for having a high level of service along with low fares, he promised to get the right resources and support to "deliver the experience you have come to expect from us." Within weeks, JetBlue had issued a Passengers' Bill of Rights and made it clear that it intended to right its wrongs—with much thanks to the passengers who had made it very clear that they wouldn't stand for anything less than a humane flying experience from JetBlue. The company's quick action averted a major brand breakdown.

While Starbucks, another brand icon, didn't undergo a specific less-than-promised branding episode, it started to see the less-than-exemplary writing on the wall in late 2007 as its profits started to sag. Its promise of delivering both a revolutionary coffee taste and a revolutionary coffee experience, modeled on the charming coffee houses in Italy, began to lose steam due to the company's rapid growth. People voted with their wallets as a way of expressing that this promise, made to them almost thirty years ago, wasn't holding together. The double whammy for Starbucks was some customers' complaint that it wasn't keeping either the in-the-box or the out-of-the-box elements of its promise. It had promised a better coffee experience. Better coffee, meaning the "in the box" promise of a coffee that tasted better than consumers could expect from other coffee brands. And, as a better overall experience, Starbucks promised to give consumers an entirely new way to enjoy their coffee, morning, noon, or night. Consumers appreciated Starbucks' promise because, at this point in our caffeine nation, most of us grabbed our coffee as we rushed out the door on our way to work, hoping that if we got to the last drop it would be good.

It might be helpful to put the whole thing in context with a bit of history. It's Seattle, 1971, and three friends with a passion for great-tasting coffee start a little business selling fresh-roasted coffee along with roasting and brewing accessories. In 1980, one of the friends sells out to the others and goes off to explore other ventures. By that time, the little business was the largest coffee roaster in the state of Washington. The two remaining partners decide to hire a young fellow by the name of Howard Schultz, a sales representative for a manufacturer of plastic drip-brewing thermoses, to help them with their marketing efforts. They send him to Italy for an industry show, where he falls in love with the vibrant culture of the Italian coffee houses and the taste of those delicious lattes. He had stumbled upon something different in an out-of-the-box kind of way; the experience of sitting within a community of people—reading, laughing, talking, and sharing the moment. And he had discovered an in-the-box difference—the taste of deliciously brewed coffee drinks. Howard Shultz brought the idea back to America, hoping that both the taste sensations and the experience of the brand would find relevance among Americans. Americans drank it up, until the brand started to slide in meeting both the yin and the yang of its promise.

The company had expanded beyond being able to deliver on both aspects of its promise. It started to sell things that didn't fit the whole Italian coffee house experience, including breakfast sandwiches that, when warmed in the microwave, made their retail establishments smell less than friendly. More than this, the company couldn't keep up with the quality of its coffee drinks. It couldn't hire employees fast enough and train them well enough to deliver the coffee drinks its loyal fans expected. Howard Schultz, who had by this point turned over the reins of chief executive to someone else, returned as CEO to oversee the reestablishment of his brand's promise. In an unprecedented move, on February 26, 2008, he closed 7,100 Starbucks establishments for three hours for a massive retraining program for 135,000 of its employees. It was just one initiative of many he would undertake to see that his company would get back on track. In a formal statement prior to the store closings, he said that it was necessary to "ensure the customer experience that we provide is the best that it can be."

The strength of the Starbucks brand has always been based on the relevantly different promise to deliver both exceptional coffee and a unique coffee experience. As blog and chat room conversations among coffee fanatics filled with comments about going to local, independently owned shops for the taste of the coffee and the quiet, communal atmosphere, as more and more people began showing their displeasure at the less-than-expected Starbucks experience, Howard Schultz took note and took action. In addition to the company-wide training, the company made a major investment in special espresso machines as well reevaluating its non-coffee product line. Starbucks is a very strong brand with a very dedicated following. Chances are good that, like JetBlue, Dell, Comcast, and other brands, it has learned that consumers have the power to tell it like it is and that it's the brand that must listen hardest of all to rectify the situation.

The Starbucks experience also points up another dynamic being magnified by the digital environment. Once you've found something that relevantly differentiates your brand, it's essential to keep it relevantly differentiated. This, as you might expect, is also harder than ever. As soon as one company gets wind of what another is doing via its own monitoring of online conversations and reviews, it can quickly up the ante. This is especially true when one organization starts hearing chatter about another's not meeting its promise as expected. It's tough out there. Not only do you need to understand consumer expectations as you frame an initial promise, you have to think about how to keep the promise fresh and how to deliver on it consistently as market conditions change. Sharpening your listening skills and using the right tools to keep on top of what consumers think and feel are critical.

The fact is, as much as they can and like to help, you don't need to wait for customers to tell you via the digital grapevine that your brand promise is not being kept. There are tools and platforms that companies can embed into their own websites and category sites that enable consumers to alert your organization before they alert the media that something is amiss. Geoff Ramsey is Co-founder and CEO of emarketer, a firm that does market research and trend analysis for e-business, online marketing, and media. He said during our talk:

Your goal as an organization operating in this marketplace should be to increase trust. Trust has been declining in the past few years, across all industries. There are lots of tools, widgets, review and recommendation applications that you can add to your site that will allow people to talk to each other knowing full well that you're listening and learning from them. What's more, it's okay to shrink your reach and get more deeply engaged with those more likely to be brand evangelists. You can't pay attention to everyone. You'll learn from listening whose commentary can have the greatest impact, either positively or negatively. The sheer volume of information online has created an interesting paradigm shift. Companies must continuously ask themselves how they can become more relevant to their customers and more helpful to their customers. The customers can tell them how. But you don't have to wait, and you shouldn't wait for something to go awry. There is no time to spend figuring things out. You've got to proactively monitor the landscape. There are a number of ways to get ahead of what's out there. Take advantage of the digital space the way it should be taken advantage of—to provide a better customer experience.

Disney is one brand that continues to keep its promise relevantly different, and, for that matter, continues to deliver on its promise above and beyond consumer expectations. Actually, as Albert Cheng said about ABC Disney, the company is not content with just delivering on the promise, but with "blowing people out of the water." Disney set the bar in family entertainment and keeps raising its own bar. Being the customer-centric company it is, and the technology savvy company it is, it has taken advantage of every online application available to hear from its customers how it can *keep* over-delivering on its promise. One of the most recent tools it created was something called the Walt Disney Mom Panel. It's an application on the Disney.com site on which moms—or as Disney appropriately says, "people who serve the mom role in the family"—can log in and talk to each other about the experience of taking families to Disney's theme parks. A rotating panel of moms offers up practical advice on everything from planning a Disney vacation to dining, shopping, and navigating the lines at the most popular events and rides. The home page features a changing list of the top five most frequently asked questions. Moms engage with Disney and, more important, they engage with each other by sharing advice and insight that only those who have been-there-done-that would know. More than that, it's common knowledge that word-of-mom is the most trusted form of word of mouth, which Disney understands and appreciates.

I spoke to Leslie Ferraro, who oversees marketing for Disney Parks and Resorts, and Chris Curtin, who oversees new media marketing. "Nine out of ten visiting families do at least some of their vacation planning online," Leslie told me. "In fact, we know our guests consume online media and engage in online applications in a very big way. When they first come to Disney.com, it's critical that it immediately reflects the magic of the Disney promise. We use assets that are uniquely our own. Our belief is that the site should stand for everything Disney, its magic and its concern for the comfort of our guests."

"We constantly monitor the user experience," Chris added. "We not only formally track what's being said about our brand on other online locations to give us insight about our guests' experiences, but we act on what we hear. Word of mouth has always been a part of the Disney experience. We have natural brand evangelists and the Mom Panel was simply a natural extension for us. There are so many people that talk about the brand; it only makes sense to harness the user experience and use the digital space to its advantage. We've been providing family vacation solutions for over fifty years. The objective is to make all experiences unforgettable."

As a brand, Disney holds itself to a very high standard. It's reflected in its theme parks, in its hotels and resorts, in its entertainment, and in its online experiences. As a result, we have higher expectations for this brand. Our expectations for anything Disney are way above ordinary. As Chris said, the fact that Disney actively engages its guests and users in online forums and review panels would only make sense. Their online presence and the way they use guest feedback to keep the brand's promise relevantly different is part of what makes Disney the cultural brand phenomenon it is.

Consumers today are massively empowered to tell organizations, and each other, how they feel about brands. Delivering on the promise of the brand is as fundamental to brands and branding as establishing a point of relevant differentiation. More important than ever, however, is thinking about your brand's promise from the consumer's perspective. Consumers don't take a brand's promise literally anymore. It's as essential to deliver what's in the box—the product or service—as it is to deliver on all of your brand's out-of-the-box associations: the quality of every branded experience and the quality of the company behind the brand. There was a conference in San Francisco awhile back, titled, "Customer Service: The New Marketing." I'd say that this title is a bit short of the mark. Servicing the customer in the digital age is the new marketing, the new public relations, the new research, the new product development, and the new anything else that enables you to deliver on your brand's promise.

A quick story before I get to this chapter's list of top to-dos. A month or so before beginning this book, I bought a new wireless printer from HP. I got up at 6:30 on a Sunday morning, when I knew I'd have some time to get the thing hooked up and operating. After about an hour of trying to get it to work I realized I was getting nowhere fast and thought about calling the toll-free number listed in the manual. While pretty skeptical that I'd actually get any satisfaction by doing this, I had no recourse. I dialed the number. Lo and behold, a real person answered. He asked me how long I'd been trying to get the printer up and running, and when I told him it had been about an hour he said, "You should have called us within the first fifteen minutes. That's why we're here." The representative walked me through the setup very patiently and very conscientiously, and we tested that it worked. It did. Before he let me go he asked that I test the printer once more, just to make sure. I did. It worked. Not only did this interaction make me feel it was okay for a guy to ask for directions, it made me feel great about HP as a brand. Here was a company that understood what making and keeping a brand promise was all about in the digital age. You've got to exceed expectations. As Faith Popcorn told me, brand organizations have to work harder in an environment where consumers are more skeptical and more empowered to demand better service. She's right. In fact, if a brand exceeds my expectations, I'll be more likely to share my story and become a voluntary brand evangelist.

Four essential rules will help you to keep your brand promise in the skeptical digital world:

1. **Think like a consumer.** Look at your brand promise from the consumer's perspective. Determine what their expectations are relative to what you promise to deliver and make sure you can exceed their expectations at every point of customer interaction. Examine all aspects of your business that are related to your brand. Remember that if anything can go wrong, it will, at the worst possible time and/or place. People are connected day and night, and have the motivation and the tools to let the whole world know when some institution screws up. Get a cross-functional team together and assess all the points of touch with your brand at which its promise may be compromised. There are multiple ways your brand promise can break down—from the way a product is packaged, to the way it functions, to the way your organization offers customer care. This means it's also

essential to assess the "who" of your brand, and whether your organization behaves in a manner that will earn people's trust based on more than just the product or service it offers. Make sure there is a code, written or otherwise, by which the people in your organization behave.

2. **Make everyone in your company accountable for their part in delivering the brand promise.** This means, of course, you've got to make sure everyone in the company is fully aware of the brand's promise to its customers. Or, as Suzy Deering, Director of Advertising and Sponsorships at Verizon told me:

> Everyone in the organization, all agency and media partners, anyone associated with the brand in any way, must work in unison to deliver consistently on the brand promise. Making everyone accountable is not a nice-to-have, but a must-have in today's transparent environment. Consumers can see everything, which means keeping the brand experience integrated is essential. It's not enough to see that TV and radio or even the websites hold together, but that the host of new touch points, including consumer-to-consumer interaction and employee-to-consumer interaction on blogs and in chat rooms hold together. Anyone of Verizon's 242,000 employees could be interacting with a customer at any point in time. The ability to ensure that the customer's experience is consistent with the brand promise wherever they interact with a brand is an even greater competitive advantage than before. It will elevate the best of the bunch.

3. **Institute a management alert system.** Be on the lookout for early-warning signs of product or service issues, and establish mechanisms for immediate response and resolution. Have people in your organization empowered and ready to act should something about your brand's lack of performance hit the online message boards or chat rooms. If you act

quickly and with integrity to address the situation, the problem should be mitigated without long-term damage.

4. **Delight your customers.** Deliver on your promise in such a way that they become brand evangelists. One quick story to share: My wife and I were at the Ritz Carlton Hotel in the Caribbean about a week after it opened. Because the hotel hadn't quite worked out all the bugs, we experienced less-than-stellar service. I met the manager of the hotel while I was waiting in the lobby and told him about the situation. He asked me to make a list of all the things that had gone wrong during our stay and invited me to share the list with him over a drink later that day. When we met with the manager that afternoon, rather than saying he'd take a certain percentage off the bill, he asked me what I thought fair reimbursement for the inconvenience would be. We told him, and he said, "Done." That alone exceeded my expectations, but then he went further. He offered my wife a day of complimentary services at the Ritz Spa in New York City. The behavior of this manager as a representative of his brand not only befitted the company's reputation for excellence but turned me from a potential negative net promoter to a positive one.

1 0

Start with a Simple Idea

I want to go back to a comment made by Michael Mendenhall, Chief Marketing Officer of HP: "In the digital age, it is absolutely critical to understand the value of each branding channel and its relevance to a particular audience." He made this comment during our conversation about the fact that marketing can no longer be driven by the engine of traditional advertising, but rather must be driven by a powerful brand idea. While it's true that television advertising still takes up about sixteen minutes per hour of network television programming, less and less people are sitting still for it. TiVo, podcasting, broadband television, and the good old-fashion remote control are some of the reasons why. The other is simply that people are spending as much, if not more, time online. We're long past the age of mass media. As I said in the first part of this book, the only mass today is the mass of different consumer populations and the mass of new ways people have to interact with brands. Smart marketers are using digital to engage consumers where they're spending time and in a way that's relevant to them.

We are in the midst of a fundamental shift in the marketing paradigm from linear to wherever. And we are starting to understand with greater appreciation what it means for branding when consumers pull in the content they want and push back on content they don't. Consumers are actively seeking out what they want to be engaged in at the time it's most convenient for them and in the way it's most comfortable for them. They have no hesitation in clicking off or away from what they don't want to experience. If you were to multiply the mass of consumer segments by the mass of branding touch points, you could very well end up with mass confusion about what people think your brand stands for. In *The Long Tail,* a book by Chris Anderson, editor in chief of *Wired* magazine, his premise is that we've moved from a world of scarcity to a world of abundance. He writes about the implications of a media environment in which there are an "endless number of possibilities to connect"—"the long tail" of ways that marketers and content providers can interact with consumers. From a branding perspective, this has also created endless ways for consumers to interact with content—if, of course, they choose to do so.

No sane organization wants mass confusion about what people think its brand stands for. That being the case, in order for an organization to ensure that the meaning of its brand is clearly understood by consumers it must be clearly understood by those responsible for the branding. Going back to Michael Mendenhall's comment, given that a brand is a promise between a company and the consumer; that branding is the way in which the company delivers on this promise; and that branding is no longer delivered en masse, but across multiple points of touch (touched at the consumer's discretion)—the idea at the core of the brand promise, the idea that must drive all brand experiences, must be simple for those doing the branding to understand. The importance of this long, but true sentence has been magnified in a marketplace whose tail continues to grow longer and longer with connectivity possibilities. To succeed as a brand in the digital world, it's essential to capture the simple thought you want consumers to associate with your brand in a brand driver. You've got to give your simple idea a handle everyone across departments and agencies can grab onto. It's only after establishing a brand driver that those responsible for the branding will know what tools to use as branding tools, digital and otherwise, to deliver the brand message in the most compelling, relevant way possible. There can be no confusion anywhere for anyone, but most importantly, for the consumer.

One of the simplest of simple brand drivers and among the most evocative is Johnson & Johnson's "Having a baby changes everything." I can't imagine a parent anywhere in the world who would disagree with this simple, but highly emotional statement. Having a baby *does* change everything. It's a universal truth obvious in meaning and globally understood. In this brand driver, Johnson & Johnson has summed up all of the tangible and intangible implications of having a new little person in your life. And capturing the idea in this simple phrase makes it simple for everyone associated with the brand to unlock its equity in appropriate ways, from research and product development to marketing. I spoke to Joe McCarthy, Vice President of Worldwide Advertising and Marketing Communications for Johnson & Johnson, about the company's brand driver and why it works so beautifully for the brand. "When the line 'Having a baby changes everything' was instituted about three years back, we knew we could own it because we have long been associated with the bond between mothers and their babies. It's believable coming from us because we have always been regarded as a trusted healthcare company and a brand trusted by mothers. The essence of this line incorporates both the soul of our brand and our brand values. While the actual line, itself, appears only in corporate communication, it drives everything having to do with our baby products on a global basis. This simple idea marries the functional nature of our baby products with the emotional aspects of being a nurturing mother. The promise is consistent with our beliefs and our products."

I don't know a person anywhere who, when someone mentions Johnson & Johnson, doesn't think "No more tears®" shampoo, or, at the very least, has very positive childhood memories of the brand—if from nothing else than having mom put a Johnson's Band-Aid® on a skinned knee. Johnson & Johnson has been the leader in baby care for the past century. The fact that the Johnson & Johnson brand driver supports its brand equity so credibly gives it traction and gravitas. In a marketplace where credibility is key, this gives the company an incredible advantage in the expansion of its franchise. It gives the brand organization permission to talk about anything that has to do with parenting and babies across a broad array of topics and brand products.

In addition to Joe McCarthy, I spoke to Bridgette Heller, Global President-Baby Care GBU for Johnson & Johnson Consumer Companies, Inc. about the company's special little brand driver and what it means to the company in light of the shift in marketing paradigms. Prior to joining Johnson & Johnson she was at Gevalia coffee, where she was instrumental in perfecting the company's online consumer experience before most companies even had websites. She began our conversation by providing her perspective on the digital environment in general. "Before I talk about the Johnson & Johnson baby story, let me go tell you what I learned about consumer behavior as a result of my experience at Gevalia," Bridgette began.

> Historically, as brand marketers, we were accustomed to the one-way communication model. You pushed stuff out and didn't expect a lot of interaction. At Gevalia, I had the opportunity to see what happens when you let customers connect with you when they want to and where they want to. Back then, we were able to provide two options, the phone or on our website. This was over ten years ago, and the Internet wasn't nearly what it is today. We thought that we'd maybe have about 5 percent of customers in-

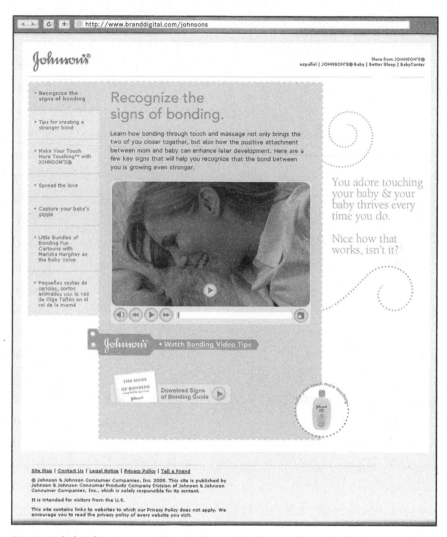

"Having a baby changes everything," Johnson & Johnson's brand driver, is as evocative as it is simple. Courtesy of Johnson & Johnson Consumer Companies, Inc. Used with permission.

teracting with us online, but within a few months of going live with our site, we had over 30 percent of people doing their ordering online. This was a powerful insight for us. If you let your customers lead the conversation in the way that's most convenient for them, they'll applaud you. Gevalia's promise is to deliver delicious fresh ground coffee directly to your home or office on your schedule. It's an auto-replenishment model. We created value for our customers by giving them the means to connect with us on their time and in their own way. As branding applications, our website and call centers were in total alignment with this simple brand idea. These tools, in effect, were intrinsic to the idea.

When I got to Johnson & Johnson, I was able to draw on this insight. It's a natural inclination for marketers to say "I want to be here or there with my branding, and I want to say this or that," but that's not the way it works anymore. You have to ask, "where are *they*, and what do *they* want?" In terms of branding to new mothers, we think about how we can make their lives easier. How can we improve their lives as mothers *and* as women? We have to think about the branding as the entire experience, but more so, where and how we can communicate with our customers in the ways that are most beneficial to them.

Johnson & Johnson's simple brand idea is expressed beautifully in many ways. We're all familiar with its iconic script logo and its clean and simple packaging. Those of us with kids are also familiar with the safety and purity of its baby products, not to mention how sweet even the crankiest newborn smells after being pampered with Johnson & Johnson's gentle lotions, oils, and washes. As a time-honored healthcare provider, these branding elements are credibly in line with the brand's promise. What are equally credible as branding signals in the digital world are the two websites for mothers that Johnson & Johnson sponsors, BabyCenter.com and Baby.com. Why two? BabyCenter.com was a much-respected independent site when it was purchased about five years ago by Johnson & Johnson as a means of providing new parents with general, non-branded information. Baby.com is the company's own branded site that provides content that relates mostly to Johnson & Johnson products. Both give new parents the means to connect with each other and with the company.

"Our brand is credible to new mothers," said Bridgette during our conversation about the company's online initiatives. She continued:

Only Johnson & Johnson could own the line "Having a baby changes everything" because as a brand we've credibly demonstrated through our product functionality and our messaging what it means to have a new baby. When we thought about our online presence it was critical to maintain this credibility. BabyCenter.com is a place where moms can gather and chat without being surrounded by Johnson & Johnson–specific branding messages. There are manufacturers who buy advertising on the site, all baby related, but there is no overt branding. It's a site where we can listen and learn. We listen to what moms have to say to each other, what concerns they share about being new mothers, and what solutions they offer each other. We use this insight to determine what type of content would be most beneficial and appropriate to those who visit our site. Visitors to BabyCenter.com are fully aware that it's a Johnson & Johnson site, but because it is basically a community, social networking type of site and not a commercially driven site, they feel comfortable sharing with each other and sharing with us. There are four million babies born in the United States each year and over 70 percent of moms have visited BabyCenter.com at one point or another. Obviously it's serving a purpose. While the content on Baby.com is mostly about our Johnson & Johnson products, again, it does not overtly sell. To be commercial in an overt way would not be appropriate to the Johnson & Johnson brand. There is product information on the site, but it's about how to use the products to take better care of your baby and better care of yourself as a new mother. Johnson & Johnson puts care for people above everything else. In order for our branding to resonate authentically, we have to keep this in mind.

Maintaining authenticity in any marketing age has always been a critical factor in a brand's success. In a marketing environment that some have likened to the Wild West it's an even greater challenge. The key, as Bridgette said, is to communicate with people in a way that links credibly with your brand idea and that offers up value in a personally relevant way. As a global brand, this can pose some interesting hurdles, but not if you do your research and talk to the people who matter about things that matter, no matter where they live.

> In the U.S., we have been learning, with increasing effectiveness, how to target our messages to our moms, and, as such, we've reduced our spending on traditional media significantly. We use the same learning to target audiences on a global basis, determining who we should be talking to and through which media. In the U.S. for example, we target our professional messaging to pediatricians. In the United Kingdom, we talk to midwives. We've created a community for midwives, in fact. This is a very critical touch point for us, because in the U.K. midwives deliver over 60 percent of the babies. Never in a million years, using traditional media, could we have a special conversation with midwives. The whole notion of the world being flat is right. Because of digital technology we're much better at taking ideas from around the globe and integrating them in different markets much more readily. Consumers are getting used to being spoken to on a more personal level, and they're learning to tune out what they don't need.

What's interesting about digital technology is that consumers have learned they can tune out things that are not important to them. It's sort of like Pavlov's dogs. We've all become accustomed to going after things that are rewarding and paying little heed to those that don't feed our desires. Consumers these days may be overwhelmed by the inundation of products and promises, but they're fast figuring out how to send marketers a message that the branding messages they're being sent had better be relevant. Smart marketers are figuring out the best ways to do this. Those that follow the lead of their brand drivers have the greatest success. Target, another company with a powerful, but simple brand driver, is among the early adopters of this digital-age branding dynamic. Target started life with a strong brand driver, and it continues to adapt its branding without missing, well, the target.

In the beginning, Target recognized that there are value-conscious consumers at all income levels. When senior management noticed Mercedes and BMWs in the parking lots of the wholesale retail clubs, its senior management realized that the company could appeal to a wide range of customers by offering great value. To differentiate itself, however, it asked one of those obvious questions: "Ever wonder why discount has to *look* like discount?" Its on-trend—and in some cases, forward-trend—merchandise offered at affordable prices ushered in a whole new category of discount shopping. Its first prototype "T–1" store was easy to shop, attractive, and full of stylishly designed, high-quality goods displayed in a clean, welcoming environment. The company discovered a way to add high design to peoples' lives at low prices. "Design for All" is the mantra by which Target works and plays. And "play" is the key emotional counterbalance to its very rational promise of good value.

I talked to Bill Melton, Vice President of Client Services at Schematic, a digital marketing firm, about Target's driving brand idea. Bill explained:

> Target is all about what we call "the wink." The essence of its brand driver is great design at great prices, but at the emotional core of this idea is a playful, whimsical nature. It's fun to shop at Target, and the branding exudes this fun. Because Target serves so many masters across a number of branding constituencies, for any branding tactic to be authentic to the brand it has to capture this whimsy, this spirit of surprise. The television ads are instrumental in establishing this tone for consumers. In addition to this, Target has found that its Sunday newspaper advertising insert, along with the online version of the insert, the "Weekly Ad," helps drive people to the store. It's one of the primary media vehicles Target uses to convey value to customers, and it's the perfect balance between playful and practical. Loyal Target shoppers know just where to find the Weekly Ad on the website and can sign up to have it e-mailed. Obviously one of the big challenges for marketers today is keeping the branding consistent across channels. Anyone who works with the Target brand knows instinctively what's right and what's not.

And thus, yet more proof of the importance of the brand driver, especially in a branding environment as channel-laden as the digital environment. In my conversation with Tom Bedecarre, whose firm, AKQA, does work for Target along with other clients including Nike, Microsoft, and Coca-Cola, he answered one of the biggest questions that seem to puzzle marketers these days: "Should we have a presence on a social networking site, like MySpace or Facebook?" In a nutshell, Tom's answer is yes: if the consumers you want to reach would find your presence credible, and not gratuitous, and if your presence and your offer are relevant to them. If you want play on Facebook or MySpace, the brand and its branding have to demonstrate a clear understanding of who inhabits these community pages and what matters to them. It has to be adapted to the style of the online community natives. Target is a brand that clearly understands what matters to people. Tom and his team clearly understand how to adapt its branding to the styles of the MySpace and Facebook communities, using the brand driver, great design at great prices, as a guide.

Our recent back-to-college initiative on Facebook for Target was adapted to the conversations taking place within this predominantly student community. It focused on how to trick out your dorm room as you got ready to go back to college. We termed it the "Dorm Survival Guide." It was all about the "box," the tiny space we've all had to inhabit at some point in our lives. The site was set up to show kids what was available from Target, the pillows and comforters, but more importantly it was designed to give them the tools they needed to talk to each other about the whole college dorm experience. It reflected an understanding on the part of the Target brand that this could be both an exciting time and a time that could generate apprehension. Kids talked to RAs [resident assistants], and they talked to each other about what they were bringing to school. "Hey, I've got a clock radio, do you have a microwave?" We created feature applications the participants could use to get design advice from Target, or to get recipes using stuff you'd likely find in a dorm refrigerator. Kids were able to post pictures of their dorm rooms and ask for input from each other. This wasn't about advertising on Facebook. It was about using Facebook in the way it should be used; to get people engaged and talking to each other about things that are relevant to them. The campaign showed that Target understood what Facebook was all about and what its members were all about. People use Facebook as a means of expressing their identity. Target's branding fit right in to the environment; it didn't interfere with it. The objective was to empower kids to talk with other kids about what their cribs were going to look like, and they felt comfortable including Target in the conversation. The venue was right, and the message was relevant to the venue and its participants.

Another important point about this initiative was that Target recognized that in order to maintain its credibility with the community, it had to dial back its more promotional ads on other sections of the Facebook site. Tom reiterated what a number of people in the industry have said about branding in the digital world. "You need to be able to talk to people first and let them get to know you before you try to sell them anything. You've got to build trust." There's no doubt that Target earned the trust of its Facebook friends by adapting to their needs through its branding style. According to an article in *AdWeek*, the brand's 2007 back-to-school sales were up 6.1 percent over 2006 sales. The most effective branding will always be in concert with the brand idea and relevant to the brand's core consumers, online or off.

Burger King demonstrated its understanding of this digital principle when it established a MySpace page for the King, himself. I'm not sure having the Burger King as my friend would do anything for my status in the business world, but for twelve- to sixteen-year-old boys it seems to be a must have. Burger King was one of the first major brand organizations to create a site on MySpace that allowed kids to virtually befriend the jolly monarch. Since making its entrance, Burger King has amassed more than one hundred thousand friends, people who want to associate with his Highness. Those who post blogs and write messages to the King continue to generate a level of brand evangelism any political figure would relish (no pun intended). In any case, Burger King, much like Target, understands that success is not based on marketing en masse anymore; it comes from one group at a time—letting them have it their way—and not your way.

Using the brand idea as the engine of the branding process could have been a very hard lesson in paradigm shifting for Procter & Gamble, one of the largest en masse branders in history. But, as I discussed earlier in the book, the organization is a quick study. As a matter of fact, it's such a quick study that 2007–2008 marked the time period in which it undertook two very interesting branding initiatives for one of its oldest brands, Tide® detergent. Before I get to those stories, let's start with a bit of historical context. Until the 1930s, people used soap flakes to clean their clothes. These flakes didn't exactly do a great job. Procter & Gamble, intent upon changing the laundry game, challenged its researchers to come up with a better answer, which, of course, they did. What they discovered was that getting clothing clean involves a two-step molecular process. The first molecular process pulls dirt out of the fabric while the second involves holding the dirt away from the fabric until it can be rinsed away. Using this science, the first product that P&G introduced using this science was called Dreft®. They found that it could do a better job than soap flakes, but not as good a job as P&G was hoping for. It went back to work, and in 1943 introduced Tide. By 1946, Tide had begun its run as the best-selling laundry detergent in history.

While the detergent's cleaning power is its ultimate branding signal, the simple phrase, "Tide knows fabric best," sums up quite well the idea the company wants the brand to represent in the minds of consumers. Inside to out, the most powerful external signal of the brand is its packaging. A logo radiating concentric rings of vivid orange and yellow, superimposed by the name Tide in bold, blue typeface, it's one of the most enduring logos on the market. According to website titled "The History of Soap and Detergent," Tide detergent was improved twenty-two times during its first twenty-one years on the market. While this might be good enough for some companies, it's not good enough for a company that understands a competitor's research and development can be responsible for quickly sending brand leadership down the drain. P&G continues to work on new and improved products that prove it does "know fabric best." Tide's driving idea, visually held together by its instantly recognizable logo, continues to connect with consumers no matter where or how they connect with the brand. And herein lies the tale of two completely different branding efforts driven by the same simple idea.

For quite a long time P&G, like most consumer goods companies, depended on traditional media as the engine of its branding. In fact, Tide, along with other cleansing products, was responsible for the "soap" in soap operas, the programs that originated on radio and eventually moved to television. Well, guess what? Soap operas have moved to the Internet. In 2007, P&G developed a new soap opera called "Crescent Heights," aimed not at stay-at-home moms, but at recent college graduates. Crescent Heights' three-minute episodes star Ashley, who is fresh out of school and fresh from Wisconsin, and now settled in Los Angeles to start a career in public relations. Tide, while it makes a couple of appearances peeking out of laundry baskets, is not the star. Ashley and her friends are, along with the clothing they wear to work and to the parties at which they want to attract the perfect guy. I spoke to Kevin Crociata, Tide's Associate Marketing Director, about the organization's choice of branding and its adherence to the brand idea. "We were looking to connect with an audience that spends very little time watching television and a lot of time surfing the Internet," he told me. "In order to connect online, where there is so much competition for attention, you have to make your message both entertaining and informative. The objective of Crescent Heights is to engage and entertain potential consumers while still conveying the Tide brand promise. The whole point is to be where they are and present the brand in a way that's meaningful to them. This is a time in people's lives when they form household-related habits. The brand, itself, plays a supporting role to the actors and the plot. If your brand promise is not interesting to the viewers you want to reach, you're not going to be successful."

This *Friends*-like series of Webisodes was a test for P&G, but the brand team started with the right priorities. First, they determined who they wanted to reach. They then identified the type of media and other branding channels this group is most likely to interact with. The team also paid heed to the type of lifestyle this audience led and how it could get across Tide's brand message in a way that was relevant and entertaining, but also conveyed the product's tangible benefits. Crescent Heights was taped in ten three-minute segments, and, as of this writing, it seems to have caught on with the post–soap opera crowd. "It's not about the laundry," Kevin said. "It's about trying to find the most effective way to communicate with a specific group of consumers. In the digital environment you have to focus on the consumer and engage them in the way that's meaningful to them without losing sight of your ultimate objective—to get them to believe in your brand promise."

This brings me to the second interesting branding initiative P&G undertook in the 2007–2008 timeframe. It goes back to its roots as a mass-market advertiser, but for a very good reason. February 2008 was the first time this marketer of brands to the masses placed advertising on one of the most massive television events of the year, the Super Bowl. The reason it did so was that it had a new product that would appeal to anyone who has ever spilled food on their clothing and hoped the stain wouldn't set in before they were able to get to a

Crescent Heights, an innovative series of Webisodes created by P&G's Tide group, was designed to get the brand idea across to a specific group of consumers in a way that would resonate with them.

washing machine. I would say that's a massive amount of people. Tide to Go is an instant stain remover that comes in a marker-size tube. Spill your guacamole dip, the jelly from your morning toast, the coffee from your too-full cup onto your nice clean shirt, dab Tide to Go over the bothersome spot, and you're good to go. P&G chose television time on Super Bowl Sunday to launch this new product because it determined that this is where the people who would most benefit from its branding message were likely to be: spilling guacamole dip onto their nice clean shirts.

In the ad, there's a nerdy guy at a job interview with a coffee stain, clearly visible, on his shirt. The guy's rambling on about his credentials. The stern fellow doing the interviewing is not listening to the nerdy guy. He's staring at and listening to the stain, which is also rambling on in some bizarre language. It's a funny ad, and totally appropriate to marketing in the digital age. It's engaging and highly entertaining. It has pass-along value. It's clear what P&G wants people to associate with its new product's benefit. It's relevant. And, it's very much driven by the product's brand driver: Tide knows fabrics best. It also knows people feel embarrassed and distracted when they've got a stain on their clothing. Because this is the digital age, P&G created a Tide to Go website, where people can write in and post stories about how Tide to Go saved the day. The company clearly knows the value of letting customers do the talking.

The best brands on the planet know the importance of basing their promise and their branding on a simple, relevantly different idea. However, the fact that it's relevantly different will become *irrelevant* if you cannot capture this simple idea in a blatantly clear and evocative brand driver. The fact that an idea is simple is also simply not enough. To generate branding that expresses everything you want consumers to associate with the brand, your brand driver must be intuitive enough for everyone doing the branding to understand and sticky enough for them to pass along while keeping its intent intact. Branding today is not linear: it's everywhere. A succinct, sticky, intuitive brand driver will ensure that your branding will be easily understood by those doing the branding and those influenced by the branding: the consumers. There are four criteria by which a good brand driver can be judged. To make it a snap, they all start with the letter *S*.

1. **Simple.** A brand driver must be, above all, simple in nature. It must capture the essence of the brand's promise in a way understandable, if not explainable, by a fifth grader. This is not a simple task. It's not that people aren't smart. Quite the opposite. It's that it's very difficult to get a roomful of smart people to agree on the one word, the one thought or notion that captures the essence of the brand. The very dynamics

of big business, small business, any business with more than three people works against you. Group decisions are tough. The bigger the room, and the more people in it, the harder it gets. One exercise that we use with clients at Landor to meet the criterion of "simple" involves building a "story pyramid." You begin this exercise by having the group members write single words, or singular thoughts or notions about the brand's attributes or characteristics on index cards. The first task for the group is to determine which index card contains the word or notion that best conveys the point of the brand "story." This exercise will force the team to make hard choices. And that's okay. Establishing a brand driver requires making hard choices. Your brand can't stand for everything. Your goal is not to end up with a run-on sentence. The second task for the team is to use the remaining cards to build the supporting argument to the story in ascending order; to demonstrate why the idea on the pinnacle of the pyramid deserves to be on top. A good test of whether you've succeeded in your efforts is to run the idea by that fifth-grader. If the kid says, "Oh yeah, I get it!" chances are everyone else will, too. On the other hand, if the precocious kid asks, "So, what's your point?" your simple idea simply isn't ready for prime time.

2. **Specific.** If you tell me your brand is innovative, I'll ask you to be more precise; "innovative" in what way? When you use boilerplate words like "innovative" to describe a brand, they can be interpreted any number of ways. The words you use in a brand driver must be absolutely unambiguous in meaning and clear in intent.

   Because it can be very difficult for people to articulate something as precisely as necessary, we often use pictures to help our clients get to the specific word they're after. Visual cues can assist people who are trying to capture the difference between innovative as in a paper clip, and innovative as in the Click Wheel on an iPod. Another exercise to help people be more specific in their articulation of an idea is to have them express it in a book title or a movie poster. A similar exercise is to have them write a headline for an ad that succinctly and accurately captures the intent of the idea. You'll find that exercises like these help people self-edit. Once people learn to think beyond the obvious, they'll be able to hone ideas to their core.

3. **Surprising.** If something is surprising, it's easy to remember. Buzz words and jargon are forgettable. That's why brand drivers or mission statements filled with buzz words and jargon are often laminated or framed to hang on office walls. People forget what they say. The objective of a brand driver is to be memorable. By giving your brand driver a clever or surprising twist, it will be easy for people to remember and it will live and grow organically within the organization. A good brand driver is meant to inspire people. If it's not inspiring on its own, it will never intuitively lead to appropriate and brilliant branding executions. To determine whether your brand driver is memorable enough not to have to be laminated and framed, tell a random group of people in the organization what your intended brand driver is. Go back the next day and ask them to recite what you've told them. If the words you hope to hear trip liltingly off their tongues, you've got it. If they don't, go back to the drawing board.

4. **Story-worthy.** In my last book, *BrandSimple,* I wrote about British Petroleum which, after changing its name to BP, became associated with the phrase "Beyond Petroleum."

These two simple words tell a story. If you were to write a story about an energy company that's about more than petroleum as an energy source, it might include content about solar energy or wind energy. Being about more than petroleum as an energy source implies that the company looks for new and innovative ways to power the world. Being an innovator in this respect means the company would most likely be an innovator in other respects: in the way it runs its retail establishments, treats its employees, builds its own buildings, does its advertising, or supports philanthropic organizations. A brand driver must be inspirational to the people who do the branding. To see if it is, get folks together and have each of them write a story about the brand driver and what it implies about the company. The objective is to see if they pick up the key factors. Use these stories to see if people "get it." If they do, the branding should be right on.

Establish a Clear Brand Voice

If you work in marketing, at one point in your career you will probably participate in some sort of workshop in which you try to tackle a challenging problem as a team. These workshops often work best if led by an experienced facilitator who ensures that the group does not kill good ideas and that new thinking is nurtured. The best facilitators begin these work sessions with warm-up activities to get people comfortable with each other and to get them thinking in fresh ways.

I've participated in quite a few of these sessions with a variety of warm-up exercises, some of which really got us energized. One exercise I remember with great clarity, and use occasionally in my current work, involved asking people to describe someone using a fictional movie or storybook character as a starting point. For example, the woman I saw in a trendy store made me think about how Scarlett O'Hara from *Gone with the Wind* would behave if she lived in Beverly Hills circa 2008. Or how the CFO of the guy's company kind of reminded me of Captain Ahab, the fanatical whaling captain in *Moby Dick*. Or how the kid who helped me in the video store could've been Cosmo Kramer's younger brother. These mental calisthenics were meant to get the workshop participants to flex their imaginations and stretch their brains to think in ways they weren't necessarily used to. Describing a person in a way that makes it possible to imagine Miss Scarlett cavorting among the shops on Rodeo Drive—reacting to the paparazzi, or taking on Paris Hilton—is so much more evocative than using a few simple adjectives.

Unlike many other warm-up exercises in the workshops I've attended over the years, this one stuck. I'm glad it did. Not just because it is an engaging way to open a meeting, but because it is a perfect exercise for any organization responsible for building a brand in the digital arena. The marketplace today is democratic, it's clamorous, and it's personal. Anyone with a digital device and ample battery power can engage in a conversation with anyone else who cares to engage. They can blog, e-mail, text, and voice their opinion to anyone who's willing to listen and get a response within seconds. We express our deepest feelings online, our most ardent concerns, and our greatest joys. Digital technology fosters communication. We use these tools to interact one-to-one. They are, by nature, relationship- and identity-builders. As such, we can express our identities and build virtual relationships with people from around the world. We can become active participants in all sorts of virtual communities. Entities that once evoked little or no personality must now define and express distinct character traits in order to be credible members of society. This includes brand entities. While brands have always demonstrated some degree of personality, today it's necessary for this persona to have greater definition and substance. To bolster its relevant differentiation, to set itself apart from all the other brands-as-people in this personal, portable, talkative, and transparent society—to carry weight in a global conversation—it's essential that consumers be able to perceive a brand as a living, breathing individual with well-defined characteristics and behavior traits. As consumers, we must be able to clearly imagine this brand-as-person as a very distinct and definitive *who,* and not just a *what.* And, this *who* must behave consistently wherever consumers come into contact with it. Like McGraw-Hill's "man in the chair" ad I wrote about earlier in the book, brand success begins with being able to define who your brand is as a person, not what you sell. Digital technology has put a strong magnifying glass on factors that are critical to building a powerful brand. Among these factors is having a distinct and distinctive brand voice, a voice clear enough and strong enough to hold all brand experiences together.

While a distinguishing brand voice has always been a critical factor in establishing long-lasting relationships with consumers, the importance of this factor has been magnified in a marketplace where one-to-one communication is the name of the game. The companies most likely to succeed will be those that realize how essential it is to customer relationships to engage on an emotional level and not simply a transactional level. More than this, because the Internet and other digital devices create social experiences, organizations must think about how their brand would behave as participants in these experiences. As such, they must be able to articulate these "human" attributes precisely and help all those involved in the branding intuit how these attributes would play out in specific brand initiatives. Once a brand voice has been established, an organization must be able to get anyone with branding responsibility to internalize the character of the brand and embed it into branded experiences in a convincingly realistic manner.

In the last chapter, I wrote about Johnson & Johnson and the simple brand idea that drives all of its brand's actions and behaviors: "Having a baby changes everything." The fact that the organization has been able to capture its relevant differentiation in such a clear, concise brand driver is one of the things that has led to its success as a brand. Another factor is that it has defined the voice, the personality at the core of this idea. This has made it that much easier for all of its branding constituencies to keep their branding initiatives cohesive and consistent with the voice of the brand. It's the glue that holds the brand experiences together. Bridgette Heller, Global President-Baby Care for Johnson & Johnson, and I spoke about why it's so much more important for brands to have a distinct voice in a digital marketplace. Bridgette told me,

> There are just so many places that consumers touch and interact with brands today. You've got to be able to articulate the brand voice very clearly for people across internal departments and across all agency partners around the world so that the brand experience is consistent and familiar at all these points of contact. The Johnson & Johnson voice is a vital factor in differentiating our brand on the emotional level on which we compete. Our brand must be perceived as genuinely empathetic to mothers. We're champions for moms, and while this comes across in the functionality of our products—the lotions, the oils, and powders—it's critical that it come across on a higher level. We want mothers to trust us, to know we are there to encourage and support them. It's essential to our brand credibility that its voice, its personality, come across at every point of touch. This means it's essential that anyone who works with the brand understands the voice, internalizes it, and expresses it in the branding.

Johnson & Johnson baby products are introduced into parents' lives at a point in time when they are very confused. Having a baby *does* change everything. It's a transforming experience. All of a sudden, a little bald bundle has taken over the house. Day and night, night and day, this tiny, vulnerable person demands full-time attention. Among the relevantly differentiating factors contributing to Johnson & Johnson's success is that its brand *is* perceived as a supportive, compassionate champion for parents at this life-altering time. And this characterization is expressed consistently wherever parents touch the brand. Bridgette explained that she and the team she works with at Lowe like to describe this brand-as-person as a sort of a "doula," a knowledgeable, experienced caregiver who provides physical and emotional support and encouragement to parents before, during, and after a child's birth. It's the warm voice and supportive personality of this doula that resides in Johnson & Johnson's branding. "We see our brand as the doula in the middle. Her presence comes through in all of our branding. The Johnson & Johnson brand facilitates the bond between mother and child," Bridgette told me. "Our brand is not the star, but rather it's there to help foster the emotional connection between parents and their children. In our advertising, on our website, we always show pictures of mothers and babies. The baby is never pictured alone as in some baby product advertising. The product is never the hero. It's always about the relationship between the mother and her child. Our brand is there to help smooth the process of this relationship."

With so many people responsible for Johnson & Johnson's branding, Bridgette explained that it was absolutely necessary to define the brand voice as distinctly as possible so that all "voice points," as she put it, come together as one person. One exercise the team used to articulate this voice is akin to the old television show, *Name that Tune*, in which contestants competed against each other to name a song based on the fewest number of opening notes played. The way the Johnson & Johnson team constructed their exercise was to see how few words or catch phrases it would take to telegraphically convey its brand's personality and how quickly the greatest number of people could pick up on it. An example of the catch phrases the team used in its voice exercise was "no more tears," "generations of trust," and "you and me." I was able to name that tune and all its inherent emotional associations after just the first two.

Another exercise Johnson & Johnson has been using to ensure that all branding members are on board with its brand voice is something the company calls Baby Camp. Because of the broad array of new constituencies now involved in branding—the various online agencies worldwide, the new media partners, and so on—it was necessary for the company to reignite the flame under its brand voice. More than this, because of the decentralized nature of its business and the importance of being able to move very quickly in a digital marketplace, the company knew it had to empower as many people as necessary to act on issues as they come up. In a marketplace where time waits for no one, it's essential for people to know intuitively how to act on-brand. According to Bridgette, Baby Camp involves four days of conversation and activities around the brand voice and everything else having to do with the brand persona. Baby Camp is attended by people from across all disciplines and departments, and from all levels. Since Johnson & Johnson is truly a global brand, this Baby Camp is held on a global basis to ensure that the branding is expressed consistently worldwide. The goal is to ensure that anyone from the outside who touches the brand experiences the same compassionate, encouraging, and supportive touch no matter where or how they interact. One of Johnson & Johnson's newest campaigns is based on the idea that the brand will "make your touch more touching." If you go to touchingbond.com, you can see how perfectly the Johnson & Johnson brand voice comes to life. And if you go to any one of its sites, pick up any one of its products, or view its advertising, you'll see how the same brand voice rings just as true.

To hold together as a singular identity, a brand's voice should ring true at both its simplest touch points—like banner ads, blogs, or the header cards at the end of retail shelving—and its most sophisticated touch points—like websites, advertising, philanthropic initiatives, and public relations. It used to be common practice for organizations to define their voice and personality using adjectives and general characteristic descriptors. What this produced was an identity a mile wide and an inch deep. How many companies do you know who define their personalities as friendly, professional, and accessible? Quite a few, I'm sure. To engage with consumers in the way in which they should be engaged today, it's necessary to define the brand voice in such a way that anyone can tell you how the brand persona would be expressed as a customer service call, a package design, or an advertisement. If Scarlett O'Hara, circa Beverly Hills 2008, was the brand persona, what tone would you expect her blogs to take? How would she design the retail space? If Captain Ahab was the voice of the brand, how would he write an e-mail or come across as company spokesperson on a television ad? If Cosmo Kramer internalized the brand, what you expect his branded video for YouTube to be like? Those doing the branding must be able to understand precisely how the brand should act in any situation or be expressed in any specific brand initiative. In the digital age of marketing, there can be no question about *who's* doing the talking and what they stand for.

In an earlier chapter, I wrote about how Apple was so sure of its brand's voice that it was able to literally hold a casting call for this character. Its series of "Mac versus PC" ads were as successful as they were because those who did the casting knew exactly what type of person to cast in the role. Those of us in the audience could tell from these ads exactly how the Mac was relevantly different from the PC. The Apple brand voice is so clear that we have no problem associating it with the person who plays it on TV. As another example, when I spoke to the folks at Burger King about its brand voice, they were immediately able to tell me that, when developing branding initiatives, they consider the voice of the Burger King brand as a cool, somewhat youngish uncle. He's the guy who's older than the age of its core audience, boys in their early teens, but not as old as their parents. He's the guy who knows why *The Big Lebowski* is the Dude, and he knows what clothes are, like, "totally money." He's also the guy who will give the kids a surreptitious wink when their folks do, "like, something so lame." We pick up the voice of this cool uncle in all of Burger King's branding: its websites, its MySpace page, its advertising, and its promotions. The cool uncle is, like, the dude, man.

While there is a real man behind the eponymous Charles Schwab brand, he doesn't appear in branding as himself, but rather as the presence that inhabits every single Schwab brand endeavor, and this presence keeps them glued together as one cohesive voice. I spoke to Becky Saeger, Chief Marketing Officer of Charles Schwab, about the tone and attitude of the company's brand voice. Becky said:

> It's simple. "Talk to Chuck" is such a simple and intuitive way to think about our brand. The idea, as both a brand driver and a voice, is so right for the transparency and communicativeness of the Web 2.0 world. It crystallizes what we stand for. Our company is based on relationships with people, not on transactions. "Talk to Chuck" is our way of putting this into words. As a company we want to know what *you* have to say. Schwab is interested in you as a person. Our doors are always open to your questions, your input, and your concerns. We're in a very complicated business. We're dealing with big decisions. Money is core to people's sense of well being. On any given day you think about your finances multiple times. How we act, how we talk, the way in which we give people the information they need is critical to building trust, which is integral to the brand experience.

Brand trust starts with *who* you are as a company and whether it is conveyed convincingly, consistently, and respectfully across all touch points. In a company as large as Schwab, this *who* crosses many departments, many agencies, and many offices. During our conversation, Becky explained the various things the company does to maintain the tone and attitude of its brand voice:

> This may sound obvious, but it was essential to start with a company intranet site and interactive activities that clearly defined the style of speech that anyone "talking to Chuck" should experience in blogs, in e-mails, direct mail, in collateral material, in advertising, or in speeches given by manage-

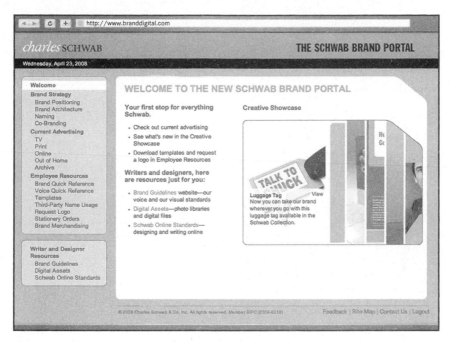

Charles Schwab works to ensure that every interaction with its customers and prospects is "on brand" and that all communications speak with the same "voice."

ment. We actually created a toolbox to give people guidelines for articulating the brand voice in everything from e-mails to speeches. Key to this voice is that it must convey to consumers that the Schwab brand knows them, will remember them from contact to contact, and respects them. When you connect with the Charles Schwab brand in any way, it will be a familiar experience—simple to understand, straightforward, and engaging. We wanted everyone in our organization to be able to understand exactly what the consumer would expect from a brand that invites them to "Talk to Chuck." We wanted anyone involved in the branding to say "I get it!"

The initiatives that the Charles Schwab organization undertook to ensure the consistency of its brand voice are *not* always obvious. People need to "get it" and be able to act on it intuitively without having to painstakingly scrutinize a forty-page set of guidelines. Tools for maintaining and facilitating consistent brand experiences are absolutely necessary, but the simpler and more instinctive they are the better. At the end of the day, consumers can get what they need from any number of places. Your objective should be to ensure there is clarity around what your brand stands for. In the digital marketplace, it's very easy for a brand voice to run amok, which is not conducive to building trust. In a transparent marketplace, trust is of the essence, especially when it comes to people's financial well being.

Among the other reasons it is so critical to define and be able to clearly articulate a brand voice is that it will enable you to become more innovative in your branding expressions. During my conversation with Becky, she said that, in the digital world, the quote by Norman Berry, a former creative director at Ogilvy & Mather, has become even more relevant for her: "Give me the freedom of a tightly-defined strategy." I agree with her. One of the ways to make innovators out of everyone in an organization is to clearly define the company's point of view, engage them in this point of view, and make believers out of them. When there is a concisely stated and compelling starting point, it enables everyone to execute against it brilliantly down to the smallest things, all consistent with the brand's definition. As new technology generates even more branding channels, more venues, and more ways to get a message across, a tightly defined strategy and an equally tightly defined brand voice become even more important. When people "get it," you get better work.

As the branding world has shifted toward engaging consumers not only in conversations, but in experiences, the old ways of defining a brand voice just aren't good enough anymore. Yes, it helps to have a real person driving the character of the brand. Charles Schwab, Apple's Steve Jobs, and Virgin's Richard Branson have helped set the tonality for their brands' personalities. But these organizations are successful as brands because the people working for them know that it's not the person that drives branding that's consistent with the voice; it is because the attributes and characteristics of this person have been captured and ingrained in everyone in the organization. There's a distinct voice that comes through loud and clear from touch point to touch point. Everything about these brands is rooted in the same culture.

If you currently define your brand's voice by way of a few adjectives, as well-chosen as they might be, this may not be enough to help differentiate your brand in a tumultuous branding world. Even taken together, these words may not be descriptive enough for all the folks who do your branding to grab onto and intuitively embed in the brand experiences for which they're responsible. Do they bring your brand idea to life? Do they clearly define your brand as the "person" with whom you'd like consumers to interact? If not, here are a few tools of the trade.

1. **Define your brand voice as a character from a book or movie, or even a blend of characters.** For example, the brand's personality is as inventive and adventurous as Indiana Jones but as confident as James Bond. Or, the brand is as rational and patient as Homer Simpson's wife, but as savvy as Heidi Klum. Once you think you've got a general personality that works as an expression of your brand, flesh out the character. What kind of books would they read? What's their favorite kind of music? What would they order in a restaurant? How would they decorate their home? What kind of pet would they own? What's in their refrigerator? Where do they vacation? What kind of relationship do they have with their siblings, their friends, their coworkers? Remember, this is the person who has to interact with your customers. To do so credibly, they have to be able to relate

to your customers. This is the person in whose voice your blogs, website, and advertising will be written. It's the person from whose point of view you'll devise a customer service or a retail experience. It's the person who will write your CEO's speeches, determine company-wide policies, and decide on your philanthropic activities. You've got to define this person to a T, and you must be able to articulate clearly. Everyone has to be able to get it immediately. We're talking "a-ha" here.

2. **Create a prototypical Facebook page for your brand voice.** Not a real page to be posted, but a page that expresses the brand voice as if it were a Facebook profile. Where did this "person" go to school? What did they major in? What extracurricular activities did they engage in? What sports did they play? What are their hobbies? What movie star's or musician's pictures were on their walls? Who posts stuff on their walls? Are their blogs well-written or are they hastily scribbled and random? People in the organization must know this person-as-brand so intimately that when this person-as-brand comes through in your direct mail pieces, your television spots, your customer service scripts, the designs of your packaging, the personality and voice are definitive and instantly familiar.

2. **Create an eHarmony profile for your brand voice.** The objective is to get the brand a date with someone who is absolutely compatible, shares the same beliefs and value systems, and has the same approach to life and partnerships. (Unlike many of these profiles, be real.)

3. **Take on the job of casting director.** If you were casting the brand voice in a movie, who would play the part? Write some scenes. Establish how this character would behave.

What range of emotions would they portray? How would they behave toward other characters in the movie? Would they be polite or self-deprecating, or would they be direct and plainspoken? Would they have a sense of humor? Would it be sarcastic, slapstick, or sophomoric?

4. **Capture the essence of this voice.** Once you've done any or all of the above, or you've devised your own process, do one more thing. See how few words or phrases you need to capture the essence of this person. Much like Johnson & Johnson did in defining its brand voice, see how few notes it takes you to name that tune and have everyone get it so that it consistently rings true from touch point to touch point.

5. **Share the brand voice with everyone inside the company.** Make sure everyone gets it. This can't be accomplished with an e-mail or an inter-office memo. Set up workshops with interactive exercises and hands-on activities. Allow the people in the organization to roll up their sleeves and try out the brand voice in a number of different branding initiatives: e-mails, website copy, corporate communications, etc. Role play with the voice. Create different scenarios: How would the brand voice be used when interacting with customers on phone calls, on a Web activities, in text messages?

6. **Build some simple guidelines and tools.** Give employees something they can refer to. Make sure you provide examples. Because organizations are constantly evolving with employees coming and going, there have to be standards to which everyone can refer. A brand voice is far too important today to let everyone in the organization make it up as they go along—especially when the whole world can listen in.

Identify Where You Can Play to Win

Mrs. P. F. Albee holds a significant place in the history of marketing. In 1886, she was hired as the first "Avon lady." David H. McConnell, who founded the business as the California Perfume Company, considered women to be an untapped resource, both as customers and as employees. He had the brilliantly prescient idea that if you asked a woman to sell beauty products to her friends and neighbors it might make for a lovely business model. His belief was that a woman was more likely to trust a female neighbor than a high-pressured salesman when it came to buying soaps, perfumes, and other beauty aids. Long before there were sophisticated analytics to prove him right, he trusted his instincts and was, of course, proven right. A fleet of Avon ladies made for an extremely lovely business model, and Mrs. P. F. Albee was the lady who helped start this multi-million dollar global business. A minister's daughter from Winchester, New Hampshire, she didn't just invite her friends and neighbors to try the products she was asked to sell; she also was asked to recruit a sales force of equally motivated housewives who loved the idea of financial independence. (For those who need a quick history lesson, 1886 was thirty-four years before women were given the right to vote.). Today Avon is a company with over 39,000 employees and 3.5 million sales representatives from every corner of the world who continue to invite their friends and family to learn about the newest Avon products over a cup of tea and some neighborly chat.

David H. McConnell had tapped into an insight about consumers that led to this incredibly effective branding touch point. These ladies didn't trust the fast-talking traveling salesmen who knocked on their doors. In assessing the journey his potential customers would take with his brand of perfumes and cosmetics, he recognized that these ladies *did* trust each other to know what was worth buying. He also recognized that having them engage with each other in their homes to talk about his products was as powerful a mode of brand interaction for this specific audience as there was. As a way of influencing consumer behavior, active engagement with trusted conveyors of information is a powerful branding tactic. Consumers who become actively engaged in a branding experience become more relevantly aware of what makes the brand unique and better. This fosters deeper relationships, more robust sales figures, and stronger brand equity. It was a concept that did not escape this 28-year-old entrepreneur over 120 years ago. What made the brand experience even more powerful was how intrinsically aligned it was with the promise of the brand: to help women feel empowered. It was a touch point that reinforced the brand's relevant differentiation in every respect. Avon is a company *for* women.

The importance of identifying the points of touch at which a brand can play and win is perhaps the most challenging factor organizations face in the digital age. Gaining someone's attention, let alone getting them engaged, is hard in any market situation. The heightened ability of consumers to control the sales and purchasing process in the digital era has created additional barriers for organizations trying to get their brand message across and understood. Digital technology shines a bright light on the many new opportunities consumers have to interact with brands. And, it shines the same bright light on the many new opportunities brand organizations have to leverage these points of contact. The trick is to be able to uncover and then take advantage of insights about consumers in order to determine which points of touch along a customer's journey with the brand will have the greatest potential to attract people and gain traction.

It's never been easy to assess with absolute certainty which consumers' interactions with a brand has most influenced their buying behavior and, until only about five or so years ago there were far fewer sources to be credited. Back in these dark ages of marketing, it was more likely than not that the creative strategy and execution, in the form of an inventive television spot, dictated branding strategy. After the TV ad was made, the media department or agency was brought in to determine where, based on the viewing habits of the target audience, the inventive spot should be placed. It was established protocol that making consumers aware of a product's benefits en masse was the way to go to market. This traditional branding process started with radio and made a relatively easy transformation into the television era. As I wrote about in chapter 4, the television ad as engine drove most of the other branding components. This is not how it works anymore, nor should it be. In a society of fragmented audiences and fragmented channels of influence, the effectiveness of this approach is not only ineffective; it's inefficient. (I once had a boss who alluded to an ill-conceived contact strategy as shoveling money off the roof. There has been a large sum of money shoveled off the roof these past few years, and smart organizations are quickly determining where to pick it up and how to use it.)

The decision about where to invest branding dollars has become a huge challenge for today's brand organizations. And, it's become acutely obvious that organizations need to think more broadly than just using paid media or advertising when assessing a branding strategy. It's essential to scrutinize more carefully than ever before all of the channels by which a specific group of consumers might pick up information or interact with brands. It's also essential to scrutinize how they behave on a category by category basis. What might work for automobiles or mobile phones won't necessarily work for diapers or soft drinks. And even more complicating, what works for soft drinks in one age group won't work for the same soft drink in another. In addition, if you go back to the idea of the customer's journey with a brand, it's critical to identify at which points of touch a consumer will stop and smell the coffee—in contrast to the point of touch where the customer will smell the coffee and then buy it. Consumers behave very differently in the digital world. We're *all* consumers, and we know how *we* behave. We search for information one way and make a purchase decision in another. The views of people half a world away can influence our decisions. The blogs or reviews of people we're never likely to meet in person can cause us to change our opinion of a company overnight. The amount of information at our disposal, the copious results of search engine proficiency, can make a once easy decision complex and a once complex decision easy. Is it better to scale back the footprint of your branding reach and attempt to reach only those people that are most likely to react? Or, does it make more sense to go large scale? Is it smart to think about going after zealous brand evangelists and count on them to spread the word for you, or should you go after those who are straying from the flock and try to entice them back?

There are no magic answers to questions like these and the other questions that marketers grapple with in relation to their branding budgets. But there are some fundamental things you should do before you develop a branding strategy. First and foremost, stand back. Take a good hard look at the customer's journey with your brand and determine where the people you really want to reach are doing most of their hanging out. Forget about the way you used to buy media or made your branding decisions. As Strauss Zelnick, Founder of ZelnickMedia and formerly president and CEO of BMG Entertainment, told me,

> Technology's influence on marketing choices will only continue to grow. The effect of Moore's Law will not be diminishing anytime soon. What you have to think about is that new media is not other-worldly. In the mid-1880s the newspapers reported on all the new ways that electricity would drive information forward. They now talk in similar fashion about how the Internet is doing this. Marketers shouldn't be thinking about whether it's either traditional channels or interactive channels, they should be thinking about the fact that given all this new technology the consumer's tolerance for interruption has been diminished. Consumers don't resist marketing messages based on the device on which they're received, but based on whether or not these messages are relevant. The focus should be on delivering the right message in the right way at the right time and monetizing it.

The good news is that marketers today have at their disposal a full range of tools and technologies with which they can decipher where and how consumers are getting their information and making their buying decisions. The key is to use these tools to observe consumer behavior—to watch, listen, and learn about what's relevant to consumers and not be tied to one type of branding solution over another. The ability to become flexible with your branding program may be more difficult for some than others, especially those who work in categories that have long been dependent on traditional media opportunities, including those in packaged goods and fast food. But, in a digital world in which consumers will engage only when and where they choose to, taking a narrow attitude won't work. Organizations that look deeper for insights about their customers' habits and desires, that don't allow themselves to be constricted by one annual planning meeting, will have a better chance of identifying where to play and how to win. There is only one thing that's set in stone in this marketplace: consumer behavior should be your guiding light. Be ready and flexible enough to go where they go and appeal to them in a way that makes sense—to them, and for your brand.

In addition to the above, identify places your brand can play where your competitors can't or won't go. In an earlier chapter, I wrote about the impact of Pepsi's decision to change its packaging, a smart move on the company's part. Using the insight that the ultimate step in the purchase process takes place in the soft drink aisle at the supermarket, the smart folks at Pepsi drew attention to their brand's relevantly differentiated brand promise by relevantly differentiating its cans. The inventive, consumer-generated designs of its cans not only signal that Pepsi is the cola of choice for a young and hip generation; it also sent a message to other generations that define themselves through their art, their music, and their contemporary cultural awareness. This point of touch on the customer's journey was where a whole lot of people were hanging out, as was the Internet on which a Pepsi website was designed specifically to let people express themselves. As a result of keen insight, this is where Pepsi decided to invest its branding dollars.

Another beverage company, this one decidedly for adults, discovered that its consumers are also a culturally aware bunch constantly on the lookout for new experiences. The brand team for Smirnoff vodka, a brand in the Diageo stable of products, takes this insight into account when assessing touch points. It looks for experiences that will reinforce what makes its brand of vodka unique. It is driven by the fact that it is the original vodka, that it *is* unique.

Those of you who are James Bond aficionados know that the line "Martini, shaken, not stirred," and Smirnoff vodka go hand in hand or rather, martini glass in hand. It was in the movie *Dr. No* that the suave James Bond first uttered that memorable line, over forty years ago. Go back even further to the product's launch in the 1860s and you'll discover Poitr Arsenyevitch Smirnov, the suave man who discovered the unique charcoal filtration system that defines the Smirnoff taste. As the story goes, soon after the Russian Revolution in the 1920s, Poitr's son, Vladimir, fled the Bolsheviks and ended up in Paris with the family brand. He changed the spelling of his surname to Smirnoff and was instrumental in establishing the brand as the number one-selling vodka in the world, which it remains to this day.

I spoke to Philip Gladman, Senior Vice President of Marketing for the Smirnoff brand, about how the organization determines where to spend its branding dollars in a world quite unlike the world in the 1920s. "It's very easy to say let's create a website," Philip said.

At best, however, you might get 350,000 visitors a month. In the scheme of things, this is a rounding error. The question is how to best to use digital to increase your reach while staying true to the idea that Smirnoff does things differently. We're original. Among the major branding initiatives we've instituted over the past couple of years is something called the Smirnoff Experience, the details of which can be found at smirnoffexperience.com. It's a series of cultural events, totally unique dance and music festivals, each tied to the brand idea of being the original vodka. We promote each of these events across multi-channels, like the web, print and packaging, but it's the event itself which powers the brand experience. For example, we did four events, one in Moscow, Shanghai, Paris, and New York, which followed the travels and flight of Vladimir and featured the music of Faithless with a Russian orchestra. A key factor in the success of these branding experiences as both awareness and revenue builders is the ability to use digital to amplify the message. Digital can extend your reach very efficiently. Yes, fifteen hundred or two thousand people attend the actual events, but it's being aware of which digital applications generate buzz with the right audience that's critical. We've been able to reach well over half a million people for each event. We've engaged in relevant media partnerships around the globe, with entities like MTV and YouTube. People know they're onto something cool, and they pass it along. Digital used properly is a powerful PR mechanism. It's an activation platform that allows you to engage with the people you want to reach on a deeper level at an incredibly fast rate. The Internet has allowed the economics of branding to change.

The Internet does allow the economics of branding to change if you know your audience's digital habits. Smirnoff definitely does. Choosing the right environment for a branding message is as essential as generating impressions. The consumer is at the center of everything Diageo does. Its genius is in being able to relevantly tie the brand's promise of being the "original" vodka to this consumer group. The brand managers at Smirnoff create content—the event—and then build on it across various branding channels to bring the idea to life in a uniquely Smirnoff way. The uniquely Smirnoff way is to promote its heritage, take the benefit of the brand to a higher level than just the charcoal filtration process. "The providence of our brand has emotional appeal. People don't bond with the vodka because of how it's made. They bond with it because of its back story," Philip said. "The intent of our branding is to get people engaged in this story as a way to gain an understanding of what makes our brand of vodka authentically different. Everything we do is authentic to the brand. We choose the branding touch points we do because they have the ability to create a sense of excitement and inclusion on a global scale. It started out as a calculated experiment. While all experiments are inherently risky, this one continues to yield maximum gain."

Experimentation is inherently risky, but there were very few people I spoke to as I wrote this book who didn't mention experimentation as a cost of doing business in the digital market. This is in no way meant to imply that all branding initiatives today should be of an experimental nature; far from it. However, following consumers as they bob and weave from one point on a journey with the brand to another makes it necessary to take some risk—although as Philip said, it should be calculated. You'll never learn where you should or can play to win if you don't look for new and innovative ways to connect with people. When I talked to Bob Gilbreath, who was a senior manager at P&G before joining Bridge Worldwide as Chief Marketing Strategist, he confirmed this belief. "I started at P&G in 1998 so I definitely experienced the early days of establishing branding plans with the digital space in mind," he told me, continuing:

> We were used to the old TV-led model of branding. Tell a story. The initial reaction to digital was to use it like you use TV, to tell a story. We had our share of pouring money into a lot of cool stuff because it was there. In one effort, P&G partnered with Yahoo to develop an online soap opera for the Pepto-Bismol brand. It was about these college-age kids who were backpacking through Europe. They carried journals with them in which they'd write about their adventures, including any stomach issues that required the help of Pepto-Bismol. It was an innovative endeavor for its time, but it didn't fit with the brand strategy or objectives. Nor did it reach the target audience, which skews much older and is not prone to backpacking through Europe. It was a case of using the technology because it was there. It's the same thing that's happening today with organizations that buy MySpace pages but have no reason to play in this space. Their core users aren't there, and they have no business being there, literally and figuratively. The starting point for any branding initiative should be to ask if it's going to provide value to the consumer. Then, does it meet the brand's business goal, and, finally, will it build brand equity? It doesn't matter what it is—an ad, a customer service effort, or a promotional offer. It has to align with both the consumer's need and what the brand stands for.

A number of the brand managers I spoke to at P&G also talked about early digital efforts. As they tried and erred, and then tried and succeeded, what they recognized was that to play and win the basic rules of branding still apply. You spend your branding budget on efforts that will attract the right people for the right reason and that will reinforce your promise to them. While there are now many more tools in the branding tool box, these general principles haven't changed. What P&G eventually did with Pepto-Bismol was to fold it in a categorical branding initiative called Health Expressions, a website filled with general healthcare information, along with facts about relevant P&G brands including Oral-B, Thermacare, Vicks, Crest, Prilosec, and Metamucil. With the recognition that these were relatively low involvement brands on their own, the company made the smart decision to create a content-rich site that would offer consumers timely and relevant content about health-related issues like recognizing the signs of high blood pressure, exercise for "tweenagers," and fixing heart-healthy family meals. Health Expressions was in no way designed to compete with medical sites like WebMD, but to respond to the growing desire of consumers to know as much as possible about their health and to take more responsibility for it. People want to be more informed prior to visiting their physicians. Searching for healthcare information is the third most common activity on the Internet. The other insight P&G derived from its research prior to launching Health Expressions was that it's usually the women in the family who carry the responsibility for keeping everyone healthy. The site is designed with this in mind, providing widgets and other applications women can use to talk to each other and share family solutions for common healthcare issues. As P&G competitively analyzed the field, the company realized that, given the equity they've earned as a purveyor of trusted household products, Health Expressions was a branding touch point where it could credibly play and win. Instead of spending huge sums of money on one individual product at a time, P&G was able to effectively brand all of these healthcare products under a single emotional topic: in-spired health solutions.

P&G, like all smart companies, knows that experimentation is part of the learning curve in any new marketing environment. In the early 1950s, it had to figure out how to make the transition from print and radio to television, and it is now making the same transition as brand-ing opportunities continue to evolve. It sets aside money for trying things out and sets aside money for the tried and true. Like all smart companies, it also knows that branding is like putting on a major Broadway show. There has to be someone in charge of ensuring that the branding touch points along the customer's journey hold together from the center. With so many new ways for consumers to experience a brand, the challenge to keep things glued together as a cohesive en-tity could be a tough one. Organizations that make the brand prom-ise the essence of all they do find the going a little smoother.

In *BrandSimple,* I wrote about a company that took the idea of experimenting with a branding touch point to a whole new level: the business model. In 1998 Sephora opened its first store in the United States in New York City's SoHo area. Until that time, there were primarily two ways for women to compare cosmetics brands. They could go to a high-end department store and walk from counter to counter asking commissioned saleswomen who repre-sented individual brands to show them a product that was kept under glass. Or, they could go to mass-market retailers, where the cosmetics hung side-by-side-in plastic packaging. Sephora intro-duced a third way. Hundreds of the same brands found in both high-end department stores and in smaller specialty retailers are displayed openly: The lotions, gels, and powders are ready to play with. This allows women to try on one color after another and eas-ily compare one brand's product to another. The simple idea driv-ing the brand is accessibility, and its store experience being as friendly and accessible as it is remains among the most dominant touch points on the customer journey. I spoke to Betsy Olum, Sephora's Senior Vice President of Marketing, about how the brand adapted its promise to a market that is more virtual than real. Betsy said:

> Buying beauty products is such a personal experience. You go into our stores and can actually try on the makeup before you commit to buying it. In the very beginning, before anyone was actually sure where the Internet was going, we felt that if we had a Web presence it would be a great place replenishment resource for our customers. What we learned as we went along, however, was that our website is an incredibly powerful way to get our message and our brand story out to the masses. There are plenty of women out there who have never heard of Sephora and don't have a Sephora store nearby. We recognized that, with the Internet, we could expand our reach. But the reason our site works so well is that, unlike a lot of other beauty sites which are pure sales plays, our site is fully integrated into our business model. To stay true to our brand promise we had to make our online presence as similar to our store presence as possible. To build equity, to maintain credibility, we deliver the same product assortment, the same level of service, and the same feeling of accessibility we deliver in our stores. Our overall branding strategy was not just to have our site be a shopping destination, but a site where women could come to research and compare products easily, to get information about the various manufacturers, to look at the ingredient listings, as well as get tips and trends from beauty experts. We make a substantial commitment to our website because we want to make sure our clients feel comfortable purchasing a product they normally get to try on.

Sephora discovered very soon after it opened its Rockefeller Center store, and hundreds of others around the world, that its retail establishments were definitely consumer touch points at which its brand (and women) could play and win. As Sephora ventured into the digital landscape, it wasn't sure what would happen. The ability to reach a broader audience was certainly appealing, but at what expense? A website is a consumer interaction at which a brand can very easily lose credibility. It can dramatically impact the perception of the brand from the point of view of people who know it well and those who don't know it at all. The insight that Sephora's brand management had to keep clearly in mind was that women love Sephora because it offers a totally different and relevant way for them to buy makeup. The competition in the retail space wasn't as much as a challenge for them as the competition they found waiting in the digital space. Beauty websites are a dime a dozen. The way Sephora kept the brand promise alive in this very busy category was to keep its site clearly aligned with the promise. It made the site as close to the store experience as it virtually could. The organization didn't allow itself to be technology led, but brand led. In an article in the *New York Times*, Donna Hoffman, Co-director for the Sloan Center for Internet Retailing at the University of California, Riverside, said that while many multi-brand cosmetic websites had shut down, Sephora, in contrast, was successful. "Sephora has invested heavily in its own brand," she said. "Sephora really paved the way in this category and showed other retailers this could work online." Sephora might have been concerned initially about what would happen as it moved to enlarge its brand footprint by expanding into the digital space. It took a page out of its own brand book to add a powerful point of touch that continues to be worth every penny of branding investment it made.

Doing a deep dive into customer insight, playing where other brands don't, doing a bit of experimentation, and keeping all branding initiatives in alignment with the brand promise are some of the fundamental things all brand organizations should do when assessing where to invest their branding dollars these days. As the world becomes more transparent, there is, however, another thing organizations should think about as they consider where they can ply their branding and win; it is in their area of philanthropic initiatives. Going back to what futurist Faith Popcorn referred to as the "goodness factor," digital magnifies everything about companies—all dimensions of their behavior, not just those related to what they sell. When we read about a company, we are more apt than before to think about its moral fiber. In my conversation with Scott Osman of brand strategy firm HFX, he mentioned that consumers don't see companies as being made up of distinct silos, the products and services, the marketing, the promotions and websites. They see companies in their totality. His idea that digital technology eliminates the friction that has allowed companies to control what's heard and observed about them is a reality. The Internet greases the wheels of information sharing. In our conversation, Scott told me that consumer data is proving that consumers are more likely to buy a product from a company that supports a cause they care about. What's more, a good percentage of them said they'd be likely to switch from one product to another (price and quality being equal) if the other product was associated with a good cause. Companies that actively demonstrate socially responsible behavior and align their social strategy with products and company marketing are not only likely to attract more customers as a result, but attract top talent and, thus, increase productivity. As Scott put it, "nice is necessary," and many companies are responding by including socially related initiatives into their overall branding mix. They recognize that the customer journey is now comprised of touch points related to their products and services, as well as touch points related to their standing as good corporate citizens.

To be most advantageous, a philanthropic activity should be intrinsically linked to what the brand represents in the minds of consumers and must reinforce the brand's relevant differentiation. Like all other branding initiatives, "good" initiatives must be as aligned with the brand's promise as everything else associated with the brand. When a company takes on a social cause based on the personal interest of the CEO or a long-standing board member, it's admirable, but it won't do much to help cement the meaning of the brand in the minds of consumers. It's more likely that the CEO's equity will rise more than the company's. On the other hand, when a company like GE gets involved in causes related to alternative energy, funding research for wind turbines, for example, it's a perfect fit. As consumers, we already associate imaginative sources of energy with GE. When P&G's Dawn brand becomes involved with saving wildlife from the ravages of water pollution and oil spills, it makes sense and helps reinforce that Dawn is the brand of dishwashing liquid that eliminates grease from dishwater. Its social consciousness makes us feel even better about the product and more likely to buy it. When a financial institution like Citi becomes involved with micro-lending to budding entrepreneurs in underprivileged areas of the world, it's a perfect fit. It helps reinforce the brand's values and lets consumers see that Citi puts its money where its brand promise is. Susan Avarde, Managing Director of Global Branding for Citi's businesses, explained the company's philosophy toward social initiatives in more detail. "A company's actions and behaviors relative to delivering on the brand go far beyond products and service and far beyond standard forms of communications. As stewards of the brand, we also have to look at the way Citi ties the brand promise to social responsibility. The way we behave as a corporate citizen is a critical part of 'holding the house together.' We don't beat our chests about what we do, or spend lots of time publicizing it. That wouldn't be genuine. We just do it because it's right." Citi helped reach 3.5 million people in 2006 and it will give an estimated $200 million over ten years to individuals in disadvantaged positions to help them build small sustainable businesses. The Citi foundation's stated purpose is to help individuals and communities build stable and rewarding lives, in effect "bringing dreams to reality." As a financial institution, this quiet but powerful philanthropic effort is a credible and very appropriate linkage to the brand's promise.

This brings me back to the first part of this chapter. When David McConnell hired Mrs. P. F. Albee as the first Avon lady, he believed that women were an undervalued resource, as both employees and as customers. Avon became a brand associated with the promise of empowering women, and it continues to relevantly play this idea forward in its business model, in its product line, and, equally so, in its philanthropic points of touch, most significantly its breast cancer awareness activities. In 1993, it launched its first Breast Cancer Awareness Crusade, enlisting over a half million Avon sales representatives to raise awareness and money with the sale of the now ubiquitous pink ribbons and through contributions from the sale of its products. In 1998 the company's first annual 3-Day Avon Walks for Breast Cancer began. These multi-city events are an opportunity for women around the country to "walk as one" in order to dramatically impact the lives of women around the world who have breast cancer. Since 2003, these walks have generated over $200 million and have included over 75,000 participants. For over 120 years, Avon has been associated with building bonds with women and enabling them to become economically independent. That it chose to align itself with a cause like breast cancer shows an incredible self-awareness of what its brand stands for in the minds of all people. Its commitment to make the world a better place for women in terms of both health and personal empowerment is clearly evident in all points of its customer's journey with the brand. It has integrated its social responsibility perfectly with its brand promise.

A number of recent studies have confirmed that "good" is good for business. Latitude Research reported that most people are willing to pay over 6 percent more for a product from a company they know is doing something good. A CSR Monitor study stated that 70 percent of college students would not apply for a job at a company considered socially irresponsible. However, it doesn't require studies to confirm what most marketers experience as true. The transparency of the digital environment makes everything visible and in real time. When nine out of ten consumers say that companies should support causes that are consistent with their business practices, it's powerful. When consumers can see whether these companies actually do what they say they do and vote with their wallets, it's even more powerful. As an organization examines a customer's journey with the brand to identify places it can make optimal branding investments, it must keep this transparency in mind. Consumers are more than willing to engage with brands they trust and that provide them with experiences that reinforce this trust over time. There is no magic bullet, no magic of any kind to establish exactly where a brand should play to succeed in the digital marketplace. However, if you keep in mind that all branding activities must be authentic to the brand, must stand up to scrutiny, and must support a brand's relevant differentiation, you're off to a good start. Here are a few more things to think about.

1. **Become a fly on the wall.** Join online communities and make use of other online sources of information to listen to what's being said about your brand by people who have the power to influence those you'd like to attract. Every successful brand has evangelists. See where they're hanging out and what your brand can do to get them actively engaged on your behalf. Use all the tools at your disposal to get good insights about your customers. Determine where they go for information, how they do their buying, whether they come back for additional information, and why. Your objective is to see at which points of customer touch you can have the greatest impact on their behavior.

Some points of contact have far more influence than others in being able to get people to think about your brand the way you want them to. Determine where you can deliver the greatest value to your customer while at the same time building your brand's equity.

2. **Experiment.** Try new things. Don't be held back by traditional ideas of media planning, including the once-a-year planning session. The biggest names in the brand world, including P&G and General Motors, learn through trial and error. The marketing communications agency, Digitas, part of the Publicis family of companies, set up a whole division just to test online ads for GM using a variety of customer criteria. They add, they subtract, they paste, and edit until they get the ad that yields the best ROI. This is not your father's media planning environment.

3. **Give someone the role of brand director.** Much as you'd like it to be, the branding process cannot be democratic. Someone has to make the ultimate decisions about whether a specific branding initiative is on-brand or not and whether it's doing what's required to convey the brand-promise. If there isn't a firm hand and voice of authority to ensure that all points hold together from the middle there's a good chance the promise will fall apart.

4. **Don't overlook social responsibility.** The Internet has created a transparent world, and consumers can see everything having to do with your brand. Consider good deeds to be brand touch points on the customer's journey. Take advantage of your good works and your brand's moral core to reinforce your brand's relevant differentiation.

5. **Unlearn old knowledge and play to win.** Take a fresh look at everything you do. When Burger King came up with its

Subservient Chicken campaign, it used all of its creative juices to ensure kids would pass it along and create buzz. When Xerox wanted to change its image from the old-fashioned black and white copier company, it built a campaign around clickable color ads for the *Financial Times* that could be viewed on mobile phones. Its market share went up 5.6 percent.

6. **Look for branding activities that will actively change consumer behavior.** Much as Diageo did with its series of Smirnoff events, your goal is not merely to inform or entertain but to engage. When a brand can get a consumer to actively engage with its product or service, its relevant differentiation becomes more apparent and understood. Determine how to use digital tools to their advantage, specifically to increase your brand's footprint or amplify its voice without adding to your budget.

BrandDigital
The Top Ideas to Remember

About two and half years ago, I was contacted by an executive at WPP who was given the responsibility to put together a program that would bring the senior leadership of the organization up to speed on the changes in the marketplace being brought about by digital technology. I was also asked if Landor could work on a name for this program. Digital Acceleration was the name our team came up with, and I was fortunate enough to join my colleagues from across WPP organizations in this terrific program. During the sessions, we wouldn't just watch PowerPoint presentations or listen to lectures about all that was going on. Rather, we rolled up our sleeves and got involved with it: setting up blogs, creating MySpace profiles, downloading videos, uploading videos, creating avatars in Second Life, sending text messages, joining the chats in chat rooms, and adding to the product reviews on branded websites. We got to experience, to a pretty good extent, the way millions of people get and share information, news, and entertainment. It was during this program that I first thought about writing this book. There are many people who work in the brand, media, and marketing industries that have a sense of the vastness of the digital world, who participate in it to one extent or another, but who don't know to *what* extent it's having an influence on the way brands are built and managed. I decided to find out.

Without exaggeration, this book has served as my personal course in digital acceleration. I interviewed close to one hundred people who work in the fields of advertising and marketing, media and entertainment, and, of course, digital technology. I talked to children and teenagers, and friends and family, about their daily routines in the personal, portable digital environment. I observed and I read, but, more importantly, I got as much hands-on experience as time allowed. The most important thing I learned from this personal course in digital acceleration was this: Much like learning a foreign language, you can teach yourself from a book or a videotape, you can take a class, but the best way to learn a language is to live in the country whose language you want to learn, to immerse yourself in the culture, to make it a part of your life. The same is true of digital. After talking to all the great people I interviewed for this book, the thing that really accelerated my learning about what digital technology means to us as brand and marketing professionals was living it, immersing myself in it, and embracing it. After reading this book, I advise you to do the same. It is only by learning about digital technology, by living it, that you'll be able to harness all the tools and tactics available to you and use them to the benefit of your brand organization.

Having said that, I'd like to end this book the way I ended the classes I taught at New York University's Stern School—with a list of the top ideas I wanted the students to take away from sessions. It was as much for the benefit of my students that I did this as it was for me. This exercise forced me to make sure I was driving home exactly the points I wanted people to bear in mind as they moved from the theoretical world to practical applications. It's with this in mind that I present the top ideas from this book that I believe will help readers move from theory to practice.

1. **To understand digital technology you must interact with it.** Digital technology has its own learning curve. It's not enough to read the countless articles about what's happen-

ing in this evolving space. In order to serve your brand well, in order to provide value to the consumers with whom you'd likc to do business, it's essential that you have a working knowledge of the space in which they and you are playing. As I said, this requires taking an active part. In the interviews I conducted for this book, I concluded each with the same question: What do you do to keep up with the rapid changes in the digital environments? Almost everyone responded with one of two fundamental answers, in many cases both.

First, they take the time to experiment and engage in what's happening. They crcate profiles on LinkedIn or Facebook. Upload and download photographs from Flickr. Post messages to a friend's MySpace wall. Advertise something on Google. Play with widgets and other mash-up applications and upload a video to YouTube. Read blogs and respond. Post reviews on a manufacturer's website. Subscribe to a variety of RSS feeds. See if they can thumb a multi-sentence text message in less than sixty seconds. Beyond just checking your e-mail and searching for stereo equipment on eBay, by engaging in online activities, you will get a good idea of what consumers are involved with on a day-to-day basis. To be perceived as a credible participant in the digital space, it's essential that you can demonstrate that you know what you're doing, that you "get it."

The second thing people do to keep up with this fast-changing technological space is to watch what their kids or other peoples' kids are doing. Seriously. Digital technology is intuitive to children. They're exposed to it from the time they are toddlers, and as far as they're concerned, it's as much a utility as electricity and the telephone service. It's a natural way for them to communicate with each other. They plug, or unplug, as the case may be, and play. For a real learning experience, ask some young teen what websites she visits on a regular basis and how she keeps up with what's going on in her world. Watch a bunch of pre-teens interact with each other as they interact with Xbox. I have a friend who stopped by with his thirteen-year-old son, who immediately asked me if he could use my computer to check some gaming competition that was taking place somewhere in the world. I invited myself to watch the action with him and was amazed at both the speed with which he was able to get to exactly where he wanted to go online and the complexity of the sites he was able to manipulate with absolute assuredness. I watch my son use my Blackberry to check baseball scores while we're out of town, and I watch my daughter interact online with her Webkinz buddies. Kids don't think about it as digital. It's just there, and they just do it. Given that these are the people we'll be marketing to sometime in the very near future—if not already—it's vital to be able to access and use the same information that they use and even to find a way to go beyond that—not just to keep up, but to stay ahead of where they get their information and why.

2. **Identify where people are hanging out and what they're doing.** Identify exactly what form of digital technology the consumers you want to reach are using to get their news, entertainment, and purchase-related information. As Bob Pittman from the Pilot Group said, "People use technology to make things they already do easier or more convenient." Or, as Esther Dyson, WPP Board member and digital guru put it, "Just as in real life, you wouldn't sell life insurance in

church, but you would sell hot dogs at a football game. You have to behave properly for the context." It makes no sense to invest money in a Facebook page if your customers aren't there. Study the dynamics of the environment in which you'd like to participate. If you waltz into a Facebook "party" uninvited and interrupt rather than engage the inhabitants in a relevant way, you'll be lucky if all that happens is that people ignore you. More than likely your brand will suffer serious equity consequences. On the other hand, it makes all the sense in the world to invest in the creation of an innovative series of brand-related videos and post them on YouTube if the folks you want to reach hang out on the Tube. Think before you jump whether it's brand appropriate to use a specific digital tool or channel to make the things people already do easier, more convenient, or more fun—whether it's shopping, signing up for car insurance, buying airline tickets, getting product reviews, or setting up a community for new mothers. Is it a relevant place for your brand to be, and does your brand have any business being there?

3. **Listen to your customers.** Take advantage of technology, specifically search technology, to learn about what consumers are looking for online and for what reason. In order to become the brand a specific consumer segment *actively* searches for and *chooses* to interact with, you've got to take advantage of all the innovative new ways you can get insights about the consumers you want to reach. The need to watch what your customers and prospects are doing and to listen to what matters to them is more important, and, luckily, easier to do. While gaining insight about what's important to consumers has always been a key factor in a brand's success, consumers today can signal what they want *before* you

deliver it. Look for these signals. If you don't zero in quickly on what matters most to the people you most want to attract, some other brand organization will. Your search engine optimization strategy will only be optimized if it yields relevant solutions to the consumers you want to target.

4. **Make sure your brand stands for something that is genuinely different and that this difference is relevant to the consumers you want to reach.** Consumers have so many more brand choices and so many more ways to see what's out there that it's critical for them to be able to discern immediately what makes one brand different from another. Because setting a brand apart based on some functional benefit is becoming harder to do, it may be necessary to take the benefit "up the ladder" to an emotional rung. Organizations that can define what makes their brand different in a way that transcends basic functionality not only demonstrate a deeper understanding of a consumer's lifestyle but can more readily own the top position in a category. It's much harder to compete against an emotional ideal than an objective based on a tangible feature that can be eclipsed in a matter of months.

5. **Make your brand promise simple to understand, for two reasons.** First, anyone responsible for the branding must be able to quickly and intuitively understand what the brand stands for and recognize how to bring it to life without needing. Marketing is no longer for masses to ask if what they're doing is right. Second, if the meaning of the brand isn't clearly and simply defined before going to market, the market will define it for you—and you probably won't like the definition.

6. **Align all branding initiatives with the brand promise.** Consumers are media agnostic. Mass media, while a player,

doesn't necessarily drive the train. Branding signals come in a wider variety of shapes and dimensions than before, and some are simply more influential with one target group than another. It's critical to determine at which points of touch your branding will have the greatest influence on the audience you want to reach. You can reinforce what makes your brand different and relevant by taking advantage of the right tools in your branding tool box, digital and otherwise.

7. **"Who" trumps "what."** The digital world is an interactive world. As such, it's important to have a clear brand voice that personifies your brand. It's essential to clearly define and represent your brand's values, beliefs, and character traits. To be perceived as credible, the brand's voice must be conveyed consistently across all points of touch, and each expression must be appropriate to the interaction.

8. **Be honest.** Don't make a promise you can't keep. But if you falter, tell the truth. It's a transparent society. If you can't or don't prove how and why your brand's promise is both different and relevant, if the brand promise doesn't stand up to scrutiny, your organization will become discredited very quickly. When you make a brand promise, you must be absolutely sure you can deliver on it. There is no mercy in the digital space. However, there is forgiveness. If you come clean and make good on your mistakes quickly and effectively, you stand a good chance of being rewarded for your honesty.

9. **Engage with customers on their terms.** Creating a trustworthy relationship with a customer has always been a factor in brand success. The digital marketplace is made for relationship building. Success is being able to determine how to engage in a way that adds genuine value to the conversations

or activities taking place. Better yet, it's being able to make the value of interaction with the brand so obvious and compelling that consumers seek you out. However, in all engagements, clearly identify your organization as "the brand." Trust is of the essence. (See point #8.)

10. **Be ready to make rolling adjustments.** It's a mad, mad world and a fast, fast world. The digital marketplace requires flexibility and a test-as-you-go mentality. It also requires an operational infrastructure primed to react when necessary.

11. **Invest in content that people want.** Create content that is functional and/or entertaining. If you create something that is fun to watch, people will send it to their friends. If you create a website with useful information, people will go back to it time and again and spend more time with it. Giving away content for free is a huge brand-building investment that could be considered part of the marketing or branding budget. This requires a serious shift in attitude. Because consumers now have the tools to pass along things they find interesting, innovative, and engaging, the value of great creative work has literally never been greater. It can spawn spontaneous distribution, which can be a boon to the bottom line. To be successful, however, the creative work must be considered interesting, innovative, and engaging by the consumers you want to attract, and not just to the creative people who created it.

I mentioned at the beginning of this section that it was during the course in Digital Acceleration that I first thought about writing this book. To be more specific, it was during a presentation by Rob Norman, CEO of GroupM Interaction, in which he described digital dynamics as the ability to "hover on the backyard fence of millions of conversations," that the spark was ignited. Even after a full day of fascinating and absorbing activities, it was this term and all the images it evoked that kept popping into my head. In a sense, it became my "brand driver," crystallizing all the profound changes that digital technology has had on marketing and brand building over the past few years.

If you think about it, and you should, Rob said, "the years between 1950 and 2000 were an anomaly in the history of marketing and branding." Television and other mass media vehicles brought forth mass marketing. Prior to this people got most of their most relevant information about products and services from their friends and neighbors—over the backyard fence, so to speak. Someone with whom you had a day-to-day relationship would tell you in a simple, personal, and matter-of-fact way why they liked or disliked a particular product. If you remembered what they had to say, it was because they were genuinely passionate about their recommendation and compelling in their explanation. And because this person knew you were going to see them the next day, they knew they had to be able to stand by their words, be credible. They knew they could be held accountable for their recommendations.

Digital technology, as Rob said, has brought back the backyard fence, albeit a fence that spans the globe. If you use the evocative idea of a backyard fence as the filter for all of your organization's marketing and branding initiatives, you'll be a good way toward understanding how to successfully use the digital space. Think about conveying your brand message to consumers in a simple, personal way. Forget the hard sell. Think about conveying the message to only those who'll find it relevant, and make what you have to say memorable and compelling so it will stick with people. Think about the fact that you must be credible because you absolutely *will* be held accountable for your message and everything associated with your message. People will see you the next day, if not the next minute.

As my final point, I advise you to picture a backyard fence, a fence of global dimensions. It's the perfect metaphor; a picture that captures all that's true about branding in the digital age. It's the perfect brand driver.

Index